# AN EYE ON CRICKET

## Gideon Haigh

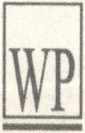

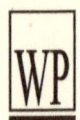

Published by:
Wilkinson Publishing Pty Ltd
ACN 006 042 173
Level 4, 2 Collins St Melbourne, Victoria, Australia 3000
Ph: +61 3 9654 5446
www.wilkinsonpublishing.com.au

National Library of Australia Cataloguing-in-Publication entry
Creator: Haigh, Gideon, author.
Title: An eye on cricket / Gideon Haigh.
ISBN: 9781925642216 (paperback)
Subjects: Cricket--History.
Cricket--Tournaments.
Test matches (Cricket)
Cricket players.

Front cover painting/illustration: John Scurry
Back cover photography: Matt Irwin

# Introduction

Some years ago now I had to fill out a questionnaire for a kind of local who's who called *Contemporary Australians*, and was invited to list my 'Major Achievements'. Unable to think of any, I wrote: 'Staying employed'. This probably still applies. I've now been contributor on cricket to *The Australian* for six years. It has been a happy arrangement, enhanced by excellent colleagues. In modern media terms, it probably also qualifies as long-term

What it has depended on most, of course, has been a cycle of event and personality. Fortunately these have abounded. The work I've selected for *An Eye on Cricket* covers a period in Australian cricket as intense as any: the regaining and surrender of the Ashes; World Cup victory and World T20 failure; the rise of Steve Smith; the fall of Michael Clarke; the death of Phillip Hughes, and also of past masters such as Richie Benaud and Max Walker. Then there have been the noises off, often very loud: the collapse and reconstitution of the International Cricket Council and the Board of Control for Cricket in India; the bull market in T20; the bearish trend in Test cricket; the threats of doping, fixing, corruption and maladministration generally.

*An Eye on Cricket* is divided into three sections. The first encompasses profiles, interviews, valedictions and obituaries — players, parents, coaches, commentators, men, women, gladness, sadness. The second comprises match reports, previews, reviews and digressions, from the daily business of cricket on the road; the third explores issues made current for whatever reason. The pieces have previously published, mainly in *The Australian*, although also in *The Times* and on *Cricinfo*. Journalism is inherently perishable — perhaps never more so. But I quite enjoyed being reminded of all the things that have excited and infuriated me over the last few years, if only to have reinforced how much fades away, despite the heat of temper, and how much remains unresolved, despite best efforts.

The title *An Eye on Cricket* is used advisedly too. There may never have been a period in the game's evolution when it has been more important while watching to keep an eye on other things: politics, economics, technology, ideology, markets, management, and the culture more generally; even history, though it is these days hardly paid more than lip service. Sometimes these 'controversial' dimensions are deemed to be distractions from the primal thrills of the contest — why can we not 'just get on with the game'? I think this less and less. A trend in cricket writing is towards ever more minute analysis, down to the level of data; rightly or wrongly, and it is an entirely personal preference, I remain partial to bigger sweeps, longer perspectives. Which may make me a bit, well, weird. But it was ever thus.

It remains for me to thank the peers who have made the last little while so enjoyable: Peter Lalor, Mike Atherton, Andrew Faulkner, Wayne Smith, my sports editors Wally Mason and Tim Hallissey; and also Michael Wilkinson, who is publishing me again after a gap of thirty years, making us both feel old, I dare say.

GIDEON HAIGH

# Contents

## Part 1 Cricket Gallery

# Part 2 **Matches and Despatches**

## Part 3 Conspiracies, Cock-Ups and a Tragedy

# PART 1
## Cricket Gallery

# Richie Benaud
# FACE OF CRICKET
## APRIL 2015

It turns out that the last occasion on which the cricket public heard Richie Benaud was the thirty-second recitation he delivered in honour of the late Phillip Hughes, played at Adelaide Oval before the First Test between Australia and India in December 2014. Benaud summed Hughes up in a few, well-chosen words, with a paternally warm concluding sentiment: 'Rest in peace, son.'

It somehow reflected Benaud's relationship with cricket. When you heard it from Benaud, that made it official, credible, true, even in the ghastliest circumstances. He had been there; he had seen it; but the sun would rise on cricket tomorrow, and the game would go on. Had a politician been able to achieve such trustworthiness, there would have been no need for elections, or even opinion polls. Benaud's was the bluechip stock in every portfolio, the household brand in every home.

He was being marketed before he was even aware of it. He was born Richard, his father's middle name, but this was too formal for down-dressing Australia, where Jack was as good as his master partly because he preferred it to John. There was a threat he might be 'Dick' until mother Rene subtly imposed her will by a quiet campaign for something a little less curt.

So Richie he became. One of the very few organs to lean towards formal address was *Wisden Cricketers' Almanack*, Harry Gee's Five Cricketers profile in the 1962 edition beginning: 'If one player, more than any other, has deserved well of cricket for lifting the game out of the doldrums, that man is Richard Benaud.' And Rene was right: he was *never* a Dick.

Did he market himself? Benaud was too intelligent a man not to understand the impression he made, and its usefulness. After all he was a professional presenter; meeting audiences was his business. But he could not have succeeded had 'Richieness' simply been a guise he adopted when the cameras rolled. No, like a stick of rock, he was Richie through and through, which fascinated those he met, like Michael Clarke at a cricket award evening in 2005: 'I remember talking to Richie on stage and marvelling at the fact that he sounded in the flesh exactly as he sounded on television. I have no idea why I was so surprised. Maybe it was the fact that he had been parodied so often, but somehow I had it in my head that the television voice was just that, and he would probably be different face to face.'

When Benaud died on 10 April 2015, there were a great many such tributes. No fewer than four books have followed, anthologising extracted writings about and by the subject: *Richie: The Man Behind The Legend,* edited by Norman Tasker and Ian Heads (Stoke Hill); *Benaud in Wisden,* edited by Rob Smyth (John Wisden); *Remembering Richie: Richie Benaud & Friends* (Hodder & Stoughton); *Those Summers of Cricket: Richie Benaud 1930-2015* (Hardie Grant). Not bad for someone who played his last cricket more than half a century earlier; not bad for someone whom most knew only as a disembodied voice, economical in expression, cool in tone; so not bad that such an astonishing consistency of appeal cries out for explanation. Benaud's media career must be described in terms of two related broadcasting revolutions in which he was intimately involved: the rise of the ex-player expert; and revolution in the commercial value of television rights.

Both lay well in the future when Benaud was playing, even if in hindsight he seems always to have been a media performer in the making — an enterprising all-rounder who became an imaginative captain and a gifted communicator, a colourful figure in an austere period. It was thought extremely unusual when 26-year-old Benaud organised with the BBC's head of light entertainment, Tom Sloan, to spend three weeks after the 1956 Ashes tour watching the corporation at work in the medium of television shortly to arrive in Australia.

As he often recalled, Benaud followed the racecaller Peter O'Sullevan at work at Newbury; he watched the Wimbledon final called by Dan Maskell; he followed the British Open Golf called by Henry Longhurst. Each was a master of a technique espoused by Seymour de Lotbiniere, the BBC's pioneer of outside broadcast called the 'pyramid': start with the core facts of the score, then broaden to discussion of weather, venue and other material. The cardinal principle was often condensed as: 'Don't speak unless you can add to the picture.' Its later influence on Benaud was obvious.

The irony is that at the time this approach had only limited application to cricket. Like the other sports, it was also the preserve of professional broadcasters: television's 'voices of cricket' were the ebullient Brian Johnston and the mandarin E. W. Swanton. But here pyramidial principles were not felt so binding: as John Arlott said, de Lotbiniere had 'no particular liking for the game, and little knowledge of its finer points.' The picture in televised cricket was not yet so good that it often spoke for itself, so commentators talked quite a lot, sometimes unpopularly so. On the occasion of Benaud's last Test in England, for example, Johnston and his Australian summariser Jack Fingleton caused considerable annoyance by whiling away the closing stages of a draw with long, rambling stories unrelated to the play, and to chatting with statistician Roy Webber about his glamorous wife.

In the second half of his playing career, meanwhile, Benaud dabbled in a variety of media, but not television. On Sydney's tabloid *Sun*, he learned basic principles of daily reporting as a junior police roundsman and of opinion making as a regular sports columnist. With the assistance of a literary agent,

George Greenfield, he published three cricket books; Greenfield also arranged his first media engagements in England, with *News of the World* and with BBC radio in 1960. He appeared on television in 1963 initially only as a summariser — it was to prove the first of eighty-four consecutive summers on either side of the world.

For Benaud had retired from cricket just at the right time. Instrumental to his rise was Bryan Cowgill, a no-nonsense northerner who had just become the BBC's head of sport. Forever associated with the institutions of *Grandstand* and *Match of the Day*, Cowgill argued that the day of the genial waffler on television was done. For one thing, television pictures were improving: the coming of the 625-line screen and of colour finally made it sensible to apply to cricket the principle of the picture's predominance. For another thing, the public wanted to hear from former players, preferably those with a bit of glamour. As first Benaud then Jim Laker, Ted Dexter and Denis Compton took up their television microphones in the 1960s, first Swanton then Johnston moved to radio, Johnston with a tart comment or two in his *It Never Rains* (1972) about the new ways not being his 'cup of tea'. 'Cricket includes so many other things besides what goes on in the middle,' he complained. 'It is a game full of character and fun and there is always laughter not far away. But not if you have a producer shouting down your ear "...Steady — no jokes — stick to the cricket!"'

Fidelity to 'what goes on in the middle' had other implications. Television was a compelling medium, immediate and potentially intimate. But its limits tended to be the edge of the screen. It was far less interested in issues requiring of deep analysis or investigation, as Benaud himself was to find when he followed the Australian tour of the West Indies for the *Sun*, also commentating for local radio and television, in 1965.

It was expected to be an exciting tour, as the first rematch of the contestants for the Frank Worrell Trophy; it was also bound to be controversial, featuring as it did Charlie Griffith, the fastest bowler in the world with most-discussed action. Benaud was typically well-prepared, having undertaken training in photography from Harry Martin of the *Sun's* broadsheet sister, the *Sydney Morning Herald*, and brought a Minolta SR7 with a Tamron lens and a hundred rolls of film. And after due consideration of the photographic evidence he collected during the First Test at Sabina Park, Benaud labelled Griffith a thrower in the *Sun* and in the *Jamaica Gleaner.*

In doing so, Benaud courted considerable unpopularity: 'I was to find out that not only was the press not keen to publish the photos but that radio and television, which I was serving, were very keen that nothing of a disquieting note should be mentioned on either medium and I was effectively gagged the following day at Sabina Park.' In a radio talk on the BBC, he scolded administrators for their inaction. 'I believed that Griffith threw in this game and I was prepared to say so. The alternative was to burn the photographs and shut up about it, but the time for wishy-washy diplomacy in this matter is long past.' But when the BBC covered the West Indies tour of 1966, Benaud and his commentary box colleagues said nothing about Griffith's action, even as it was extensively debated in print.

So emerged a characteristic of televised cricket, a kind of tacit restraint, that while it might dwell on moments of telegenic conflict, it has tended, at least in England and Australia, to shrink from controversy towards...well, 'wishy-washy diplomacy.' As Jack Williams notes in *Cricket and Broadcasting* (2011): 'Televised cricket has not followed the example of televised football and rugby in replaying in detail foul play and making this an important aspect of recorded highlights...Radio and TV have not gone out of their way to uncover instances of poor sportsmanship.'

Benaud fulfilled all the early expectations of Bryan Cowgill, and his

BBC producers Nick Hunter and David Kenning. No commentator was more respectful of the nostrum about only speaking when necessary, on which he developed his own variations: 'If you can add to the pictures do so'; 'No-one ever complained about silence'; 'Silence can be your greatest weapon.' This last Benaud liked so much that he believed in it not only for broadcasting but for 'my general organisation, working in the office and in business.'

Silence didn't only express the superfluity of comment. After that early brush with trenchancy in the Griffith affair, Benaud seemed to agree that television was not a place for debate or contention. In *Richie*, the golf commentator Jack Newton remembers Benaud counselling him that in the event of an on-air colleague airing a debateable sentiment, the best response was none: 'If it happens you don't agree, don't say anything.' Newton followed the commandment to the letter, 'essentially doing what I was taught by Richie.'

Benaud was also ever wary of the commentary of the first person, where it involved mention of his own career or era. One day, Doug Walters recalls in *Richie*, he attempted to draw his colleague on the subject of the turning pitch with a cheerful jest: 'Gee Richie, I bet you would love to be bowling on this sort of wicket.' He got no answer. He repeated himself. He got no answer again. At last came the ad break and a gentle reprimand: 'I don't answer hypothetical questions.'

Why such self-denying ordinances? Why not a bit of disputation or contradiction? Why not a telling anecdote from personal experience? Might they not have 'added to the picture'? Not, thought Benaud, if they were a distraction from the action. From outright criticism of players, especially that which might involve 'in-my-day' comparison, he recoiled completely. And the breadth of Benaud's appeal while observing such tenets of commentary suggest an acute understanding of the preferences of his audience.

So did the boldest step of Benaud's broadcasting career: his involvement in Kerry Packer's World Series Cricket, to whose success he was among the most fundamental ingredients. Cricket was a primly shockable game in 1977. To WSC Benaud imparted a patina of respectability. If it *was* a 'circus', at least one was aware of an undeniably competent ringmaster.

Television coverage of cricket in Australia had traditionally lagged that in England, the Australian Broadcasting Corporation a pale epigone of the BBC. WSC changed all that. Australian coverage became the standard, in technical proficiency and narrative verve, and viewers embraced it — more of them, indeed, than before.

At the same time, while Nine's modus operandi is often interpreted as a profound break with the past, with its lavish array of cameras and compelling use of replays, Benaud was never other than himself. All the novelty was presented with the moderating influence of a man who believed that commentators should behave as a guest in the viewer's home. His less-is-more habits withstood even Packer's injunctions. In *Richie*, Benaud's old confrere Bill Lawry recalls their boss's telephoned complaints during an early WSC fixture:

> He informed us in very clear terms that this was not the BBC, most of the people watching didn't have a clue about cricket, and we were supposed to be telling them what was going on. Richie wasn't going to change or in any way dilute the commentary lessons he lived by: you only spoke if you could add to the pictures. So the next over was again virtually word-free. After that, I thought keeping Kerry on side was a bit more important, so I started rattling on. The pattern sort of stuck.

Indeed it did. If such an audit were possible, a study of Benaud commentaries down the years would reveal a word ratio growingly in favour of the garrulous colleagues with whom he shared a microphone.

In fact, Benaud's natural vein made him the perfect commentator for the new order. Under the Nine regime, commentators had less time: commercial breaks deprived them of twenty-five seconds every over; the previous convention of the forty-minute stint was shortened to half an hour. The subtly smaller canvas played to Benaud's strengths. Nine also gradually relieved commentators of mundanities like repeating the score or reciting statistics by presenting these on-screen. Benaud could confine his scrupulously rationed remarks to what mattered, which probably no commentator has done so well.

The great change that WSC presaged, of course, was economic. It hastened the end of a world in which cricket was covered by national broadcasters — since as his first employers, the BBC — as a kind of public trust. It ushered in a present day when the game is funded by the sale of the rights to televise it.

In some ways that involved a continuation of television's tendency to exclude considerations outside the screen, which was now about the conservatism of commerce. The modern commentator became not simply a critic but a promotor too. With his natural moderation and understatement, Benaud balanced these roles as effectively as anyone in history: you bought Benaud's wares without even realising they were for sale, and, as with the best salesmen, the transaction left you feeling enriched. Because he always looked for the best in cricket, he entitled one to optimism. Because he never mentioned his own career, he remained startlingly contemporary. His presence was a certification of quality. When cricket at last left BBC television behind, Benaud's continued presence assuaged all concerns, even that of the former corporation pillar Swanton. 'I don't despair of Channel Four at all,' he said. 'After all, they've got Richie Benaud, the great arbiter.'

There was a degree of artificiality about this great arbitration. From the 1980s on, cricket seemed to lurch from one crisis to the next: rebel tours, match fixing, illegal actions, ball tampering, aggression that trembled on the brink of cheating, commercial chicanery that skirted the bounds of legality, rock-bottom standards of governance. Yet none of this intruded on a Benaud commentary stint, the supersmooth succinctness of 'super shot' and 'marvellous' interrupted only every so often by an oracular comment or an inscrutable silence that might, or might not, convey displeasure. Indeed, it may have further enhanced his appeal — that while Benaud was at the microphone, externalities were always suspended, and progress was generally benign.

It's tempting when a great presence is lost to opine about the qualities the next generation would do well to emulate. Yet while Benaud was extraordinarily adept at accommodating change, he was *sui generis*. Cricket's biggest audiences are now young, Indian, well-informed and social media savvy, brought up on short-form cricket and shouty current affairs television. What to them is the commentator dispensing terse advices between silences from an Olympian remove? The televised cricket of the future will increasingly be geared to their values, their expectations.

Benaud, one suspects, would not have been uncomfortable with that. In *Richie*, Nine's head of sport Steve Crawley recalls the circumstances of his last on-air words, and of presenting Benaud with a script that ended 'God bless you, son.' Benaud amended it to 'rest in peace' with a polite but firm: 'I don't do God.' Good thing too.

# Max Walker
# O LUCKY MAN
SEPTEMBER 2016

Max Walker belonged to a very small subset of Australian cricketers recognisable only by their Christian names. For forty years 'Max', or even 'Maxy', usually prefaced by 'Big', summoned up the image of a bowler who did much spiritedly right while seeming to do almost everything biomechanically wrong, and of a preternaturally amiable figure in a sunhat with a sunny smile framed by bandido moustache and sideburns.

Walker was a fine, unflagging medium pacer, suited by temperament to the role of auxiliary in an attack led by Dennis Lillee and Jeff Thomson. He became, improbably, a sporting brand *avant le lettre*, with a personality, a catchphrase, a fund of stories, and eventually a literary oeuvre that sold more than a million copies. The max is what he extracted from his talents on field and off.

Funnily enough, Walker was reticent about calling himself 'Big Max'. That was his father, one of nine children, a gregarious master builder and publican whom his son worshipped: they later collaborated on a book, *A Chip Off The Old Block* (1996), brimming with devotion and reverence.

Walker's first cricket games were on North Hobart's Hill Street, bisected by tram tracks, lit by streetlamps. His first sporting loyalties were to Lansdowne Crescent State School, whose cricket team had no cap and whose jumpers were heavily patched hand-me-downs, but which he nonetheless led with pride. His first hero remained so: his father. He owed him, Walker felt.

Big Max, a fine all-round sportsman, had resisted the siren song of the mainland. When Melbourne Football Club's talent scouts sought Young Max's signature, it was an opportunity not to be foregone. A half century's association with the MCG began when Walker worked there as a maintenance man and scoreboard operator while studying architecture at the Royal Melbourne Institute of Technology.

Walker was eighteen when he played the first of 94 games for Melbourne, mainly as a ruckman, wearing number 1 — which, as he self-deprecatingly pointed out, was exactly the number of Brownlow votes he polled. But if he was no champion, football ensured that Walker would bring to cricket unusual fitness and stamina, and capacity for forebearing injury: five times did he break his nose representing the Demons.

The cricket took longer, although that was because it involved a second string becoming a first. Walker arrived at the Melbourne Cricket Club as a batsman, but was born to bowl, even if he required some convincing of this by chairman of selectors Clive Fairbairn.

Those who wish to illustrate the concept of bowling 'off the wrong foot' often have recourse to the example of Walker. His ungainly jump cost him momentum through the crease. He looked inside his left arm, so struggled to bowl the outswinger other than 'for show'. He got by on immense physical strength, a wrist that cocked naturally for the inswinger and leg-cutter, and an appetite for work.

In their pomp, the great English photographer Patrick Eagar took side-on studies of Lillee, Thomson and Walker in their delivery strides. Lillee's front leg is thrillingly parallel to the ground, Thomson's right arm wound back like a ancient ballista; Walker resembles a biplane trying to take off into a fierce headwind. Yet as many children would have imitated Walker in the backyard as his colleagues, and with perhaps more enjoyment. I played with two boys in under age cricket with wrong footed actions, and both were nicknamed 'Max'.

The tri-cornered bowling partnership was arrived at almost by accident. The first time the trio bowled together, at the MCG in December 1972, Pakistan made eight for 574; first Thomson then Lillee succumbed to injuries. Walker first made his way on his own, closing out the Sydney Test against Pakistan with five for 3 in thirty balls to conjure a 52-run Australian victory, then taking twenty-six wickets at 20.7 in the Caribbean. On that tour Walker bowled 375 overs in nine matches in enervating heat and humidity. It was hard yakka even with his footballer's physique. 'I used to think Barassi was a hard man,' he said to his grateful captain Ian Chappell one day. 'He's got nothing on you.'

Another superb Eagar picture shows him dismissing Alvin Kallicharran at Port-of-Spain in that series, arms upraised, roar reverberating, to commence another unlikely Australian victory march. Captioning it in Eagar's *An Eye for Cricket* (1979), John Arlott saw the photo as an embodying Australian spirit: 'Australians, throughout cricket history, have been quick to strike back even from a position of apparently imminent defeat.'

Walker settled into the up-the-hill, into-the-breeze role with which he's now identified at the Gabba in November 1974. Lillee and Thomson were back; Walker ensured there was no escape, sealing up the exits with long spells of patient denial. When injury hit Lillee and Thomson again during the Sixth Test, Walker bowled 42.2 eight-ball overs and took eight for 143. He also made runs, extending a long front leg and offering a broad straight bat, finishing third in the batting averages with 221 runs at 44.

By then he was a character in the making. Reckitt and Colman Australia used him to promote their insect repellent Aerogard, features softening into a broad grin under the questioning of a young fan who wishes him an Australian *bonne chance*: 'Avagoodweekend Mr Walker.' His first book, *Tangles* (1976), then almost trademarked his nickname. At the time he was being courted by the agents of his home state, who were pressing to join the

Sheffield Shield. Lillee urged him not to act too hastily: other opportunities might be about to arise.

Though he was not to know it, Walker was ending his Test career by signing for Kerry Packer's World Series Cricket. All he knew was what it represented. For all his visibility, he was still designing planter boxes and public conveniences for the State Public Works Department, and jogging over to the MCG for Victorian training sessions twice a week.

'For the first time in my life I, in common with the other Packer players, have financial security,' Walker wrote in *Cricketer at the Crossroads* (1978). 'My only problem is to stay at the top for the next 3 years. After that, who knows? But at least I will be in a position to practice architecture in my own right.'

It did not work out that way. If he was not a front rank performer during WSC, he was an identifiable presence in a game craving them. 'Mr Walker's playing havoc with the bats,' ran the relevant line in *C'Mon Aussie C'Mon*, identifying him by his advertising moniker. He slipped affably into commentary, prolifically into print. 'Retirement' was the wrong word for the end of his cricket career: although architecture went by the board, he worked harder than ever, and more profitably.

The experience of the establishment's disdain during the WSC years remained a somewhat painful recollection. The Melbourne Cricket Club cut ties with him, its captain and a Test player, without so much as a by-your-leave. Before WSC commenced, Walker underwent a phase of internal exile, reduced to playing park cricket with the likes of Old Caulfield Grammarians, Carltonians and Prahran Police. Yet, as was his habit, Walker managed to make of the experiences a funny story. From Sir Donald Bradman to Kerry Packer, everyone became grist to his raconteur's mill. When he recalled the 'explosion of noise' at the MCG after he yorked Tony Greig during the Centenary Test, he could make it seem like yesterday.

When I circulated among WSC's sometimes suspicious participants twenty-five years ago to put together what became *The Cricket War* (1993), Walker was among the most generous, propping his feet on a desk, taking his phone off the hook, and talking for hours, his yarns as involved and idiosyncratic as his bowling. Even his signature, which must have been appended to hundreds of thousands of books, was a tangle of loops and flourishes.

'Everyone loves 'em, even my mum,' Walker said of Billy Birmingham's Twelfth Man comedy riffs, although they took a modicum of piss from his genial everyman shtick. He was modest about his reliably affable books, but they solved many a Father's Day dilemma. Above all he looked on cricket with great gratitude. It had been a challenge, but never an ordeal, and remained an abiding joy. His last book, *Caps, Hats & Helmets* (2006), ends with his favourite cricket poem, by Alison Uttley, concluding with the line: 'I still have that ache of beauty when I hold a cricket ball.' 'Max': it also reflected his pleasure in the game.

# Martin Crowe
# THE PERFECTIONIST

MARCH 2016

The first thing that struck me on meeting Martin Crowe, even in the shadow of illness, was his physical presence. Strong frame. Broad shoulders. Deep chest. Direct gaze. This was a little unexpected. I identified him with a cricket of elegant classicism, of economy of movement, of touch and precision rather than brawn. But then I also remembered how he pervaded a crease rather than simply occupying it, and how he obtained such power from such a minuscule backlift, barely a flex of the wrists. Though illness had taken its toll, the latent strength was unmistakable.

The second thing that struck me was how completely alive he was, how dedicated to getting the most and best out of every encounter, his utter humility and insatiable curiosity. Some cricketers never cease being cricketers. Even after retirement they are still at the crease; they can't stop taking guard. Martin was past cricket in the two brief years we were friends, and perhaps the least guarded man I have ever known, utterly frank and giving of himself, healthily in touch with his feelings, and so present in all his dealings that, despite knowing how completely reconciled *he* was to his mortality, I find *myself* strangely unprepared to write about him in the past tense.

It was not always thus with Martin, as he was the first to admit. It's 20 years since he published his first autobiography, *Out on a Limb*. In hindsight, he thought it a failure — too self-protecting, too self-justifying. That same year, a controversial, unvarnished "unauthorised biography" by Joseph Romanos was published, *Tortured Genius*. "He did me better than I did me," Martin said. When I ventured that I thought I might have liked him back in the day, Martin looked momentarily very serious. "No, you wouldn't have," he said. "No, you wouldn't have."

Maybe Martin had more admirers outside his homeland than in it, or at least enjoyed more unleavened admiration. Peter Roebuck described him as "always at war with his own publicity" in New Zealand. As the country's premier batsman, captain designate, then captain, he was known for wanting, and for getting, things his own way. His occasional ruthlessness with others reflected a ruthlessness with himself.

He was first chosen against Australia, aged 19. He was not ready. It hurt him. Sometimes it's said that young players are toughened up by being blooded early, experiencing failure and fighting back. Martin would not have agreed. Strong emotions and deep anxieties lay beneath the surface confidence. He was quick to judge others as "not good enough", not because he did not know what it was to struggle but because he did. The world he later hugged to his breast he kept then at 22 yards' length, and it worked: after 13 Tests, he averaged only 21; across the decade in which he was New Zealand's first and best hope, he averaged in the mid-50s.

Young fans trying to get a feel for Martin the batsman will probably have recourse to the annals of YouTube, on which he is well represented in various highlights packages. In doing so, they will miss what I thought was his most memorable quality. Highlights transact in fours and sixes; what they won't show you is the compact, impassable certainty of the Crowe defence. Rare were the circumstances that allowed Martin to bat with true abandon. Often he was husbanding an innings or leading a regrouping. He would be behind the ball and in a position to defend so early that it was almost as emphatic a statement as striking a boundary. His theory — and he had many theories, logically reasoned — was that getting in line opened up the leg side, where there were always fewer fielders.

Whatever the case, the period of his long peak coincided with an unprecedented depth in fast bowling round the world: Wasim Akram and Waqar Younis, Malcolm Marshall, Joel Garner, Courtney Walsh and Curtly Ambrose, Kapil Dev and Allan Donald, to name but a few. The capacity to outlast counted for more than the yen to outhit. He played spin from the crease, with defensive hands as soft as down. Roebuck once wrote that had Viv Richards chosen simply to block, nobody would ever have got him out; you had a similar feeling when Martin got in his groove, shoulders perfectly aligned, bat coming through like a plumb bob, so absolute was his control.

Thirty years ago at the Gabba, Richard Hadlee led New Zealand to victory by bundling Australia out twice in short order on a sporting pitch. On the same surface, Martin batted eight hours against an attack led by Geoff Lawson and Craig McDermott for 188. I can see him now — tight, upright, playing pedantically in the V, the sleeves buttoned to the wrists, the distinctive white headband beneath the distinctive white helmet, as understated and soaringly magnificent as a Doric column. Martin's one little touch of flamboyance was his penchant for the hook, which he played fearlessly, despite eschewing a face guard on his helmet. In Christchurch a few months after Brisbane, he retired, bloodied and groggy, after a blow to the jaw from Bruce Reid: he returned in a fine fury, his 137 laced with 21 boundaries.

Other injuries were harder to surmount. The back. The knees. Touring Sri Lanka in 1984 and distracted by the pain from a broken thumb, he ate two mussels off a plate, and contracted salmonella that lasted on and off for four years. Three years later, he was struck down with glandular fever. When the lymphoma that finally overwhelmed him was diagnosed in October 2012, he determined to live until he died. Resolving to tell his story again, he unconventionally asked his unauthorised biographer Romanos to help.

The result was *Raw*, an unflinchingly honest self-appraisal, which is what caused me to contact him in the first place, not something I would normally do, but which the book seemed to demand. Martin proved to be an astonishingly assiduous correspondent, hugely motivated to become a better writer, always wanting to know what you thought of his work, endlessly encouraging of your own. Physically confined by ill-health, he had time for philosophical discussion and personal reflection. With Martin there was no such thing as a trivial contact. Perhaps because it was his own aim, he made you want to be your best self.

Martin's love of cricket was fathomless: so passionate he needed to break from it from time to time; so profound he always found his way back to the fold. His great theme in the last while was anger and ill-feeling on the cricket field. The world was so full of it; why could cricket not provide some sort of refuge, a better example? In the last messages we exchanged, he was playful, funny, happily watching the game, even though his physical presence was entering the past tense. That invincible spirit endures.

# Bishan Bedi
# EXCLAMATIONS APLENTY
## JANUARY 2012

Every now and again, I swap emails with Bishan Bedi, whom I met some years ago in England, and who of all cricketers whose paths I have crossed is perhaps the most spontaneously effusive and joyful.

Bishan is enjoying this series. He applauds good cricket whomever is playing it, and he loves Test cricket, which he regards as everyone's mission to preserve. 'I hope U r doing yur bit to keep the game alive — Tests I mean!' read a recent email sign off: which was actually quite understated from Bishan, who seldom uses one exclamation mark where two are permissible.

'The most Indian of Indian cricketers and the most international' says Suresh Menon in a splendid new biography published by Penguin entitled *Bishan: Portrait of a Cricketer* — and it was ever thus. When England's Dennis Amiss was struggling against spin in India back in the 1970s, Bishan famously consented to bowl to him in the nets, and coached him back into form. When the Australians played their 2008 Tests in India, Bedi was invited to talk slow bowling with Jason Krejza, who went out and took twelve wickets on debut.

But how it grieved Indian Bishan, rather than international Bishan, when his countrymen went into their recent Test in Perth without a spinner. Virender Sehwag bowled the only spin, seven overs of off-roll, and India's slow-motion over rate, 76 overs in 362 minutes, has cost them their captain for the final Test.

When Bishan captained India in Perth thirty-four years ago, they picked three spinners, and Bishan himself took twelve wickets at a time when the pitch was at the zenith of its reputation as the fastest and bounciest in the world. No other left-arm spinner has improved on his 31 wickets in an Australian series.

Watching Bishan that summer was a part of my cricket education for which I will be ever grateful. Children of the 1970s were born into a world of pace; from the reverent distance maintained by ABC television cameras, slow bowlers looked rather soft and floaty by comparison. That is, until I saw Bishan during the Melbourne Test.

My friends and I were sat square of the wicket, so that it was possible to discern the arcs of the Indian spinners. It was Bhagwat Chadrashekar who took the figures, the terrific whiz of his arms seeming to whirl him off his feet. But ah, Bishan: every ball the same, every ball different; some that hovered, some that dropped, some delivered with a tiny pant of extra effort, some held back so long that it was hard to believe they would make it to the other end. So *that* was what slow bowling was all about.

It was especially cunning for being so beautiful. Menon writes feelingly of a personal affinity for his subject's bowling, describing how he was once bed-ridden in intensive care following surgery and incapable of reading or watching television. He could think of nothing lovelier than Bishan's trajectory — soothing, exciting, weightless, various. 'The rainbow makes a beautiful arc, but it is predictable,' Menon says.

All of it, too, came wrapped in this marvellously exotic package: the colourful patkas, the love handles, the action so easy yet so inimitable. Bishan was naturally robust. Playing marbles as a boy had strengthened his fingers; wringing his clothes dry after washing them from a young age had hardened up his wrists and forearms. But he never seemed to expend an ounce of effort. There is an exquisite photo of him taken at Lord's by Patrick Eagar in 1974: about to enter his delivery stride and connected to the ground by just the outside of the toe of his left boot, he appears to be not so much bowling as levitating.

About the scandalous falling off in Indian cricket evident this summer, Bishan is disappointed rather than surprised. For years he has been something of a lone voice in deploring the carpet baggers and parish pump politicians who run Indian cricket, excluding himself from the rich pickings available to ex-players prepared to cosy up to the regime. 'All his deception he kept for his bowling; outside the cricket field he is neither deceptive nor tricky,' writes Menon in *Bishan*. 'He never bowled defensively, so he didn't see why he should talk defensively either.'

Nor is this a new grudge. Menon proves Bishan and the Board of Control for Cricket in India to be old antagonists. Australian cricketers of the 1970s who complained of administrative high-handedness and parsimony had nothing on their Indian counterparts, and Bishan as captain was every bit as much the shop steward as Ian Chappell.

Rather than lodge Bishan's team in a proper hotel for a Nagpur Test, for example, the BCCI once put them in an MLA Hostel in which only captain and manager had running water. So fiercely did Bishan excoriate the local association representative that he was charged with insubordination, and summonsed to appear before a five-member disciplinary committee — sitting, by the way, in a five-star hotel in Bombay.

After his reprimand, Bishan learned that the BCCI had failed to book him return tickets to Chandigarh where he was due to play a Duleep Trophy match. There being no seats left on the train, the captain of India bunked in a luggage rack for the 1400km journey to Delhi, then took a bus for the last 250km.

Bishan, nonetheless, was too much the traditionalist to be tempted by Kerry Packer's inducements, and it was thanks to his influence that India alone did not provide a player for World Series Cricket. A Packer emissary who visited Bishan in Pakistan pushed a cheque book aggressively across a table: he could name his price. Bishan pushed it back: he would have nobody put a price tag on him. Next week many of the world's top cricketers will queue for just this privilege in the Indian Premier League auction. A curious business, Bishan thinks.

Today Bishan runs a charitable foundation and a cricket school on Delhi's outskirts that has produced a dozen Test cricketers and fifty first-class players. It features twenty-five turf wickets and a kennel for his dogs. His enthusiasm remains boundless. 'First enjoy!' he says. 'Technique can follow!' You will win and lose, he believes, but you must always love the game. 'Have a good New Year Gideon & Godbless now & ever!!' he signed off in his last mail. God bless you too, Bishan.

# Bishan Bedi
# DINNER IN DELHI
SEPTEMBER 2014

As I described in a column not so long ago, I met Bishan Bedi in England just over five years ago, and at once was his friend — and I suspect am hardly unique in this, given his enormous natural warmth. Catching up with him was therefore a date to which I looked strongly forward. We chose the Delhi Golf Club, a storied 220-acre oasis in India's capital. Bishan is no less an institution — as evinced by the steady stream of fellow patrons coming to our table to pay respects during the evening. He is getting about on a walking stick these days. But mentally...well, he's uncompromisingly modern. 'Gideon, are you on The Twitter?' he asked at one point: 25,000 follow the peppery views that abound @BishanBedi.

Indeed, it's almost as though Bishan's still playing. It might have been forty years ago, for example, but he recalled bowling to Barry Richards for the first time as though it were yesterday. Richards was then at his Himalayan peak; Bishan's Northants teammates, he recalled, built the encounter up to such a degree that he experienced a rare degree of apprehension, even nervousness. His plan became to wrong foot the batsman with close fielders: a slip, silly point, short mid wicket, leg slip. It got an immediate reaction. 'This will be interesting,' Richards said to the Northants keeper George Sharp. The South African came down the wicket to Bishan's first four deliveries and smashed them to the boundary. On the fifth, a little slower, a little shorter, he also advanced, but was beaten and stumped. 'Batsmen have egos, Gideon,' said Bishan. 'Egos!' Even Sachin? Even Sachin. On one Australian tour of India, he tried explaining this to

Shane Warne: 'I told Shane that he had to make Tendulkar think. That there is nothing you can do about a straight six. You cannot set a field for it. You can only applaud.' But Warne, he sensed, was already somewhat in dread of Tendulkar, and loath to throw down any gauntlet that might be picked up.

Bishan recalled everything from the first remark his future Australian wife addressed to him when they met on the 1967-68 tour ('Do you take the turban off when you make love?') to the business of touring with Bhagwat Chandrasekhar ('I shared a room with him on so many tours. But, do you know, I never saw him with his shirt off'). His chief heroes were Tiger Pataudi ('The best captain I ever played for'), under whose leadership he took 84 wickets for 25 in 22 Tests, and Sir Donald Bradman, with whom he had an extensive correspondence ('I will keep his letters forever'). One exchange he particularly cherished. Before leaving Australia in 1977-78, Bishan wrote to the Don soliciting an article for his benefit brochure. Bradman's reply reached him in Pakistan, agreeing on one condition. There were rumours that Bishan had signed with Kerry Packer: if this was true, said Bradman, there could be no piece. When Bishan hastily assured him otherwise, the contribution was forthcoming.

Such was the torrent of stories that I kept my driver out half an hour longer than arranged. As we emerged from the bar, however, said driver recognised Bishan, leapt from the car and rushed to genuflect before him — a spontaneous and rather beautiful tribute. 'Sorry I kept you waiting, Naveen,' I said as we then drove away. 'Sir!' he said with deep seriousness. 'It was *Bishan Bedi*!'

# The Gilchrists
# FOR LOVE ALONE
## JANUARY 2017

During Adam Gilchrist's farewell Test match nine years ago, Daryl Harper offered some friendly parting advice: "Thank your parents for bringing you up the way they did." The umpire probably had in mind Gilchrist's sunny disposition and exemplary courtesy, yet the remark was perhaps truer than Harper knew. In Goonellabah, a suburb of Lismore, you can still see exactly where Australia's finest keeper-batsman was brought up, and his 75-year-old father Stan is happy to explain how.

On the family's arrival in 1984, the backyard of the quarter-acre block, looking out over a peaceful valley, had three terraces, centred on a tall camphor laurel tree. The top terrace was selected as the site for a pitch, contoured with pick and shovel by workmates, family and friends, concreted with barrows from the street, covered by a half-pitch length of artificial turf and screened off with 40m of netting secured by tent poles. The tree, happily, survived: as Stan explains, it "saved a few lost balls".

That's just the setting, of course. The true tale lies in the care, the thought, and the love, of family and of cricket — a reminder that, for all the tens of millions now allotted to professional preparation, still the most significant and formative cricket coaching in Australia is done by fathers.

The story starts in Stan's childhood. The son of a rabbit trapper on the western plains of NSW and Queensland, he lived with his family in a tent for his first 10 years, regulated by the weekly arrival of the freezer truck from Dirranbandi to collect the carcasses.

Stan was introduced to cricket one day when his father Bill, clad in white shorts, shirt and boots rather than his usual khakis, drove the family Ford for what seemed like hours to a clay pan where a cricket game was to take place on a coir matting pitch: blood flowed when Bill hit the opposition's opener in the face with a bouncer.

When the family finally settled near Inverell, one of Bill's first steps was to lay a cricket pitch enclosed in chicken wire, although Stan's tutelage would be largely from cricket books by the likes of Denis Compton and Peter May, and above all by Donald Bradman, whose *The Art of Cricket* (1958) he filled with underscores and annotations.

Stan was a leg-spinner, good enough to play first grade for Paddington, then for newly minted Sutherland, to take 17 wickets at 21 on a tour of Malaysia and Singapore with the fabled Emus in July 1959, and to dismiss Springboks Graeme Pollock and Colin Bland when he represented Australian Universities in December 1963.

He was handicapped, he suspects, by a tendency to introspection: "One of my great faults, probably why I didn't go further, was that I overanalysed myself. I was very serious, probably too serious." Certainly, his conviction was that other pleasures took second place to the game: Stan's first 'date' with his future wife, Maroubra girl June, was an invitation for her to watch him play cricket.

After they married in January 1964, Stan's career as a science teacher took them to Cabramatta and Heathcote, then Dorrigo in the Northern Tablelands, where their brood swelled to four: Jacki (born 1966), Dean (1967), Glenn (1970) and finally Adam (1971). Relocation soon after to Junee blessed them with the first of several sizeable backyards for the children to exhaust themselves in.

Stan never stopped playing cricket, undertaking a 100km weekend commute to Wagga Wagga to represent Lake Albert CC, where he played alongside Chris Rogers' uncle Derek and the rangy teenaged Geoff Lawson, then, when the family moved again to Deniliquin at the end of 1978, joining West CC.

By then his children's sport was pushing him ever more concertedly into coaching roles. He obtained Level 1 and 2 certificates in cricket, and something less formal but equally challenging in soccer. "I became a soccer coach when Dean asked if he could play in the under-10s one week," Stan recalls. "I said, 'What's the deal?' He said, 'We just have to be at the post office at 10am on Saturday'. So I drove down there in the Kombi, opened the door and 10 kids got in." Elected unanimously.

Dean was a talented and determined cricketer, destined to represent NSW at under-16 level, and to compile first-grade centuries. In hindsight, however, Stan faults himself for overemphasising technical excellence.

"Dean became a victim of my idea that you must groove skills," he says. "With Dean in his formative times I was on about him playing a perfect backward defence and a perfect cover drive, head over the ball, on and on with all the hackneyed same-old, same-old. Unconsciously, I may have been creating a barrier to his progress.

"Dean has a personality like mine — very serious, very controlled, very designed for everything to work properly. He was too analytical, worried like crazy about failure, dwelled wonderfully on his successes. Changing a person's personality isn't possible. But if I was starting again with Dean, I'd approach things very differently. Players need a point of difference, and Dean was perfectly 'in the mould'."

In Deniliquin, Stan thought that Glenn, blessed with natural athleticism and uncanny ball skills, would be the prodigy. But his commitment was as wavering as Jacki's was acute: she became West's first female player, if mainly to prove that there was nothing the boys did that she couldn't.

That left Adam, who conforms to a theory posited by English journalist Scyld Berry that it is younger siblings who come to the fore in cricket, enjoying the benefit of measuring themselves against their elders. He had by now discovered wicketkeeping, gloves acquired from Super Kmart in Shepparton, and come by a bat, a polyarmoured Slazenger inherited from Dean. He also led his Deniliquin South Public School to victory in the Taber Shield, a statewide primary school competition, just before the Education Department moved Stan, now a school inspector, to Lismore.

Stan recalls: "When we got to Lismore, Glenn said, 'I'm going to do athletics. There are more girls there'. He won a national long jump title, played for Wollongong Wolves in the National Soccer League, and having done that didn't want to train so hard. He preferred concentrating on his studies." Adam, by contrast, could think of nothing but cricket. And Stan, having read about leadership as a preparation for his inspectorate, had rethought some of his old coaching nostrums: bringing Adam up would be about establishing and nurturing that "point of difference". Their sons, the Gilchrists had come to believe, were variations on their parents: Dean was a chip from Stan's introverted block; Glenn was more like free-spirited June; Adam, with elements of both, craved both a strong framework and room to express himself.

So Stan began to dream up exercises. Adam, for example, was a natural right-hander in everything but batting. Stan consolidated that top-hand strength with a "speed ball" drill that involved Adam hitting 50 balls in a row, one rapidly after the other, with top hand only: first using a bat and cricket balls, then using a cut-down half-bat and cricket balls, and lastly using an old stump and golf balls. There was also, at the end of each session, a time when Stan told Adam: "Just hit it". Adam was exhilarated by the combination of delayed gratification and complete freedom.

Stan gestures to two pictures on the wall of his study: Dean, in whites in the nets, executing a perfect off-drive, fit to be sculpted; Adam, in his colourful one-day motley, picking a ball up off his legs, as close to motion as a still image can capture. It reflects their father's own coaching journey.

For Stan became as much an improviser as his youngest son. The backyard net was an alternative to the journey to Goonellabah Primary School or laying waste the immaculate lawn of their Deniliquin greenkeeper neighbour Ray Jeffries. Exercise routines involving weights improvised with water-filled oil bottles, ropes and broom handles for the forearms and keeping drills with his upper legs horizontal to build the haunches were alternatives to a gymnasium. There was no treatise to follow; just a boy who could not get enough cricket.

Family ties, of course, can constrict as well as bind. Stan became regional director of coaching for Northern NSW which, although the role was honorary, offered him nominal influence over Adam's progress through cricket's levels. As a result, he scrupulously avoided conflicts. Had Adam to be advised of a youth fixture or championships, Stan would write him a formal letter, as he did for every boy. He stood back from all selection roles, and remains nettled by the only occasion he was accused of nepotism. "Only one other person ever suggested that my kids were getting on because of my involvement, and he was a bit of a scatterbrain, but that hurts every time I think of it," he says.

At games, Stan would stand scrupulously to one side, and communicate any advice anonymously through the appointed coach. And he took care that his one-to-one instruction remained at Adam's volition, to which Adam pays tribute in his autobiography: "It wasn't Dad pushing me, it was me pushing him." Yet even this may miss a step, for Adam also notes how he pushed Stan to push him: "I don't know if even the Australian team was training as systematically as we were in the mid-1980s."

In some ways it anticipates the catchy rubric Cricket Australia for many years applied to its strategic plans, From Backyard to Baggy Green, for it is hard to imagine any family working so strenuously to shorten the relevant distance. The seminal decision came when 17-year-old Adam, school captain at Kadina High, was offered a Big Brother scholarship, endowed by John Swire & Co, to play cricket in England's summer. Because cricket had impinged on Dean's last year at school, June was resistant to the idea, while Stan as an educationalist was at least a little conflicted. A compromise was reached: Adam could go, providing he attended to his studies by correspondence. Stan recalls: "I said to Adam, 'This is going to be your university. And if it doesn't work out, then we'll do something else'." It's unlikely Adam derived as much from his studies as he did from playing 77 games for Richmond CC in 149 days, but he married the tasks successfully, and returned matured; a part-time scholarship at the AIS Cricket Academy under Rod Marsh followed the next year.

It was now merely a matter of time before Adam became a fully fledged cricketer, and Stan was there when it happened. Adam was helping his father run a coaching clinic for juniors at Lismore's Woodlawn College in January 1993 when NSW selector Steve Bernard rang to advise of his Sheffield Shield baptism.

Some attributes of Adam Gilchrist evidently run a little deeper. He would become famous, for example, for balancing flamboyance and fair play. Yet when I ask Stan if he ever offered his youngest son explicit moral tuition, he demurs: "walking" was all Adam's own work. Well, almost all. Because the funny thing is that Stan *was* a walker, while never discussing it with his son. "Yes, I walked," he says. "Although even now I'm not sure that Adam has ever been aware of that. It's like working in a gym, isn't it? If you ease off, you're only cheating yourself. If you nick a ball and you're given not out, you've got to feel guilty." Pause and smile. "Except if you're KP, maybe. Then it's a God-given right."

In Stan's reckoning, it is cricket that offers the moral instruction, whether or not the player chooses to absorb it. "The nature of the game is that it exposes you, those you play with and against," he says. "Adam has very close friendships with other international players, and an incredible bond with those who played in that long run of Australian victories — they're closer than brothers. To me, cricket offers leadership, followership, development, improvisation, tradition and heritage."

This reflects, perhaps, a deeper sharing, that has kept the Gilchrists close, while leaving each member free to live their own lives. Stan and June, herself a teacher of disabled children, have never lived vicariously: they have busied themselves with extensive community work, for which Stan was recognised with a Medal of the Order of Australia in January 2015.

This decade, Stan has launched and built up Australia's busiest branch of the Lord's Taverners, the venerable cricket-based charity which provides funding and other opportunities to disadvantaged youth. The Northern NSW branch has six times as many members as the NSW branch, based in Sydney; last year Stan became national executive officer in an attempt to draw the Taverners' far-flung branches closer together.

Adam is the organisation's patron, personally funding one of its initiatives: a scholarship for a young cricketer to play an English season patterned on the one from which he benefited in 1989. Daryl Harper may have had the half of it those years ago, with the other half contained in a reference Rod Marsh wrote for Gilchrist after his stint at the Cricket Academy: 'He is the type of lad you would be proud to have as a son.'

# James Hopes
# OLD FAITHFUL
## MARCH 2016

*Cricinfo* has not updated James Hopes' player profile for five and a half years, more or less the point at which his international career ended. Since then he has kept on keeping on, averaged 34 with the bat and 23 with the ball for Queensland: day-in, day-out, the most consistent all-round cricket in Australia, seldom leaving a game having not made some impact with his enterprising strokes and pawky medium-pace. Now Queensland will have to do without him. It will be like replacing two cricketers.

There were no cheering masses for his farewell at the Gabba yesterday — it was a standard Sheffield Shield day, and a disappointing one too, for Queensland were exiting. But there was an honour guard of cricketers composed of teammates and West Australian opponents, applauding Hopes and fellow valedictee Michael Hogan — a nice glimpse of the camaraderie among interstate cricketers. There was also Hopes' wife, now relieved of ministering to his various aches and pains. 'When I turned up this morning after bowling 20 overs the day before, I could barely walk,' Hopes said candidly.

Today Hopes seems to belong to a different cricket era. His father was a bank manager. Early on he worked a second job in a childcare centre to stretch his meagre cricket income. But he was always fun to watch. Turn on the livestream of any Queensland game in the Sheffield Shield any time in the last few years and it always seemed to be Hopes walking back to his mark, sweat-soaked duds clinging to his flanks, then trundling up into the breeze, nagging away against whatever brassy youngster was making his way at the other end. In those last six seasons he was never mentioned in connection with higher honours. What was missing? A touch of class? A bit of zip? In part he just seemed on the wrong side of fashion, in a game hung up on X-factors and athleticism, with his plumber's physique and that stubbornly unchanging hair-do, like he'd just stepped from the shower. Asked to sum his career up yesterday, he said succinctly: 'I had to train my ring off.'

Nominally Hopes has a readymade successor in the promising Jack Wildermuth, who bowls at a clip and already has a first-class hundred to his credit. But more than a sum of abilities is lost when a player such as Hopes calls it a day — it is their experience, their example, their capacity for knitting a dressing room, their connection to an inspiriting heritage, which is not measured in figures, and eludes the pen pics. It is not just Queensland that is poorer for his departing but Australia, even if onlookers may not notice.

# Shane Watson
# OLDER AND WISER

OCTOBER 2016

Shane Watson thinks he's probably as happy as he has ever been. It's partly because, towards the close of his international career, there were phases he was as unhappy as he'd ever felt.

Things happened so fast. There was the tragedy of Phillip Hughes, and the emotional stress of the subsequent Border-Gavaskar Trophy. Losing his place then bouncing back in Australia's World Cup triumph. Losing his place then not bouncing back in Australia's Ashes. Test cricket seemed almost to give him up before he did it.

And the harder he tried, the worse things grew. 'I just kept digging and digging,' Watson says. 'No matter what I was trying, I got deeper and deeper. And it comes to the point where you say: "I know what I've got deep down inside of me. I've shown it before. But I can't do it any more." '

Watson sought not to consume media about himself, but it was almost like he could feel what was being said — a clinician might have called it hypervigilance. 'In theory if your mind's where it needs to be all the other things should bounce off you,' he observes, then laughs. 'The theory's not always the reality.'

The experience caused Watson, who has spent three years on the executive of the Australian Cricketers' Association, to reflect very deeply. He feels he is strengthened for having bounced from that bottom, but laughs again when asked how easy it is to seek help in a masculine environment privileging toughness and aggression, and a sports structure unsentimentally professional.

'That's a very good question,' says Watson. 'Because it was something, towards the back end of my career...well I knew I couldn't do it. Or I didn't feel comfortable doing it. Because you say: "You know, I'm really struggling here." And the reply is: "Well, we feel for you, but you're out. You're gone. We'll find someone who doesn't feel that way." '

Few players felt so strongly the vacuum in the Australian team left by the retirement of Ricky Ponting — and Watson wonders if it has been, or even can be, filled. 'Ricky's just a good human being,' he says. 'There were a number of times in my career where I sat down and chatted to him about important things. But when leaders change, environments change. The best environment is where a player can say those things and not feel judged, where they feel supported. But the system today is about creating good cricketers not good human beings. The good human beings get in by chance.'

Maybe the system can't work that way any more. 'I believe it needs to,' Watson says. 'Because that's the way you get the best from people. It's them feeling like they can be open rather than having to put up a brave face all the time. You shouldn't have to hit rock bottom before you start working your way back up.'

His Australian career did not end so badly. In contrast to almost all his teammates, Watson had an excellent World T20. 'It was just a celebration,' he recalls. 'Everything came together at the right time.' Did he feel like he was going too soon? 'No,' he answers quickly. 'I cherished every moment I played for Australia. But there were also things I knew I was not going to miss. One is the relentless schedule, because there are points where you go: "I just don't think I've got it in me to keep going." And the scrutiny. Compared to playing for Australia, playing for different T20 franchises is pretty relaxing. Sometimes I miss international cricket. But I'm not envious.'

Nor should he be: in demand wherever there is domestic T20 to be played, unencumbered by the need for No Objection Certificates, he enjoys an enviable lifestyle. But after some long conversations with Mike Hussey while they represented the St Lucia Zouks in the Caribbean Premier League in July, the pair decided to chart a fresh course.

The mentoring business they are establishing is based on simple reasoning: that players receive a lot of advice about their techniques from coaches, and about their careers from agents, but little impartial counsel about how to deal with the new cricket world's extreme highs and lows.

Watson has ample experience of extremes. He began his own career with all good intentions of leading a 'balanced life', commencing courses in business and human movement at Queensland University of Technology, continuing them by correspondence when he was recruited by Tasmania. But as international cricket beckoned, something had to give, and that was study.

'It was good in the sense that I knew I left no stone unturned in pursuing my goal,' says Watson. 'I look back and know now I did everything I could to get the best out of myself. I was obsessed with it. But it meant that I rode the highs and lows, more so the lows, than someone for whom cricket wasn't the be-all and end-all.'

When injury struck Watson, as it did all too often, the isolation could be desolating: 'You're in the thick of it one minute, then you're gone. No one contacts you. In fact, I understand now that it's just they're so busy in the present it's hard to think about anything else. But at the time it seems like they don't care. The train rolls on, you're left in the dust.'

Watson worries now that the train is running express. 'It's got that there's just no off-season for players,' he observes. 'That Australia A series felt like it went for three months. There'll be a few guys who go into the Sheffield Shield...well, pretty cooked.

'When I started, the A series were infrequent and not so long. It was just about getting a bit of cricket into you, with the priority being to be fresh for the domestic season.

'I understand the theory behind giving players opportunities and helping them grow. But sometimes the best way is to let them get away, to give them the chance to work on things they want without being in game mode all the time.'

Watson faults an attitude that professional athletes need to be doing something every day, which he believes is partly an outcome of increased remuneration: 'The hierarchy see the players being paid more and think: "Well, we need to get our money's worth. We can't give you time off." That's even with Test matches. Somehow there always needs to be three days training leading up to every match, even when players have been playing non-stop for twelve months. That's just practice for the sake of it, not because it's making you better. You need time off even in a training block, to mentally refresh if not physically.'

Is it also about the huge retinue of support staff needing to be seen to contribute? 'Job justification,' Watson laughs. 'I've said that a lot over the last few years!'

This perspective is integral to Watson's critique of the relationship between international and franchise cricket.

Watson likes T20. Playing it continuously, moreover, has enhanced his abilities: 'I'm a better player because I'm non-stop in the one format, and using certain skills in constantly different situations. My bowling is better than ever, and even the things I've been exposed to mentally over the last 12-18 months have helped. So I'm still learning and evolving.'

But Watson was above all passionate about Test cricket: 'It was always the priority. That was the way I was brought up.' He would love to have excelled in it, accepts that he didn't quite, is consoled by the knowledge that he did his best, and now worries that players' priorities are shifting.

Batsmen and bowlers, Watson believes, will see it a bit differently. He mentions a talented young batsman entering Australian calculations: 'He will push as long as he can, I'm sure, because he has that burning desire to have a crack at Test cricket. But if he doesn't make it by, say, his late 20s, early 30s, there'll be a point where he goes: "Well, maybe I'll just become a shorter form cricketer." Especially if the English league gets up and running, it's going to get more lucrative.

'The bowling will shift sooner, because of the physical demands of bowling fast which you see in Pat Cummins and James Pattinson. Guys will say: "Why should I push my body to the limit, bowl 30 overs in a day, when I could bowl four overs, fast, and have fewer injuries.

'At some stage in the next three or four years, I believe there will be one or two higher profile players who elect not to push the Test cricket dream...I think it's inevitable. They'll be a pioneer, but once one or two do it it'll open the floodgates.'

It won't, Watson says, only be about the money. Players aren't that simple. 'After the Argus Review, Cricket Australia brought in all these [financial] incentives like what happens in the corporate world,' he remembers. 'That did not succeed at all. People didn't try harder to win because of the possibility of extra money. It didn't motivate them. You're playing for your country. Nobody says: "Gee, I'll get another $100,000 if we win this game, I'm going to try harder." Within a year that sort of died down. I think the hierarchy realised it made no difference.'

Even now, Watson thinks only a minority of cricketers are materially motivated, and of these there have been 'some in every generation.' This may be the fond projection of a young man lucky enough to have few financial worries, but Watson's experience of the Zouks, the Rajasthan Royals and Royal

Challengers Bangalore in the Indian Premier League, Islamabad United in the Pakistan Super League and the Sydney Thunder in the Big Bash League convince him that factors of the future will be enjoyment and empowerment.

'What excites me now is going into a really good team environment,' says Watson. 'Getting to know people I might only have played against or never met. Sure, for some guys it is all about getting the highest bid. But others want to go somewhere that will help them get the best out of themselves.

'Younger guys at the Thunder last year with opportunities to go elsewhere were prepared to forgo more money or a higher profile team because they liked what we were doing.' Because it's easier to influence the culture of, say, the Melbourne Renegades than the Victorian Sheffield Shield team? 'Exactly.'

How about influencing the culture of the Australian team? It contains many forceful characters. Unfortunately, none of them are players. When some are saying that clouds hover over as many as six members of the Test side, the environment is hardly conducive to organic change. And just because Shane Watson's experience is that challenges are survivable does not make them much easier to face.

# Steve Cazzulino
# THE LONG GOODBYE
## OCTOBER 2016

For Australian cricketers, October is a month like no other. For most it is about returning to the game after the lull of winter; for some it is when the reality of their decision to give it away sets in.

Left-handed opening batsman Steve Cazzulino grew up an elite cricketer. He played thirteen first-class matches: fewer than 1000 men in Australian history have played more than a dozen. Yet the elite of that elite proved too difficult to crack.

In the off-season, in his thirtieth year and without a state contract, two years having elapsed since his last Sheffield Shield appearance, Cazzulino decided he could stave the future off no longer. He retired from all cricket to concentrate on a coffee business he runs with erstwhile teammate Ed Cowan, and to complete long-delayed university studies.

'There's a great group of 21-22 year-olds coming through at St George,' Cazzulino jokes. 'But there's only so many shagging stories you can listen to before you start wondering what other 30-year-old guys are doing with their lives.'

Tripod Coffee — disclaimer alert: writer is a heavy consumer — has been both a stimulating experience and a bit of a godsend. In the job market, Cazzulino observes, others have a significant head start: 'Cricket has enriched my life in many ways, been a great teacher of life lessons. But when you are up against guys of my age who've ten years' greater work experience, it can almost be a hindrance that you've dedicated so much of your life to it.'

Cazzulino is such a bright and personable young man with such a healthy perspective on the game that it comes as a slight surprise when he describes times he struggled with it. This is actually the second time he has quit. A prolific junior who played under-17s and under-19s for New South Wales, he abandoned cricket at nineteen after wintering with a club in Scotland.

'It was a great life experience, but the back-to-back seasons took their toll when I returned,' he recalls. 'On Monday I'd go to work and train; Tuesday I'd have a day off; Wednesday and Thursday and Friday I'd work and train; Saturday I'd nick off in the second over, be down on myself the rest of the weekend, which would carry on into Monday, into Tuesday, and start again.

'It was this excrutiating merry-go-round where so much of my happiness was dictated by whether I was making runs. I got into this vicious habit of looking at the paper on Mondays and seeing Phil Hughes and Uzi Khawaja plundering 100s and just thinking: what on earth am I doing this for?'

Cazzulino worked, none too happily, as an estate agent for eighteen months, before resuming cricket, peaking in 2009-10 with 1289 runs at 71 in Sydney first-grade. Relocating to Tasmania in a successful search for first-class opportunities, he suddenly had status, direction, money...for as long as he was playing, anyway.

'As a 23-25-year-old, taking home $80,000 a year, you're doing better than contemporaries,' Cazzulino observes. 'But where a contemporary's income is on an upward trajectory, mine was either going to grow exponentially or stop. So where property was concerned, I was never prepared to take a leap of faith. I was always wary of being delisted and not having the income to support a loan.'

Family values stood him in good stead: 'It can lull you into a false sense of security. I remember one month where there were two Shield games and a 2nd XI game, and I got my pay cheque and my gross was $16,000. I thought: "I've made it, this is what it's like!"

'It would have been very easy to go out and have a good time with that. Fortunately, as the son of Italian migrants who came here with nothing, I always had my dad's voice in the back of my mind saying: 'Save up''. A few other guys in the squad took a rather more cavalier attitude.'

Yet while Cazzulino followed the sensible route of undertaking a marketing degree, he felt conflicted about it: 'I always wondered if going to uni was detracting from my performances, or my recovery — whether I shouldn't have been hitting more balls at that point.' He saw others, heads down, talented, focused — who still weren't getting a go. And he worried.

Is it difficult to be a rounded person at cricket? 'Absolutely,' says Cazzulino. 'I think you either need to be incredibly smart or incredibly thick-skinned. I was neither. The reason Ed [Cowan] has succeeded is because he is able to learn from his mistakes; the reason James Faulkner has succeeded is because it's almost like his mistakes didn't happen.' Otherwise, he says, setbacks have a way of reverberating: 'Usually getting dropped in first-class cricket is the first time it's happened to you. Some guys even manage to defer the experience until they play Test cricket. But it's a whole new dimension of the game for which you are unprepared.'

Cazzulino speaks from experience. Having averaged 35 for Tasmania in 2011-12 and batted most of the first day of the Shield final, he suddenly lost preferment, and felt 'the lowest I've been in my life.' Worse, Cazzulino felt he had almost nobody to turn to: 'If you're struggling, you might ask a senior guy what you're doing wrong. But when it's moving away from a form slump into a minor form of depression, it's something that, realistically, is very hard to get advice on. And it's a bit of a taboo to seek it.

'I remember one day saying to a respected coach: "I don't know what's happening. I'm miserable. All day and every day." He said: "Well, that's 'cos you're not scoring runs." And he drew this ridiculous parallel. He said: "Imagine if you were a lawyer and losing case after case. That would be bound to affect you." I look back and I think: "What was I doing listening to that?" But you're in this tight little bubble and it's very difficult to break out.'

After delisting by the Tigers, Cazzulino returned to Sydney two years ago and his beloved St George, but then went nineteen innings without passing 45 — a waking nightmare that originated, he says now, in a tiny, morbid anxiety. Cazzulino was afraid, he says, not so much of failure as of ignominy. 'It wasn't that I couldn't score a run; it was the fear of getting dropped to second-grade having been a first-class cricketer — although you probably could have put me in fourth grade and I wouldn't have scored a run.'

The harder Cazzulino tried, the worse it got, culminating in a harrowing pair in February 2015. He confronted his fear, and asked to be left out; the club backed him, and were proved right. The rest of the year, he averaged 53: 'I was playing as well as I'd ever played, with freedom, and felt completely on top of my game.' And by now he was looking on, sometimes with an almost anthropological detachment, at what seemed like versions of his younger self.

'There are some blokes you see and it's obvious they're unlikely to progress beyond a certain point and you just want to say: Get out while you still can,' Cazzulino observes. Young men playing sport, working menial jobs, not studying: 'You wonder if they'd be better off focusing their energies on something more productive.'

Cazzulino wonders because he started doing the same about himself. 'Late last year I had a realistic think about where I was headed,' he recalls. 'Ed [Cowan] and Maddo [Nic Maddinson] were opening for NSW. Daniel Hughes and Nick Larkin were averaging over 100 in first-grade. I thought: "Realistically I'm going to struggle from here." I went to Fiji for Christmas, kind of let myself go, and averaged 20 in the back half.'

Now the game is moving on, and so is Cazzulino. Will he miss cricket? 'I'm grateful for everything it's given me,' he says. 'The person I am today is in large part due to the people I've met and the places I've seen through cricket.' But he laughs that he's intrigued: 'Every October I've strapped on the pads and put myself through hell for six months. I'm curious to see how I cope without it.'

# Chris Hartley
# KEEPING IT REAL

OCTOBER 2016

When Chris Hartley was poised to break his state's wicketkeeping record a year ago, Cricket Australia's website adorned its report with a well-chosen image — not a spectacular catch, or a quicksilver stumping, but a glimpse of Hartley poised to accept a return from the outfield, eyes intent on the incoming ball, gloves perfectly positioned, having set himself just ahead of the stumps to make a half-good throw look a little better.

One rarely sees such photos, as one seldom registers such moments, which somehow sums up what 34-year-old Hartley has been bringing to Queensland, and to first-class cricket, for thirteen years: not just the example of utmost professional reliability, but those tiny, unobtrusive excellences that lift a team almost without them noticing.

Not being noticed has also been Hartley's problem. When he leads Queensland at the MCG on Friday, the crowd will be in the hundreds, as has been the way of it his whole career. Many inferior players have represented Australia. But that, says Hartley, is the keeper's lot: 'That's advice I heard very early: "The third best bat is in the Firsts, the third best keeper is in the Thirds." '

It's required Hartley to develop a technique not taught in any coaching manual: that of processing disappointment. Three years ago, for example, Australian chairman of selectors John Inverarity extemporised at a press conference about depth in local keeping ranks, and managed to reel off the name of every state gloveman — except Queensland's.

Hartley's admirers were dismayed, and so, briefly, was he: 'I'd be lying if I said there wasn't part of me that deep down was a bit peeved. I remember reading and thinking: "Gee, can't even get on the list now let alone get in the team." But I also remember turning around pretty quickly and saying: "You can dwell on it, or you can use it as motivation to become better. I'd better concentrate on making sure they do know who I am." '

At the same time, it's caused Hartley to reflect on cricket's cardinal virtues, and how they might be changed by a post-T20 preoccupation with X-factors and game impact. 'The way the game is played, and the way it's being consumed by people as entertainment, I definitely think the concept of consistency is seen as less valuable,' says Hartley.

'It's about players grabbing the game, taking it from the opposition, and if that means you go blob blob blob blob then score a sparkling 100 off 50 balls, then that can take you a long way. It's sometimes as though consistent excellence can hurt you because it becomes an expectation and is taken for granted. As a keeper I'm particularly conscious of that.'

In hindsight, Hartley suspects, it's as well he took the precautions of cultivating a life beyond the game. He was captain of Brisbane Boys College, an outstanding sportsman but also a hard-working scholar. Unsure what he wanted to study at tertiary level, he delayed a decision when he accepted a place at the AIS Cricket Academy, and subsequent played league cricket in England. But in 2002, just before he succeeded his keeping mentor Wade Seccombe at the Bulls, Hartley commenced an undergraduate course in journalism and management at University of Queensland. It took him eight years to finish: 'I got used to being the oldest in most of my classes.' Today, though, he owns and runs a writing and editing services business, Wordsmith Group.

Not only has he enjoyed it, but his cricket has benefited. 'I've always been a strong advocate of having something completely detached from cricket, whether it's study, or a trade,' Hartley says. 'A hundred per cent it's made me a better player and person.

'I'm the kind of person who is completely focused on whatever he's doing at any time, sometimes to my detriment. So if ever I was holding on a bit tight with cricket, if I was just trying too hard, study enabled me to get away to freshen my mind. If cricket's your passion, you're never going to give it up.'

Hartley reasons that cricket is a more forgiving game than when he began. 'Players, when I started, it was life or death,' he says. 'There was a real feeling that if you didn't get it right, it could be the end. You cherished it when you had it, and when things went against you it was more painful.

'It was definitely survival of the fittest. Any sign of weakness was not good for you as a player or an individual. You'd grit your teeth and get on with it. There was probably a lot of talent that got wasted because people didn't understand different personalities.

'I certainly don't want to think players don't value their opportunities today, but the system provides them with so many more, so you don't get as down in the dumps as you did 10 years ago. There's a Big Bash League coming up, an IPL auction I can go in — there are always ways to reinvent yourself.'

Maybe, Hartley feels, cricket's not quite ruthless enough. Eight BBL franchises draw on the resources of six states. All those opportunities can be deluding. 'If I was a kid now, I'd want to have made it in my early 20s,' he says. 'And if I hadn't I'd want the system to spit me out so I could get on with my life. The game provides so many opportunities you can hang around the periphery for a long time, and get through to your 30s without much to fall back on.'

Are the players different as a result? Hartley thinks that individuals are readier to open up about their vulnerabilities — even if they may not be open as they ought. 'Interestingly, this off season through the Australian Cricketers' Association we've done a lot of work with psychologists and people with expertises in mental health and dealing with life challenges,' he says.

'I was talking to one of them after the session and she said: "Gee, you guys are so closed." I laughed and said: "Really? I actually thought the boys were pretty open in there." So we've come a fair way, but there's room for improvement.'

Cricket's small picture, Hartley has always found, has been simpler than life's bigger one. 'On-field stuff isn't difficult,' he says. 'It's easy to sit down next to someone in the dressing room and complain how unfair life is.

'The bigger and harder questions are the ones you sit on longer than you should. Toughest for me has been being away from home, missing milestones, not being able to support my friends and family when they've spent so long supporting me. It's one thing to have a support network that looks after you, but you have to repay the favour, and sometimes I haven't been good enough at that.'

Hartley had unexpectedly more time in the bosom of family and friends recently when Queensland's selectors plumped for Jimmy Peirson, ten years his junior, in the Matador Cup. He was, typically, philosophical: 'Unfortunately, even for someone who has kept themselves very fit, time catches up with the body! So while I didn't officially tell the selectors I was stopping playing one-day cricket, I was fine with the direction they wanted to head in.'

If not one-day cricket, where does his future lie? Hartley's answer is unhesitating: 'I wouldn't want to hang around for the sake of it. But my goal is still to play Test cricket. And I feel like I've got good cricket in me.'

# Nick Buchanan
# BACK FROM THE BRINK

NOVEMBER 2016

Being deemed a 'talented' athlete with 'potential' is seldom an unmixed blessing. Sometimes, Nick Buchanan will tell you, it can almost be curse. For the last five years as a fast bowler in the squads of the Queensland Bulls and the Brisbane Heat he has been unable to move beyond initial rapturous notices.

Standing 198cm, with a 107cm chest and a 90cm waist, 25-year-old Buchanan is built like a Greek god, yet has felt at times like a crash test dummy. On him cricket has inflicted an almost conceivable range of injuries: since suffering stress fractures in the back while he was at school, he has had problems at almost every pivotal point in his anatomy, including multiple hip, groin and ankle operations, reconstructions and rehabilitations. A powerful striker, he once even put his shoulder out hitting a six.

It's made him weirdly expert on his anatomy. During pre-season at Gold Coast Dolphins, for example, Buchanan twinged a groin taking off for a run. The coach asked if he wanted the physiotherapist: 'I said: "There's no need. I know the injury. I know the rehab. I know how long it will take".' At the same time, who is a cricketer when they cannot play cricket? Buchanan has learned the hard way.

As a boy, Buchanan had a privileged view of cricket's possibilities. Father John was Australia's coach for eight years; brother Michael played state cricket; regional coach Vic Williams was a vital mentor; Nick was a member of the Australian under-19 World Cup team in 2010, led by Mitchell Marsh, and including Josh Hazelwood, Adam Zampa, Nic Maddinson and Kane Richardson.

It fixated him on the game. He detoured briefly into rugby, represented Australian Schoolboys and was pursued by the Reds. But Buchanan always preferred cricket, and Test cricket in particular: 'I want to sing the anthem on Boxing Day. That's always been my goal.' He bowled with such pace and menace at state practice that he was recruited by the Queensland Academy of Sport, being described by Matthew Hayden in October 2011 as an 'Australian Freddie Flintoff.'

That season was his most successful at first grade: he managed eight games for University, taking 15 wickets at 13. But after the first two years in the rehab room, the cycle of inactivity and frustration began taking toll: on training days where he was an onlooker, he felt like 'a shadow'.

'It's the loneliest you'll ever feel in a team sport,' says Buchanan. 'You're standing there, and you feel like all eyes are on you. The days your teammates are being belted, you imagine them thinking: "Look at him, he's so precious." You wish they knew how much you'd love to be out there.

'The mind's very powerful and it can make stuff up. Even just walking into the Queensland staff area was hard. The first question I'd be asked was: "How's your body? What is it this time. How many weeks?" Never just: 'G'day, how are you?"'

You wouldn't meet a nicer fellow in a day's march than Nick Buchanan. He's affable, courteous, the epitome of the genial giant. But even that persona proved a kind of burden: 'You didn't want people to know you were struggling, didn't want them to see the weakness in you. I guess when I went to training everyone saw me as this big fella who should be super strong. I smile 24/7. That's just the way I am. But wearing that smile at training, it used to absolutely kill me.'

The worst moments were when he was almost there, such as two days out from a Big Bash League he had been picked for. 'I was bowling as quick as I've ever bowled, just felt amazing, a million dollars. Then just one ball — bang. I said to [physiotherapist] Martin Love: "I think I've done my side." ' He had completely torn the muscle from the ribs: 'The physios say that when I do something, I don't do a half-arsed job.'

Unable to feel fully part of the playing group, Buchanan distanced himself and sought solace in alcohol: 'My friends were out partying Friday and Saturday nights and because I knew I wasn't playing cricket the next days I would join them. It was horrible. I'd wake up Sunday feeling horrendous, battle through training Monday and Tuesday. Thursday I'd be feeling ok, and I might put in a great session on Friday, build the credits. Then it would all start again. I wasn't an alcoholic. I was looking for something to take my mind off things. But the problems didn't vanish.'

If he was ever to have a chance, Buchanan realised he would need to confront his demons. In March 2014, he awoke to another horrendous Sunday, and experienced a wave of fury. 'I felt so angry. I felt like I'd let my younger self down. I thought: "You can either give up cricket, or give it everything possible to become as good as you can be." '

Abstaining from alcohol opened a welcoming side door. He was recruited to act as an ambassador for an anti-binge-drinking charity Hello Sunday Morning; he enjoyed a renewed social cachet, being able to act as a designated driver. He felt great — maybe even a little too great, for fitness became a kind of addiction. And when he suffered the inevitable injury setbacks, he had to face them stone cold sober, which was a new challenge.

Two years ago, Buchanan broke down again. He had had trouble with one hip, due to a congenital malformation; now he broke the other hip, bowling. 'Yeah,' he says, almost as though he can't quite believe it himself. 'I broke my hip...bowling.' Scheduled for another operation, he decided he might as well keep at it until then: dosed with painkillers, he bowled like the wind in a T20 final *with a broken hip*. Worth calling to mind next time you hear that modern fast bowlers are just big softies.

Convalescent again, Buchanan was disconsolate. Ruled out of the BBL, he spent Christmas/New Year with his family on Stradbroke Island: 'I was on the beach with dad and I was saying: "I just can't do it any more." ' Another listless summer passed into winter, and the pressure grew too great.

'I was in such a really horrible place, that I decided was going to run away,' Buchanan recalls. 'I was going to pack a bag, didn't know whether I was going to get in a car or on a flight, but I just had to get away. But I also knew I couldn't, because mum and dad would freak out, so I rang mum. I just felt so embarrassed. It was the lowest of lows. What was so hard was that I knew what I could do. I just kept getting let down, and by then I'd had five years on this merry-go-round.'

Then the merry-go-round, or at least a part of it, stopped: Buchanan lost his state contract. He wasn't bitter. It was almost a relief: 'For five years I'd been paid good money while offering nothing. And as much as nobody blamed me for that, it had really hurt me.'

There were other positives too: 'As a state squad member, you're looked after by the best people, you have the best coaches and the best facilities, and some financial security. Outside the system, though, there's flexibility. I could train the way I wanted to, rather than being constrained and asked about my body — could just go to gym where nobody know who I was or what I'd done.' He had a fine example of a self-directed athlete in his new girlfriend, 28-year-old ironwoman Courtney Hancock, winner of twenty-two individual and team events at the Australian championships, and recently of the Coolongatta Gold.

So clarified was Buchanan, in fact, that he felt able to decline the offer of a two-year contract from Western Australia. 'None of it is about money for me,' he says. 'I'm chasing my dream and I've backed myself. I said to JL [WA coach Justin Langer]: "My goal is to play for Australia. And if I'm not good enough to get out of club cricket and play for Queensland in order to do that, then I'm not good enough anywhere." '

Buchanan felt further affirmed in his choice by the example of Mitchell Johnson, who in his new autobiography describes being cut from the Bulls squad in 2004 as 'the best kick in the teeth I ever had.'

Moving to the Dolphins, he relished his recent pre-season, and before his recent groin injury was in the frame for Queensland's Matador Cup squad. 'It would have been a great challenge to go to Western Australia, and I think JL is a great coach,' he says. 'But I don't need someone to motivate me. I know where I want to get to. I've learned so much about dealing with disappointments.

'I know that when I do get back I'll get dropped, I'll have bad games. But for me, knowing how much cricket I've missed, I'll love it all.' This week he has his eye on selection for a two-day game, another tiny step to putting 'talent' and 'potential' behind him. Wish him luck — he deserves it.

# George Bailey
# LATE BLOOMER
### DECEMBER 2016

George Bailey has cricket in his blood. His great-great-grandfather represented Australia. He and his father are on the lookout for three volumes which will complete their sets of *Wisdens*. Yet five years ago, that lineage looked in danger.

Bailey had accumulated 5000 first-class runs at a creditable average, led Tasmania to a Sheffield Shield and a Ford Ranger Cup. But he was also in his thirtieth year, had neither qualifications in his past nor certainty about his future. If national honours were not a possibility, he had also quietly committed not to lingering in the game for the sake of it.

Five years on, Bailey has represented his country more than 100 times in different cricket formats, leading it in one-day and T20 internationals: with the Test team in disarray, a powerful Sheffield Shield hundred last week could hardly have been more timely. He has appeared, too, for three English counties, three Indian Premier League franchises and two Big Bash League clubs.

Is he surprised? 'Absolutely.' The more so, perhaps, because self-belief has never been his strong suit: 'I've found it very easy to look at someone else and say: "Gee he's a good player." While I can't see that in myself.'

Sometimes it shows. Few Australian batsmen are so handsome in full flight. There have also been phases of tentative introspection. A 'lazy perfectionist' is his half-humorous self-description: 'I like the idea of perfectionism, then I can't be bothered.' But it's also a form of self-regulation, guarding against trying too hard or wanting too much: 'I was first conscious of that in myself when I was young and playing tennis. The tournaments I really wanted to win were the ones in which I never performed.'

To talk to Bailey, in fact, is to be reminded to the trickiness of modern multi-format batting, which can be missed in all the talk of fat bats and flat pitches. Bailey broke into white ball cricket in January 2012 by excelling in red ball cricket. But as he enhanced one set of skills, others deteriorated. In first-class cricket he went from an average of 55 in 2011-12 to an average of 18 in 2012-13.

'That was purely the weight of effort I was putting into white ball cricket, while my first-class games became more sporadic,' Bailey says. He admires those players — Kohli, Warner, de Villiers — who adjust only minimally between formats. He is not, he believes, one of them.

In 2013, Bailey led Australia in a one-day international series in India, making twice as many runs as anyone else, averaging 95, and building a mandate for his selection in the subsequent Ashes series. He played all five Tests, but averaged a disappointing 26.

It figured. 'I knew when I was picked to play Test cricket I wasn't playing all that well in the four-day format,' Bailey says. 'I was certainly working as hard as I could to rectify it, but I look back now, and it was such a simple technical issue I was having: what with the amount of white ball cricket I was playing, I was trying to run good balls down to third man, which when there's four slips and a gully is generally not a great option. But you're not going to tell the selectors that, are you? "Thanks for the opportunity, but I'm not batting particularly well at the moment!"'

That Bailey has remained a short-form specialist since actually belies his own preferences. He enjoys T20; he is amazed at the virtuosity of its most skilled practitioners; but it's four- and five-day cricket that stirs him.

'For me, it's much more significant,' Bailey says. 'I don't think I've ever walked off a T20 ground absolutely devastated or elated. It's a win or a loss, but so often it's down to one performance — one person batted amazingly, we dropped that guy, he got 80 etc.

'It's also so difficult to make judgements — to evaluate the guy who makes 20 off 20 in the middle versus the guy who makes 10 off 2 at the end. You can get to the end of a tournament and might have faced 20 balls. It's just so difficult to work out how you're going.

'With four-day cricket, Test match cricket, there's that ebb and flow. You can find a way back. You can knock a team over who are stronger, then you have to find a way to do it again when the wicket's better. Winning a Sheffield Shield, looking back on what you did right, where you were lucky — that is still for me the ultimate satisfaction, and what I want desperately to achieve.'

Bailey's respectable T20 record — international strike rate 141, domestic 131 — likewise belies what he feels are innate inhibitions. 'How you play T20 is still a reflection of your inner cricketer,' he believes. 'I've vowed to have seasons of T20 where I just go out and blaze the ball. Then I find myself in the contest, and I cannot play that way. I'm forever thinking: if I just wait one more over; if I just have a look at this bowler. And however much I try to play with complete freedom and go from ball one, that takes over.'

Earlier this year, Bailey accepted a last-minute contract to replace an injured Faf du Plessis at Rising Pune Supergiants. It did not go well: 'I was at the stage where I thought I wouldn't play IPL again, and I wasn't even sure I wanted to. Then on a whim I thought: "I'll go. And I'll play the way I've always wanted to."

'But after a month of not wearing shoes up at Noosa and not

thinking about cricket, I was completely unprepared, and my instincts were to fight and survive and scrap. So my scores and strike rate were abysmal. And I was thinking at the end: "You were so clear on the plane over about how you were going to play. You've ended up doing none of the things you wanted to." '

Filed now by selectors under the heading 'batsman, ODIs', Bailey feels keenly about the format's curious status — still the financial driver of international cricket, still the nearest to a determinant of champion status through the World Cup, yet the format most often derogated or downplayed.

'I think it [ODI cricket] can be very meaningful still,' he says. 'The series against India last summer was a real spectacle, and that meant it mattered. I know we've been absolutely hammered in South Africa, but that didn't feel as meaningful, because I didn't understand where it fitted in the scene. It was very early in their season, felt squeezed in.'

Then there are the selection caprices: 'That series in India in 2013, we played seven ODIs — which is a ridiculous number. It ended up 2-2 going into the last with two washouts, and Cricket Australia took Mitch [Johnson] out of our team.

'I'm not having a go at the sports scientists. But it had been a really challenging series, we were missing a few senior players, and there we were, game seven, on the line, and our best chance of winning was taken away from us. It just deprived that series of all the meaning we'd built up.

'It was one of my frustrations as captain of the T20 side too. There's only so many times you can hand caps out to guys telling them "you've earned this, you deserve it, it's an honour", when you're doing that for three or four guys in the same game. 'It wears thin. The players know it. They're not stupid. Yet at the same time the Australian cricket team is expected to win. Like it or lump it, that's what makes people follow the game."

When short-form cricket did matter, during last year's World Cup, it was the stand-out moment of Bailey's career. He was anxious ahead of time, causing a dip in form: 'It's the only time I've really, really wanted to be in a cricket team. In the lead I was thinking: "How lucky to have a World Cup in your country, what an opportunity, I'm at the perfect age" And that really threw my cricket.'

Success then underpinned a desire among players to socialise that good fortune. Bailey was part of the executive of the Australian Cricketers' Association that allocated $13 million of World Cup revenues to what will be a $28.7 million investment in funding health, wellbeing and welfare programmes for current players, past players, and those transitioning.

'The word that came up through all the playing groups I was part of was legacy,' says Bailey. 'There's that idea in cricket about wanting to leave the game better than you found it. We recognised that whilst having having a World Cup was huge and a great boon, there were generations past and future who deserved to share in it.'

How did Cricket Australia respond to this magnanimity? Bailey chooses his words carefully. 'I didn't get the impression they were that happy about it. Personally, I thought it showed that we were serious about the game being stronger going forward, and had a commendable long-term vision. But I'm not sure CA saw it like that.

'When it was first floated, CA were quite strong in telling us where they thought our money should go, including to funding female cricket. There's obviously huge scope for growth there, but I found that interesting. All their literature was about pushing the female game. But they weren't, at that stage, backing that up with money. They expected the male players to pay for it, and tried to turn the male and female playing groups against each other, which we were disappointed about.'

Yet the ACA programmes, says Bailey, address serious concerns — including a fear he nurses, based largely on his observations as captain of Tasmania, that the game has grown so all-consuming as to impair enjoyment. 'One of the things I am constantly on the lookout for is how guys are travelling,' he says. 'I'm not concerned with how they're hitting their cover drive or whether they're swinging the ball, but how they're coping with the pressures and uncertainties, and are they enjoying their cricket for however long it lasts.

'Because it should be a really enjoyable time in your life. But I worry that there are young guys coming through for whom it won't be, and that they'll be spat out the end and left unprepared for the real world. I feel like we're so well-resourced now that players, particularly those identified early, lead such a structured upbringing that they never have to make a decision for themselves.'

Enjoyment poses its own issues, meaningful to a thirty-four-year-old who dropped out of an undergraduate commerce degree as his cricket expanded. Today Bailey is working slowly towards an MBA when cricket and a ten-month-old daughter permit: that decision about what comes next, deferred five years ago, cannot be staved off indefinitely.

'The thing that scares me most is when people say: "Oh, don't worry about life after cricket, because you'll be fine. You've captained cricket teams." I just don't think the world works that way. You have to have a bit of a plan. And it scares me that I've loved something so much from such a young age.

'My fiancée often says: most people spend their lives trying to work up to their ambition. You found it at 18, and you now have to find something you'll be just as passionate about. That scares me more than what it is. I can picture myself doing lots of things post-cricket. But I can't imagine loving any of them like I've loved cricket.'

# Chris Rogers
# LOOKING BACK, LOOKING FORWARD

DECEMBER 2016

It was touch-and-go for a moment. Chris Rogers had brooded at length about his decision to retire from international cricket. But when he went to inform his coach Darren Lehmann on the eve of last year's Oval Test, he felt suddenly equivocal. What if Lehmann asked him to stay, given he was Australia's best-performed batsman of the Ashes tour? When the coach smiled and said 'well done', it came almost as a relief.

'Darren was right,' says Rogers. 'I didn't want to keep going. The only reason I might have was if they'd really, really wanted it, if there'd been a really distinct role for me. But I was happy to move on. You live in that bubble, and it's hard. Even though I look back now and remember fantastic times, it can also get you so down that you wonder: "What am I doing here? This isn't what it's meant to be like." '

Fresh in the memory as a cricketer despite his year behind an ABC Grandstand microphone, 39-year-old Rogers still looks ready for the call-up. He approaches our meeting place with the busy bow-legged strut that grew so reassuringly familiar at the outset of Australian innings; sun-conscious, he does not remove his expensive shades while we're speaking. But through them he's already looking back on himself, the outcome of producing an autobiography, *Bucking the Trend*, which among summer's many titles is a thoughtful and readable stand-out.

'One of the refreshing things about the book is that you look back and you realised why you made decisions,' says Rogers. 'In hindsight I'd regretted a lot of things. But when I was doing the book I realised that there had been reasons.

'Something that occurred to me reading the books by Michael [Clarke] and Brad [Haddin] was how meticulous they were about where they wanted to go and what they wanted to achieve. I never thought of it that way. I was in the moment — maybe too much. But I just wanted to enjoy it, milk it for all it was worth. And I did. I look back and know that's what made me what I am.'

In that sense, Rogers suspects he might represent a discontinued line: 'I think that to play three forms now, you will have to have grown up in that world. I don't think guys who come in late will be able to enter into that environment, because they'll get to moments where they'll just say: "I've got to go and be normal again." It's only manageable if that's what you've come to think of as normal.

'There were times I finished Test series where I said: "I have got to get away from this, just to get centred a bit." I gave everything when I played, but the last thing I wanted to do when I wasn't playing was think about the game.'

Yet Rogers was different even in his own time. A recurrent theme of his autobiography are the sensations of feeling misunderstood, misaligned. 'That was me a little bit,' he agrees. 'It was how I felt a long way through. I'm quite opinionated, which serves me well on the radio. But that ability to be more compassionate, more of a listener, I've found harder at times. I've got great friendship through cricket; other relationships where it's maybe just a bit weird.'

The opinions? Rogers is not shy of expressing them. A disturbing aspect of the coaching of Australian batting, he argues, is its uniformity, almost to the point of monotony. Rogers was never one for offering a stationary target: his book is full of instances of technical problem solving, against specific bowlers, in different conditions.

'I'm curious about that [the coaching],' Rogers says. 'Even when I watch guys train, they'll do the same things over and over again. Whirler, bowlers, whirler, bowlers, whirler, bowlers. Even if things are going wrong: there seems no thought of changing things, maybe doing some drills, breaking it down. There seems this real fear of tinkering, and I'm happy to say that I think that's bullshit.

'Unless you're prepared to take a step back for the sake of two steps forward then you'll never get where you want to. You look at the greats, and all of them have worked on their techniques at every stage of their careers. [At Somerset] I played with Marcus Trescothick, who's 41, and he's still looking for ways to do things better.'

Rogers recently gained his Level 3 coaching certificate, but about many modern nostrums he is decidedly agnostic. 'I understand there has to be testing and measurement,' he says. 'But I heard recently that a state had a training session that was screening in the morning, then gym, then nets, then running, and if you tell me that's common sense then I'll laugh my head off.

'That's a six-hour session. And I find that unforgivable. All you're doing is draining people. The great thing about cricket is the lifestyle. I used to love that you could train hard in the morning, do what you had to do, then join your mates for lunch and relax. It's such a mental game you actually need that switching down. You've got to leave something in the bag for game time.

'In all the years I played I never once said I was 'going to work'. I was 'going to play'. There has to be that mentality, where it's about the love of the game. Lose it and you can't really succeed. I firmly believe that.'

That Rogers has the benefit of a long view he regards with a wry amusement: 'When I started it was all about the old blokes. When I finished it was all about the young blokes.' But one tendency of preferment that causes him abiding annoyance — which may be of renewed relevance — is a lack of respect for consistency.

'One of the things that used to frustrate me about selectors was that they'd see a player make an attractive hundred and immediately identify him as the next big thing,' recalls Rogers. 'What they'd overlook would be the next three or four innings in which that player would do nothing, because they had a technical flaw only overcome once they were 'in'.

'They'd evaluate a player by their best performances, rather than the norm — what do we get out of this bloke *more often than not*? I got frustrated with that. Because it meant that the guys performing day-in day out were not rewarded. I say to young openers now: "You've got to contribute. Doesn't matter how. You cannot get two low scores in a game; you've got to face a minimum number of balls. Even if you get 15 and 22, you're doing a job for the side. In hindsight that's what I'm proudest of: that I very seldom failed twice.'

When I begin asking whether Cricket Australia in its incessant tinkering with the Sheffield Shield displays insufficient respect for the integrity of first-class cricket, Rogers answers 'yes' before I have finished getting the question out. 'You've got to get back to the Sheffield Shield being about winning,' he says emphatically. 'If two of your 20-year-olds average 40, that's not a successful year. A successful year is winning games, and also developing younger players one step at a time. Because then guys buy into that — they see themselves as part of something bigger. You have to make players earn the right to be a part of it. That's winning culture, not just opening the doors and letting everyone in. You've got to knock it down mate. When you've earned it you make the most of it.'

On Rogers' observations over his 25 Tests, Australian cricket has this summer paid the price of players who have not really had to 'earn it.' 'I looked at a few of the guys on the periphery and, while very talented, I didn't think they'd quite experienced how hard it could get,' says Rogers. 'Fighting England in the Ashes in England, South Africa in South Africa, spin in the sub-continent, even playing county cricket when the ball swings — there wasn't the same skill level as there had been. There needed to be improvement. And watching those games last summer on roads — with all due respect to Usman and Vogesy, I'd never seen them dominate that way. So I kind of felt: if this is indicative of the standard, then there's something missing.'

The trim physique and trenchant views notwithstanding, retirement rather becomes Rogers — perhaps a little better than at times seemed possible, his late-blooming Test career having requited his love for the game in the nick of time. 'Yes, I can look back without bitterness,' he says. 'Whereas there were times I was bitter and I'm happy to admit that; it was part of being a competitive person.'

Seeing the whole field now from the vantage of the commentary box rather than merely his own corner of it has changed his outlook but in other respects deepened his sympathies. 'When you're involved in it, it's all-consuming, which I don't think is well understood,' says Rogers. 'Guys out there aren't robots. They're humans. They make mistakes. As a player you get caught in the moment a lot. All you're thinking is next ball, next five minutes. As a commentator you see a bigger picture. You see when there should be calmness. A guy will feel like he's in the tough spell and it feels like someone is going to bowl forever because you're caught up in the moment. A commentator knows he won't. He has the luxury of seeing further ahead.

'When you have more infrastructure around you, more coaches, more social media, and everyone seems to be a critic or a commentator, there's no doubt the guys think this is the most important thing they'll ever do. But you walk away and you realise it's just a game. And you wonder: why didn't I enjoy it a little bit more?' Chris Rogers is looking forward to making up for that.

# Sam Harper
# THE KID
## DECEMBER 2016

Tomorrow at Adelaide Oval, a baggy green cap will be presented to bonny Matt Renshaw on the occasion of his first Test. At twenty, he will be the same age on debut as Bradman, Ponting and Steve Waugh; also, for lovers of the obscure, Les Joslin, Ernie Bromley and Graeme Hole.

And if the 'put-in-a-bunch-of-kids' whims persist at the selection table, chances are you will soon hear more of names like 19-year-old Victorian keeper-batsman Sam Harper. He has ticked every box with the National Performance Squad and Cricket Australia XI lately, and wants to play Test cricket. No, I mean he *really* wants to play Test cricket, an ambition formed when he was five, and lays out now with earnest emphasis: 'Getting a baggy green is all I've ever dreamed of.'

Harper has also been with the Melbourne Stars for two years, training, sitting in dug outs, attending team meetings. 'It's amazing,' he says. 'So much fun.' But it hasn't diverted him. 'Twenty20's always going to appeal to the public, it's three hours and it's over, and I love it too,' he says. 'But Twenty20, one guy gets on a roll, or one guy bowls four cheap overs, and that's the game. We play the Renegades. Luke Wright makes 100 and we win; if he gets out, we lose. Pretty simple.'

The highlight of Harper's brief career was making his Sheffield Shield debut in February, taking nine catches, conceding no byes and batting handily. 'Once you get into state cricket,' he says, 'there's just nothing more rewarding — getting together for four days, getting the job done and celebrating it.'

Of this week's Australian revamp he has been a second-order beneficiary. As Matthew Wade and Peter Handscomb ascended, Victoria's wicketkeeping berth reopened, and Harper will resume his first-class career against South Australia at the MCG on Saturday.

Harper already speaks a little like a Test veteran, staccato sentences strewn with expressions like 'at the end of the day' and 'training my backside off'. Yet he is also disarmingly astute, not so deeply indoctrinated that he cannot distinguish the system's potential pitfalls; occasionally he refers to 'young players' as though, while sympathetic to their struggles, he is somehow looking on at them, old beyond his years.

Priorities, Harper acknowledges, may well be changing: 'The question is asked sometimes in our groups: "Put your hand up if you're here for the baggy green." Everyone will put their hands up. I'm not convinced if you asked those same people anonymously without the coach looking whether you'd get the same answers. Some people probably say what they think the coach expects.

'Most of my good mates want to play Test cricket. Which I think is great. I mean, we've grown up playing junior red ball cricket over two days. But it will be interesting for us to have another coffee in five years with an 18-year-old. Look at Milo cricket: it's all about hitting the ball as far as you can, learning to hit a reverse sweep or a slog shot, or bowling a slower ball.'

Harper's beginnings were more traditional. Father Brian is a legend of sub-district cricket with Caulfield and premier cricket with Melbourne; uncle Laurie was a state stalwart in the 1990s. Yet Harper has also enjoyed opportunities via the pathway system at under-14, under-16 and under-18 level of which his elders would never have dreamed, has toured England, Dubai and Singapore, and would have added Bangladesh had Australia not withdrawn from the under-19 World Cup.

Since then he has spent three months at Brisbane's National Cricket Centre, much to the envy of Melbourne clubmates: 'Queensland cricketers are so lucky. June-July they're out on turf. We were calling our mates in Melbourne, and they were going: "It's 8 degrees here, blowing a gale." '

That intensity of incubation, Harper notes, poses its own challenges. I ask him about all the coaching influences he has come under in the past year, and he reels them off readily: 'At the Vics, we have Andrew McDonald; we had David Saker. Assistant coach Lachie Stevens, bowling coach Mick Lewis, batting coach David Hussey; I've got my keeping coach Dallas Lyons. I'm a big one for talking to blokes like Cam White, Rob Quiney, Aaron Finch. Also Marcus Stoinis and Peter Handscomb, who've established themselves: you want to find out how they got better quicker from 19 to 25.

'At the National Cricket Centre, Greg Chappell, Graeme Hick, Ryan Harris, Joe Dawes, Stuey Law, David Bailey, Michael Lloyd and the other psychologists. With the Cricket Australia XI there was Brad Hodge, Greg Blewett, Rob Cassell; at the Stars, Steve Fleming, Trent Woodhill, Tommy Simseck, Adrian Mott; at Melbourne, Andrew Walton and Julien Wiener. [Pause] Yes, there are a lot of coaches.'

What are the implications of that? 'Overthinking,' Harper says quickly. 'It's a big one. Coaching is great. Then you look at Bubba Watson, who never had coaching and did everything naturally. That's his game. And at the end of the day, that walk from the dug out to marking your guard is a lonely walk. The bowler runs in and it's just you, your mind and your batting.'

Harper diligently keeps a diary in which he summarises the fruits of every coaching interaction, in pursuit of 'one-percenters.' But it can also get confusing: 'If you try to listen to all the coaches, while they've been great players in the past and are great people, one person might tell you one thing about your grip, another might tell you something else, a third might be telling you about your head position while a fourth is talking about your cover drive or how to play the short ball.

'Your mind is just racing. You can be walking out to bat and thinking: "If I have my grip here, put my head here, play my cover drive this way and the short ball that way..." Well, how can you do that while playing a ball coming at you at 140kmh? Good luck.' Fortunately, says Harper, his filter is fining down: 'If someone tells you to change something and you change it, then you're doing it for the wrong reasons.'

For him, refreshment has come from casting his own training regimes. During pre-season, for example, he sought to learn better diving through classes at BTYC Gymnastics in Springvale Road: 'At times it was just me; at other times the foam pits were full of people. Once I got to know the coaches, we got dive mats out and I was bringing tennis balls for them to underarm to me. The movement of my body really improved. If there were eight days in a week I'd probably try to do more of it during the season.'

But ultimately, Harper says, it's about games. 'I love the game of cricket and I love preparing to play,' he observes. 'But, y'know, today we trained on pitches with nets on each side, no fielders, no keeper, no umpires. How is that even close to replicating what we get in matches?

'As a golfer you can play Augusta, exact same eighteen holes, you have a white ball in front of you that you have to hit. Stick to the same thing and you'll hit it 250 yards every time. We train a lot but very seldom in the same environment we play in. Even centre wicket training at Allan Border Field, if you got out, the sun kept shining, you just marked centre again and kept batting. In training you don't have to cope with disappointment.

'The most I've ever learned is when I've had bad games, bad weeks. You learn when you're going well, but that's also when you take things for granted. You make a score, forget how you did it. If you're not going well, you have to work out why. And it's so full of randomness. Look at the last few months Joe Burns has had: he hasn't done a heck of a lot wrong. This is a game where you can make a beautiful 18 and an ugly 72. That's why it's so fascinating.'

One other thing about Harper: taking after his mother, he is a young man of faith, part of an apostolic congregation in Scoresby. 'I grew up with mates who go to church who've become lifelong best friends who know me very well,' he says. 'So although I think about cricket a hell of a lot, it doesn't take up 100 per cent of my thinking.

'Every person has their own story, their own struggles, their own situation. As a 19-year-old, I don't have all the answers, but it doesn't stop me believing what I believe. I think faith helps me when times do get tough.' That might also be true of the Australian team that takes the field tomorrow.

# Daniel Christian
# EVERYWHERE MAN
## DECEMBER 2016

Not quite six years ago, Daniel Christian was in a Canberra hotel room about to represent the Prime Minister's XI, and on the phone to his Redbacks teammate Shaun Tait while his laptop furnished updates of the Indian Premier League player auction in Bangalore. Presently his name flashed up — 'D. Christian, South Australia, all-rounder: reserve price $US50,000.' In minutes his life would change.

It turned out that three franchises were pursuing Christian on the basis of recommendations from their Australian coaches: Darren Lehmann at the Deccan Chargers, Greg Shipperd at the Delhi Daredevils and Geoff Lawson at Kochi Tuskers Kerala.

Christian and Tait began refreshing their screens every thirty seconds in an atmosphere of growing hilarity, and even now Christian can barely keep the laughter from his voice recalling it. 'It just kept going up,' he says. 'It got to $400,000, then it stopped for a minute. And we're both, like, what's going on? Then it came back at $800,000.' He was finally knocked down for $900,000 a year for two years, with a third-year option: 'It was literally like winning the lottery.'

At the time, Christian was 27. Despite slipping quietly into three T20 internationals, he had never seen much money from cricket, and was living in rental accommodation in Adelaide. Hectic raising of paddles on the other side of the world had now nudged him towards multi-millionairehood, although paradoxically it made him feel almost like an amateur. 'Something like that takes the pressure off,' says Christian. 'It means you're not playing for your next mortgage repayment. You can actually almost afford to play for the love.'

Of course, the Chargers weren't looking for a gentleman visitor; they wanted a match-winning all-rounder. And when Christian contributed consistently without dominating, his price tag became something of a burden.

'If I'd got 70 off 30 balls and taken 3 for 15 every match, maybe I'd have justified it,' he recalls. 'And because I didn't really understand the expectations, I probably took them on a bit. I'd just got on Twitter, so I heard a lot about: "How's this bloke worth $900,000?" It did get to me a little.' He's grateful all the same for his two seasons at the Chargers and a third at Royal Challengers Bangalore: he bought a house, an investment property and shares recommended by an investment adviser.

It was also a reward for a player characterised by a willingness to back himself in any company. Christian is Australian cricket's everywhere man, having been part of dressing rooms in every state bar Western Australia: three state teams (New South Wales, South Australia and Victoria) and two Big Bash League franchises (Brisbane Heat, Hobart Hurricanes). T20 has also provided a passport to four counties, plus his last representative honours, during Australia's only win of the 2014 World T20.

This year in England, Christian had his most consistent season yet, averaging over 40 and striking at almost 160 per hundred balls as captain of Nottinghamshire in the T20 Blast. 'I wouldn't say I stumbled on a formula, but it's the first time I've really trusted that I could catch up,' he says. 'Maybe the conditions help over there, the grounds being smaller. You say: "I'll just knock it round here, wait for the spinner, and then I've only got to hit it 60m to the short boundary and I can get back to where the run rate needs to be."

'I made a couple of little technical changes working with [twice-sacked England coach] Peter Moores, who was assistant coach. He's fantastic to talk to about cricket. He was just flinging balls at me in the nets, and I started walking across my stumps to knock it into the leg side. He'd set me little scenarios like: "It's the 13th over, you need eight an over, the field is here, you're not allowed to hit it in the air."

'That's a really good game for me because my pressure reliever has always been try to hit a six, and now I wasn't allowed to do that. So I started fiddling round with getting across and it kind of undid some of the rigidness in my technique that I might have slipped into in the last few years. Loosen the arms up, get the bat going back to gully rather than trying to straighten it, just hit the ball.'

A weirdly fascinating game, this T20. Australia, Christian notes, has been slow to assimilate the format: 'I played in the first Big Bash. It was obviously going to be huge.' At the same time, he understands ambivalence about it. Although T20 has underwritten his financial well-being, he finds it vaguely unsatisfying, and continues preferring four-day cricket.

'Sheffield Shield cricket you've got ten games,' he says. 'You train for 12 months. There's a big build up. You can get into a Shield final and win it and it's amazing, fantastic, the best experience.

'The Big Bash League, you get together on 10 December for the first time, spend a week together doing some planning, have a couple of nights out getting to know your teammates, then by the 20 January you're finished. And it's such a momentum game. Last season at the Hurricanes we started well, playing decent cricket. Then within a week we'd lost three, and everyone was meant to be out of form even though it was only a week. Just gone like that, in a week.'

The matches, he finds, are also curiously indistinguishable and perishable. 'There's always another game,' Christian says. 'We've lost? No worries, another game coming up. Because it's news today, fish and chip paper tomorrow.'

If Christian sounds like an old salt, that's because he is, and in good company. Victoria is defending the Sheffield Shield robustly this season because of what he sees as a bodyguard of experience (White, Siddle, Quiney, Hastings) around its nucleus of emerging talent (Wade, Handscomb, Stoinis, Boland) and youth (Dean, Harris, Tremain). Its famously clannish dressing room is the most enjoyable of the many Christian has been part of.

'Nothing is off limits,' Christian says. 'There's no dancing around. Everything is out there. We take the piss out of each other a lot and about anything at all — you can't get offended, you can't get upset, everyone takes it. But there's a real mutual respect, of ability, of what you bring.'

Since joining the Bushrangers from the Redbacks in 2012, Christian has filled a utility role fitting his temperament: only one player in the competition has hit more sixes, while he has given up only 3.25 runs an over.

'I've never played sport for personal success or gratification,' says Christian. 'I always played team sports — rugby league, cricket — where it's been about winning as a group. I love the role I play in Victoria: come in at 7, hopefully push on when the guys at the top have done the job; bowl second change in the middle when it starts reversing. It's probably not a role that's going to take you to the next level. But it's what the team needs, and that suits me.'

On the field this summer, the Bushrangers have been merciless, men against boys when they recently clobbered youthful Queensland. 'We bullied them, pretty much bullied them,' says Christian. 'That's something we're good at. We get a bit of a sniff of vulnerability and away we go. You never used to be able to do that with Queensland. I haven't beaten them like that for a long, long time. James Hopes was part of the reason. He'd counterattack, or block an end and get a quick three-for. Harts [Chris Hartley] is still one of the hardest blokes around to get out. They'll improve as they get older but they're very young at the minute.'

Not surprisingly, Christian is unimpressed by the recent atmosphere of experimentation in domestic cricket. 'We're guinea pigs,' he says. 'It's first-class cricket. Last season we had a game where Chris Tremain bowled like the wind in the first innings, then we subbed in James Pattinson in the second innings who did the same. This season we're using four different kinds of balls. When they're trying to get blokes ready for Test cricket and talking about them banging out 1000-run years, it's ridiculous, absolutely ridiculous.'

Nor does this apply only in first-class cricket. Christian is another voice critical of the Cricket Australia XI in the Matador Cup: 'They're not trying to win the Matador Cup. They're trying to do well for themselves. I don't think it's a good concept at all. If players are good enough they're going to be in the state teams anyway. They might win one every so often if someone has a day out. Otherwise they'll get flogged every game.'

Christian sees a contradiction in a wealthy sport accenting youth when factors that used to be held against older cricketers no longer apply: 'These days if you need something, there's someone. There's no reason for being a poor fielder when there's a fielding coach. There's no excuse for not being fit when there's a fitness bloke. You shouldn't be overweight because there's a nutritionist. So there's no reason now why age should matter. If you're playing well and you're fit, who cares how old you are? Why can't the [Australian] top order be all 30-year-olds who know their trade, who've all made 5000 runs?'

Funnily enough, that puts Christian on the same page as his erstwhile state and national coach Darren Lehmann, who in his new book *Coach* calls '33 or 34 a team's ideal age profile' where 'players know their games inside out, have been around the block and know how to cope with pressure' — although apparently out of kilter with the reconstituted national selection panel, of which Lehmann is a member, recently mandated by Cricket Australia CEO James Sutherland to 'invest in youth.'

Yet the irony of his overnight IPL riches is he feels a better cricketer than he was then. 'I know my game better. You play when you're young, you don't quite cut the mustard and you're on the scrapheap quickly while they look at the next bloke. Cam White and I were talking about this a few months ago, how it would be great to play [international cricket] again, because we know so much more. Everyone who's played would say the same.' Argue if you like, but Christian has played with more of them than most.

# Jess Cameron
## A BIT OF EVERYTHING
DECEMBER 2016

This time last year, Jess Cameron was not playing cricket. She was not playing anything. She attended round one of the inaugural Women's Big Bash League at St Kilda's Junction Oval as a fan. It was fun. But more fun was sleeping in her own bed that night, without the sense of 'having to be somewhere all of the time.'

Today, Cameron is back in the thick of it: the hard-hitting 27-year-old batter stepped out at North Sydney Oval for round one of the second Women's Big Bash League at the weekend, playing in Melbourne Stars' six-run victory over title-holder the Sydney Thunder.

Yet she might not have been there at all had she not elected to 'step away' from cricket last season. She would certainly not have returned as twice the athlete, having used her break from cricket to get serious about Australian rules, and to vault into the Women's Australian Football League.

Her hiatus was not, says Cameron, a case of burn-out so much as a glimpse of that possibility. A Vic Spirit player for a decade, an Australian regular for five years, she had been feeling unsettled for some time.

'Physically I was fine,' she says. 'It was definitely mental at that stage — trying to fit everything into my life. I was dealing with a part-time job, was on the road all the time, training all the time. I had to fit my family in, my partner. I was getting annoyed with the fact I was never home and I'm a big family person.'

Cameron liked her job too, the only one she had ever held, handling spare parts for Werribee Automotive Group. They had been generous supporters of her career, but she lived daily with the risk of becoming a spare part herself. 'That's one of the things around the women's contracts,' Cameron notes. 'They're only one-year deals, so your future is never guaranteed. If they want to dump you, they can dump you any time.'

Cameron played last season's Women's National Cricket League for the Western Fury with the intention of joining the Perth Scorchers. 'That was me trying to work out whether it was cricket or the environment that were causing all these question marks in my head,' she says. 'But it was to do with the game. I wasn't even looking forward to going out to field. And I wasn't going to stop anyone else pursuing their dream if I couldn't give it 100 per cent.'

At length, Cameron wrote a list of the pros and cons of a break from the game, and consulted her parents, her partner Chris Duffin, her coach Matthew Mott, and Cricket Australia psychologist Michael Lloyd. 'I didn't want to talk to too many people,' she observes. 'Because obviously the more people you speak to, the more views you get and the more confusing it can be.' You get the sense, in fact, that it was not advice she was seeking so much as support for a resolution already made. She certainly took comfort from the example of her Australian teammate Delissa Kimmince, who also took a break from the game a few years ago.

The 'indefinite break', announced in October 2015, made for a stark change. Because the best women's cricketers tend to come to the fore earlier than the men, Cameron had been an elite cricketer more than half her life, having gone along at a school teacher's encouragement to a Victorian under-12 training camp and achieved selection.

Aged 17, she was an Australian under-21; aged 21, she was a Test cricketer; aged 24, she was a Belinda Clark Award winner; she had played 50 one-day internationals and 64 T20 internationals; suddenly, she was an onlooker, a face in the crowd, if not for long.

Cameron had always played football, where time had permitted, latterly with her sister Andrea at Port Melbourne in Division 4 of the Victorian Women's Football League. After Christmas, she joined the later stages of the AFL Women's Academy overseen by Darren Flanigan.

When she started asking round about which bigger clubs might be looking for a key forward, Steph Chiocci connected Cameron with VWFL Premier Division club Diamond Creek, for whom she kicked a bag of nine on her first appearance in April.

In May, Cameron joined the tiny number who have played both elite cricket and football on the MCG, kicking five goals for Melbourne against Brisbane in an exhibition match. When the AFL issued the eight licences for the Women's AFL the following month, her further rise was almost foreordained.

By then Cameron had returned to cricket, having kept in touch by playing seven T20 matches for her club Prahran, scoring 578 runs. 'I had no responsibility,' she says. 'I didn't have to worry about selection. I didn't have to think about playing for Australia. I think that's why I played so well — I had no expectations of myself. It was a good experience for me to have. I wasn't thinking about things I can't control. I was thinking, am I playing well, am I happy?'

Satisfied she was ready, Cameron resumed training with the Vic Spirit, and signed with the Melbourne Stars for WBBL2. When in October she was picked up in the Women's AFL draft by Collingwood, she obtained the decidedly unusual distinction of having Eddie McGuire as club president for both summer and winter games.

The regime awaiting Cameron, and also other footballing cricketers like Emma Kearney, Natalie Plane and Kirsty Lamb, is daunting.

And for somebody who set such a store on balance that she wanted to play no sport, playing two seems a counterintuitive step. It has certainly required a good deal of cooperation, from Stars coach David Hemp and Collingwood coach Wayne Siekman, in partitioning Cameron's time.

'I've had nothing but support from the Stars and Collingwood,' Cameron says loyally. 'At the moment Collingwood are training Tuesday, Thursday and Friday. As much as I can, I'll train with them. Except when the Stars are training I'll train with them.'

When they clash? Here, she sounds a little less sure, talks about possibly starting training with Stars and finishing with Collingwood. When I sound skeptical, she laughs: 'Well, the Stars are training at the MCG and the Holden Centre is just across the road. Anyway, there's obviously going to be a lot of training and I'm prepared for being tired. But you've just got to be as ready as you can.'

Interestingly, Cameron has found cricket and football pleasingly complementary games, similar in their demands on hand-eye coordination, different in their latitudes of error.

'With cricket you know that you're only a tiny mistake away from having nothing to do,' she observes. 'You can be seeing it like a beach ball and get out for 5. That's why it plays on people's minds so much.

'With footy you can fix any mistake you might make. It's a four quarter game. You can have a bad first quarter and a good last quarter. It's not like you have to wait until the next match.'

Yet the happiest aspect of playing two sports, Cameron thinks, is that one prevents you expending too much emotional energy on the other. In particular, football has lightened cricket's burdens. 'When I was playing football for Diamond Creek, I wasn't thinking about cricket,' Cameron notes. 'In the past I might have been sitting home thinking: I should be down the nets now. Instead I was on the football field. I certainly I didn't have to think about my football the way I thought about my cricket. It was a real refresher.'

The slight paradox of Cameron's position is that having enjoyed her life's new variety, she looks forward to the day it ceases — when women's cricket and football are so professionally consuming as to demand that participants choose one over the other.

'Women will be better off when they can make that decision,' says Cameron. 'Because it will mean that there's enough money for them to concentrate on one sport. I don't see down the track how women can't be paid enough by either. As much as you can play both sports, that's great. But at the end of the day we want to be professional athletes, and that's about being able to train for that one sport every day, like what the men have.'

If it was one, what would it be? What would happen in the event of an Australian cricket recall during a Women's AFL season? 'To be honest I haven't really thought about it,' answers Cameron. 'I would have to have a really good Women's BBL season to come up for selection. But if there was a clash, my loyalty would be to Collingwood. Certainly my point of view is that I'm tied to football. We'll have to see how it pans out.' And things have panned out quite well already.

# Georgia Redmayne
# DOCTOR IN THE HOUSE
JANUARY 2017

Most athletes faced with the prospect of being interviewed will assume from the journalist at least a degree of familiarity with their performances and back story.

Georgia Redmayne is a little different. A few days before we are due to speak, the 23-year-old keeper-batter with the Tasmanian Roar and Hobart Hurricanes sends a bullet-pointed personal summary of her cricket, education and family background — not in a boastful way, for it is humbly and gratefully couched, but in a spirit of helpfulness. It might, she explains, save some time.

Time, yes: fifth-year University of NSW medical student Redmayne has little to spare. When we finally meet, it's at Coffs Harbour Rural Clinical School, where she is on a rotation in the emergency department. Fortunately neither her pager nor the wallphone rings, even if she is obviously on duty — carefully groomed, papers handy, eyes darting occasionally to her iPhone. Once leave is factored in, her summer's cricket has cost her a net nine days of university, which she's making up at nights and weekends. "I do try to keep on top of things," she says briskly. "My diary is pretty full."

Her career is a novel mix of old and new. Where most players tend to talk of developing lives "outside cricket", Redmayne is developing cricket outside her life. Medicine has been her passion, sport her addition.

The two have historically been very hard to reconcile. In 1886, Henry Scott gave up the Australian captaincy to become a country doctor; the last owner of a stethoscope and a baggy green was George Thoms, who played a single Test in 1952.

Women prolonged the tiny overlap a little further: the legendary Faith Thomas was a nurse; Margaret Pickles, who played against England in December 1968, became a psychiatrist; Olivia Magno, who appeared in the last of her five Tests just over 15 years ago, became a general practitioner.

The irony is that it's the slight shift in the women's game from semi-amateurism to semi-professionalism that's kept Redmayne in the game, greater opportunity turning her from a peripheral state squad member into a potential international, in the running for a place on the Shooting Stars squad to tour Sri Lanka next month. "If you'd asked me a few years whether I'd have a future as a professional cricketer, I'd have laughed," she says. "I played because I enjoyed it. Now it is a possibility."

Life is crowded, but not uniform. "They [medicine and cricket] are similar in that they're both really full on, and if you're only doing one you might go a bit crazy," she says. "There are times you need to get away from cricket; other times you need to get away from medicine." She smiles: "I'm probably in a bit of denial at the moment, just thinking it will always work out."

It has so far. The youngest of three from Alstonville in the Northern Rivers district of NSW, Redmayne learned the game from her dentist father and club-cricketer brother — dad and daughter, aged 16, played men's second grade together.

By then, Redmayne's technique of balancing studies and sport was established. She largely stood out of cricket in her final year at high school, searching for the marks that would guarantee a university place; succeeding at that, she deferred her medical degree in order to play a season in Worcestershire, with financial support from the north NSW branch of the Lord's Taverners. A century in her first innings on English soil justified earlier sacrifices, and made her new friends. "They thought I was pretty good after that," she says.

The biggest obstacle to Redmayne's progress at the time was not the demands of her studies but the demography of her state. Drawing on ranks chock full of internationals, NSW have won 18 of the 21 seasons of the Women's National Cricket League. Although her grade performances earned her a place in the squad, Redmayne felt out of place in such exalted company, especially with Australian batter-keeper Alyssa Healy ensconced.

"It seemed so far away — all these great names I'd heard of," she recalls. "It felt like I was moving into something very big, but I also felt a bit lost too. I never thought I'd play in the National League. I was just a reserve, doing uni."

In 2015-16, Redmayne had a breakout club summer: 656 runs at 82, and 19 dismissals, winning her the First Grade Player of the Year Award. But her advance was stymied. If anything, the NSW Breakers' well-publicised embrace of fulltime professionalism was a further obstacle, placing additional demands Redmayne felt would be difficult to meet but offering no guarantee of more opportunities.

Ten years her senior, Sara Hungerford of the ACT Meteors and Sydney Sixers had just called it a day to concentrate on a job as a cardiologist at Sydney's St Vincent's Hospital. Redmayne was almost reconciled to a similarly clean break. "I'd had my best season. And I thought, 'If that doesn't get me a WBBL contract, what else can I do? Maybe I've achieved what I can; maybe it's time to focus on other things'."

Just then, however, Redmayne had a call from Cricket Tasmania's women's coach Julia Price, offering her an assured place as keeper and batter in 50- and 20-over cricket. To this day, Redmayne is unsure whether Price had, in fact, ever seen her play; what she remembers clearly is the sweet pang of the invitation. "It wasn't until I got the call from Tasmania with an offer to be in the starting line-up that I realised it was something I *really* wanted to do," she says. "I surprised myself just how excited I was when the opportunity came."

Redmayne liked Tasmania straight away, the shorter distances, gentler customs and make-do-and-mend optimism conducive to feelings of togetherness. In her serious and modest way, in fact, she began worrying whether Tasmania were investing too much in her. "All the way through pre-season, I was half expecting them to go, 'No Georgia, we think you should go back to NSW, we think someone else should come in, or we think you should drop down the order', or something. But in Tasmania I found that they really back you to perform, even when you don't back yourself."

This was put to the test when Redmayne started the season slowly, and the Roar extended a losing streak to nine games. Returning from a fortnight's hard uni yakka in Sydney, however, Redmayne walked out to open against the ACT Meteors on October 28 feeling strangely relaxed: creaming a few through the off-side, she began building Tasmania's first WNCL century.

Tasmania needed 12 from the last over, six from the last two balls, and two from the last after Redmayne stepped boldly outside off to loft the penultimate delivery into an on-side gap. Mid-pitch with Sasha Moloney, Redmayne admits she was thinking less of winning than of avoiding defeat. "I said to Sasha, 'What I don't want to do is get out. If we get one to tie, at least we can't lose. And if I hit a gap, cricket's a funny game, everything will need to go right for them to get us out.'"

Cricket duly showed its funny side. The Meteors' keeper broke the stumps in her haste to gather the return as the batters returned for their second, and Redmayne recalls being swallowed in the embrace of her 87-year-old grandfather, who had come to watch the game and vaulted the fence in his excitement. "I said, 'Grandpa, I'm not sure you're meant to be out here.'"

In six matches for the Roar, Redmayne averaged 59, took three catches and made no fewer than seven stumpings. Seven catches, five stumpings and 278 runs at 23 followed in the WBBL, where the Hurricanes rather surprised the competition, if not themselves, by advancing to the semi-finals. Afterwards, having arrived with her luggage, she hitched a ride from the Gabba to Alstonville with her parents, and was back to work next day.

The WBBL? "It was so much fun," says Redmayne. "In terms of building the women's game, we wouldn't be where we are if not for the T20." Yet she does not entirely share Cricket Australia's infatuation with the format, to the degree that some at Jolimont have urged women's cricket become a T20 game alone.

"Everyone in women's cricket really values the 50-over competition, the WNCL," Redmayne reports. "There has been talk of cancelling it and that has been met with a lot of backlash. Because that's the time you're able to develop your skills." For while T20's brevity is a commercial advantage, it can also be a competitive hindrance. "With T20 it's sometimes like you don't get a lot of cricket. You might hardly get a bat, you can only bowl four overs, you can end up playing almost as a fielder. You can finish a whole match, and it feels like only three people have done anything."

There's an impact on skills also, Redmayne believes. "The T20 mindset has affected 50-over play, because people get into that mentality where they don't think they have time," she says. "Sometimes you can get too obsessed with power and mistime in the attempt to hit really hard — I've been guilty of that. You're in that moment and you think, 'We need 10 an over. Just need to whack it as hard as I can'. You forget how many runs you can get simply by hitting gaps."

You have, as they say, more time than you think — and maybe what goes for cricket goes for life too. Although, Redmayne would probably say, that depends on making best use of the time you have.

# Trent Woodhill
# FINDING A WAY
## JANUARY 2017

When the time comes to write the history of this era in Australian cricket, a jumping off point may be the evening eight years ago when David Warner, on debut for Australia although uncapped in first-class cricket by his state, lit up the MCG with 89 from 43 balls in a T20 international against South Africa.

It was cricket, but not as we knew it: the following morning a newspaper front page juxtaposed an image of Warner with an old-timey photograph of a baseball slugger.

For another man it was also a quiet affirmation. Watching the innings, Warner's long-time batting coach Trent Woodhill heard the incredulity in the commentators' voices: 'Mark Taylor was saying things like: "That's almost a proper cricket shot!" And I thought: "Maybe what I do *is* a bit different".'

These days the 46-year-old Woodhill, list manager at the Melbourne Stars and Royal Challengers Bangalore, is quite a lot different: a coach sceptical of coaches, a familiar of world-class players with the humblest of cricket pedigrees, a vibey voice on Twitter in a good-areas, execute-our-skill-set age. In a recent article describing Woodhill's deep delvings into T20 data, *Cricinfo* recently called him a thinker 'as new-age as cricket will tolerate.'

Sitting in the MCG's Trumble Café, he freestyles cheerfully, buoyant about favourite players he has worked with like Warner, Steve Smith, Virat Kohli, AB De Villiers, Shane Watson and Virender Sehwag, caustic about the Australian culture of coaching and its consequences.

'Per capita there are more coaches in this country than anywhere else in the world,' he observes. 'Yet while Virat Kohli's made centuries all over the world, we're pretty much crap everywhere but here.'

The support staff around the Australian team leaves him profoundly unimpressed: 'This coaching structure has been given a lot more power than any previous coaching structure, but instead of giving it up and handing it off, they're trying to get more. They're building the Death Star.'

To Woodhill, coaching should not be about fitting players to a template, but helping them arrive at a robust and repeatable natural technique, suited to their instincts, personality and physicality. He accents not footwork, or backswing, or 'moving the game on', but 'contact', which he says is 'far easier to groove.'

'I train volume and sustainable tempo with the objective that they make contact in the same place every time,' Woodhill explains. 'With Shane [Watson] it might be 25 minutes, with AB [De Villiers] it might be 15 minutes, with Glenn [Maxwell] it might be seven minutes. But if Glenn hits the ball the right way for seven minutes a day, form is not going to be very far away.'

The overriding objective is enabling players to find their own way, rather than on mining his personal experience: 'I come to the ground wondering how I can help, what I can do. I don't come having to remember what I did.' Because, Woodhill says candidly, he didn't.

Woodhill was a 'good second grader, average first grader' with Bankstown who flamed out aged 24: 'I had a sales job, and getting out for 0 on Saturday morning nicking a ball I should have left didn't put me in best frame of mind for work on Monday.' Woodhill also, he says, suffered depression and anxiety, which he has worked to overcome. 'I really miss my panic attacks,' he jokes. 'I used to get a lot of stuff done.'

After three years out of the game, Woodhill returned, at Sydney University, at Sutherland, and in England, Ireland and Scotland, playing for pleasure, enjoying opportunities to coach. Sutherlander Steve Rixon offered Woodhill a job as an 'analyst' at Surrey; Sydney University's Alan Campbell recruited Woodhill to run junior teams at Cricket NSW.

In the latter role, Woodhill's path crossed with the likes of Warner, Steve Smith, Nic Maddinson and Adam Zampa, all hugely talented, all technically homespun, all under immense coaching pressure to conform to an orthodox ideal. 'People were hung up on beauty and looks, and I understand that, it's human nature,' Woodhill says. 'But it's also what cricket does: it squeezes you into a box and you can't get out.'

Where boxes were concerned, Australia's captain was a veritable Houdini. Woodhill was present at the now-famous 2006 conference at Menai High School that discussed 17-year-old Smith foregoing further education to pursue cricket. 'I got a rushed phone call from Tony Lewis [Cricket NSW welfare officer] asking if I wanted to come to the school,' recalls Woodhill. 'So I rang Steve and said: "Do you wanna go to school?" He said: "Nuh." I said: "What does your principal think?" Steve said: "He doesn't think I should be going either." I said: "OK, leave it with me."

'So I went to this meeting. The principal spoke, Tony started waffling on about Steve finishing his education, and I said: "Steve needs to leave school. He's going to make a million dollars a year out of this game." I've said to Steve since: "Gee I was wrong, wasn't I?" Because he makes a lot more than a million.'

What impressed Woodhill about Smith then has gone on impressing him — a capacity for doing his own thing. 'He was driving balls from fourth stump through wide mid-on,' Woodhill recalls. 'And the coaches at the Centre of Excellence were saying: "No that's got to go through mid-off." And I kept trying to protect him.'

Not, as Woodhill says, Smith needed much protection: 'Steve came back one year and he was hitting the ball great. I thought: "Gee it's finally worked." I said: "What you learn up there?" He said: "I learned to nod my head and not listen to a word they were saying".

What was dawning on Woodhill was the difference between how much coaching could improve a player ('10 per cent') and damage a player ('100 per cent'). Zampa, he recalls, stood out at once for his accuracy and his coolness, yet was scorned by the Centre of Excellence for failing to meet the cookie-cutter specifications of a leg-spinner.

'Adam comes back and I'm in tears,' recalls Woodhill. 'His report says: "Needs to spin the ball more." But he tried and his action just broke down. Luckily for Adam, I was close to his mum and dad — they're lovely people. And I said just to stay away from everyone for a couple of months, don't bowl a ball, and he was lucky things came back.'

Both Warner and Maddinson, meanwhile, were natural attackers pressured by convention to develop defensive techniques. Woodhill is modest about his role in Warner's rise: 'I didn't teach Davey anything. We just worked together.' But he did intercede at one critical inflexion point, during the 2013 Ryobi Cup, which Warner started hesitantly with 4, 0 and 17 from 52 deliveries.

Woodhill recalls: 'I said: "What the fuck are you doing? You're the Bull. You're not this defensive person." We sat in a café in Paddington for an hour and a half, and I unloaded, not on Davey, but on the system, how one of my players had been corrupted, technically and mechanically.' That Warner found the argument persuasive can be inferred in his next five games, in which he plundered 520 runs from 414 balls, leading into a breakthrough Ashes series.

Yet Woodhill is conscious of owing Warner too. It was after Warner's night out at the MCG that Woodhill was recruited by the Delhi Daredevils in the Indian Premier League, then coached by another figure integral to his progress — shrewd, laconic, evergreen Greg Shipperd. At first, the experience was terrifying: 'I sat down in Capetown, opened up the laptop and...didn't know what the hell I was doing. Made it up as I went along. I mean, I'd done the job with Surrey, but computers and I don't mix. Didn't really believe in the data crap anyway, not because I thought it was wrong, but because the stuff we were collecting wasn't all that meaningful. Had to make videos. And I'm doing 20-hour days. Because whereas some people can do stuff like that in two hours, it was taking me eight, then it would crash and I'd have to start again. But Shippy and I hit it off. Shippy's a teacher, so generous with his knowledge, just a brilliant bloke. I'll ring him if I want to have a laugh; I'll ring him if I'm not feeling great; he's become one of my best friends.'

Working with the likes of Sehwag, Kevin Pietersen, Ross Taylor and Mahela Jayawardene further consolidated Woodhill's view of the coach as skilled helpmate: 'One day I was with Viru [Sehwag] on the synthetic wickets outside Feroz Shah, and throwing him half-vollies so he felt good. Suddenly he says: "No no no. I want you to throw length balls. I want to drive off either foot, and your job is to stop me scoring...Make it a challenge."

'Viru knew more about technique than any other cricketer I've worked with. He did a great job of bluffing bowlers with his alleged inability to move his feet and transfer his weight, but his mechanics were as good as anyone's — just small compact movements, easily repeated.'

Woodhill is himself unusual among coaches in owning up readily to his mistakes. I ask if coaches, like players, go in and out of form. He nods vigorously: 'I did. With New Zealand [where he was assistant coach from 2010 to 2012] I lost my way big time.

'A lot of it was personal. My partner Yasmin and I were five years into IVF. I was frustrated. I thought I knew the players, felt like I should have been in charge, lost that sense of relaxation, sense of soul. Everyone needs to be sacked, and it was the right decision, because [coach] Mike Hesson was the right person for [captain] Brendon McCullum. Whether he's the right person for [Kane] Williamson time will tell.'

Ironically it is New Zealanders with whom Woodhill has struck up his firmest current relationships: Stephen Fleming at the Stars, and Dan Vettori at RCB, to where he moved after five years with Delhi. His son bears Vettori's middle name, Luca.

More than any other role in cricket, a coach lives and dies by their relationships; their security is tenuous; they must follow the work on offer, then be judged by the performances of others. It's hard, says Woodhill candidly: 'I'm drained and tired and I miss my kids and I can't wait for my mortgage to be over and to ride off into the sunset.'

But then, since that night at the MCG, he also has a front row in the batting revolution. Who could not vicariously enjoy the feats of Kohli, de Villiers, Watson, Chris Gayle and KL Rahul at RCB and Peter Handscomb and Glenn Maxwell at the Stars?

When Channel 9's commentators then found fault with Handscomb's technique on his Test debut, Woodhill felt instantly protective: 'Peter's one of the best people I've ever met in my life, and I like to think I've helped stick up for his technique, which is often getting pulled apart. He's got the only technique in Australia that repeats consistently outside the big two. And he's the most resilient cricketer in Australia. Michael Clarke was the last debutant to look so relaxed.'

With the maverick Maxwell, Woodhill feels a natural empathy: 'According to the system, Davey [Warner], Steve [Smith], Starc and Hazelwood are Australia's only world-class players. But in an IPL auction, only Davey will go for more money than Glenn. Glenn's interested in golf, his friends at Fitzroy-Doncaster, and the Stars, because he can be as vocal or quiet as he likes. He can just be himself.' And it could be Woodhill talking about *himself*.

# Sarah Coyte
# LOST IN CRICKET
MARCH 2017

Although she made it to the very top and excelled, Sarah Coyte isn't sure how much she ever enjoyed cricket. Yes, there are happy memories of constant childhood games in the backyard with her older brother Scott, who played Sheffield Shield, and twin brother Adam, who played interstate under-19s. As a teenager, she virtually lived at Campbelltown Sports Centre.

But to watch, Coyte finds cricket a bit dull. And to play, well, it grew into a source of more or less constant stress — until now. On 1 March, Cricket Australia distributed a press release quietly advising that Coyte had retired, aged just 25. Honouring an international record of more than 100 wickets at an average less than 22, James Sutherland saluted her 'fight and passion' — yet much of that had actually been directed inwardly.

Two weeks in to the next stage of the rest of Coyte's life, which at the moment involves working as a personal trainer for Healthwise Global, her chief sensation is something like relief. 'It feels like a weight has been lifted, to be honest,' she says. 'I've been talking about not playing for a while now.

'Two years ago I was in a camp on Surfers Paradise and I was talking to [teammate] Megan Schutt, who's my best mate, and I said: "I don't know if I can do it. I don't know if I want to play." Mentally I was in a bad spot and physically I just didn't think I could cope. I'd get to training and part of my body would shut down, like it didn't want to do it either.

'There was this fear of judgement: what is everyone going to say? I felt pressure from family and friends, although that was me putting pressure on myself. I'd say: "Would you still love me if I didn't play cricket for Australia?"

And the answer every time was: "We'd probably love you more." Because they knew the toll it was taking on my physical and mental state.'

About six months ago, Coyte made public aspects of that toll, starting a weblog, operationrebuildblog.wordpress.com, in which she divulged, over a series of painfully honest posts, having been plagued by an eating disorder and chronic anxiety almost the duration of her career. It was a form of therapy; it was also an outlet for nervous energy with which she has always felt oversupplied.

'I don't know how to switch off,' admits Coyte. 'I don't know how to do nothing. Even now when I'm between clients at work I find myself wracking my brains for things to do. I spend unnecessary money because I'm bored and don't know what to with myself.

'When I'm up and about, I feel like I should be doing something. I don't know why. I've always liked achieving things, and being the quiet achiever, but if I'm not doing something for me, or for someone else, or to be better, I lose it. I can't even watch a TV show without thinking: what's next? what's next?'

Seven years ago, that question was an exciting one for all-rounder Coyte. In her first weekend of Women's National Cricket League with NSW, aged 18, she took four for 25 with her medium-pacers and made 39 not out with enterprising strokes; a little over a year later she was playing for Australia, picking up two wickets and executing two run outs against New Zealand on debut.

Around that time, however, Coyte began experiencing anxiety about fitness and nutrition. 'When I was growing up, I hadn't had the mentality around fitness playing cricket,' Coyte recalls. 'I thought, oh, you just bat and bowl.

'But then I got a gym membership. And once I started to progress, in my mind I was saying: "You can do more, you can do more." People started saying: "You're looking well, you've lost weight." And I started thinking: "What else can I do?" She began running after every meal. She began, surreptitiously, vomiting.

Anorexics devote immense energy to hiding their symptoms; Coyte's camouflage, a classic instance of hiding in plain sight, was to blend into a system that praised and rewarded the results of her obsession.

'My skinfolds had never been all that good,' Coyte recalls. 'Suddenly mine dropped dramatically, from 90 to the 60 mark — and to this day I sit at 45-50. And there was this response: "Well done, whatever you're doing must be great."

'They didn't know what I'd done to get to that point. All they saw was a number. Boom: you get that tick of approval. That was one thing that I think drove me more. Pushed me even further downhill: "I'm 60. I can get even lower".'

It was during the 2012 World T20 in Sri Lanka that Coyte began to realise she had a problem. She could not keep food down. Team management were convinced that Coyte was suffering from an upset stomach, and she was flown back to Australia, troubled by divided thoughts.

'The next morning after my decision, when I was going home, there was a WSG [gym session] and weigh-in. So I did it, and I looked at the scale and I was 2kg down.

'Regardless of how sick I was I thought: "That's so good. I'm losing weight, I'm losing weight." Then another part of me was saying: "Omigod. This isn't good." By then I'd lost 5kg in 2 weeks and it wasn't in a good way at all.'

Yet nobody would broach the subject with Coyte until a fellow employee at the NSW Education Department, where she worked with the Premier's Sporting Challenge in schools, expressed curiosity about about her regular trips to the toilet.

Ahead of Australia's visit to Bangladesh for the 2014 World T20, the team doctor referred Coyte to psychologist Paul Penna, who recommended coping strategies, then consulted with her daily by Skype while she was away.

Coyte had an outstanding tournament. In the semi-final, she spiked the guns of West Indian stars Stafanie Taylor and Deanna Dottin; in the final against England, her three for 16 included the key wickets of Charlotte Edwards and Sarah Taylor, and won her the individual medal. Big occasions, in fact were a stimulus Coyte always welcomed: 'If there was a pressure situation, I was, like, 'give me the ball'. I loved it when my mind was totally involved.'

Off the field, Coyte was at war with herself, subsisting on protein bars, coffee and duty-free alcohol, while mainly keeping her teammates at arms' length: 'They knew bits and pieces. They're not silly. A few clued on quicker than others. But again they were at that "I don't know what to say to her" kind of stage. It was a tricky period for everyone.'

The on-field success subtly worsened the pressure: 'I was thinking: "You know, you could do so much better if you were healthy right now." At the same time, because I was having success, I didn't see any reason to change, and that threw me deeper into the hole.

'The uniform just felt like it was stuck to me. I'd think: "Everyone's going to see you on TV, what are you going to look like?" I was too scared that if I did start doing things the right way, I'd put on all this weight, look different to people, and play different to how I was playing.'

Then there was the continued approbation that came with perception of Coyte's 'work ethic'. 'In the gym, I was referred to as "the freak"', she recalls. 'When we'd have a 2km time trial, the others would go: "What are you worried about? You'll smash it." And I'd think: "That's awesome. I've got this great reputation for always working hard." '

At the time of her conversation with Megan Schutt a year later, Coyte was preparing for a 2015 Ashes tour that was stalked by doubt. 'It was a tough trip,' says Coyte. 'There was probably once a day for all seven weeks that I'd go through at least an hour contemplating how much I wanted to go home, whether I shouldn't go to the coaching staff and tell them.'

Australia prevailed; Coyte felt defeated: 'That's when I knew that sooner or later I was going to pull the pin.' That she lasted as long as she did is testament to the welcoming sorority she found on moving to the SA Scorpions and Adelaide Strikers in September 2015, where she spent two successful seasons, including breaking the NSW Breakers' stranglehold on the Women's National Cricket League.

Coyte shared a house with visiting Englishwoman Sarah Taylor, with whom she discussed her future, whether a break should be temporary or total: 'I remember talking to her a lot about how I was feeling, how I didn't want to play, wanted to walk away. We came up with a list of pros and cons, what I liked and didn't like about the game.

'A couple of years earlier she [Taylor] had taken a break from the game and said it was the best thing for her. And she said if that's what it takes you should do it. So she was a good voice of reason.' Ironically, Taylor has since taken another longer break from the game, dealing with her own issues of anxiety.

So Coyte began working on an exit strategy with Australian Cricketers' Association professional development officer Matt McGregor, with an eye on a career in personal training. As if reciprocally, cricket grew finally unbearable. In February last year, Coyte withdrew from a one-day international series against India for what was reported as a 'medical reason': in fact, it was 'a bit of a breakdown.'

Says Coyte: 'It was anxiety-based. Depression-based too. I found myself not wanting to do anything cricket related. Play, go to training. I was just miserable really. I felt like I didn't have control over things. Cricket had become an environment I resented.'

At last Coyte agreed to medication, which she had previously rejected as a 'sign of weakness'. She also decided to talk about her condition with those friends whom she'd worried about letting down: Coyte's weblog faithfully charted the last stages of her career, a mix of hesitation, resolution, confusion and candour.

Coyte speaks in the same frank and intelligent voice, about blackouts, and body checking, and the stress of hewing to a path of recovery now she has returned to Sydney to live with her older sister. She is neither morose nor self-pitying: occasionally there is a sigh of bemusement. Is it hard to make sense of the last few years? 'So hard,' she says. 'It doesn't make sense to me now. That's what I tell my sister. I know right from wrong. I know what I should do. But I'm just not doing it.'

She sees potential pitfalls for others, however, with great clarity. Something as routine as a skinfold test, for instance, has a social dimension. 'I think that now skinfolds are like regular testing they're something you have to be really careful of,' observes Coyte. 'Particularly in this day and age, with younger girls so impressionable. It's becoming a big problem with younger girls — how they look, how they train, the way that they see food, I think it's a dangerous path...It's the society we live in.'

The experience is intensified by social media's hall of mirrors: 'You take a good photo and you think: "Yeah I'll post that up." Then you discard five bad ones. 'I still find myself body checking all the time. Looking in windows, feeling around my neck, my hips, round the wrist sometimes, anywhere really. Even when I've had my best days, I still don't know how to break that cycle.'

Some days, in fact, normality feels a long way off. 'Someone asked me the other day: "What's your favourite meal?" I don't even know any more. I eat the same stuff every day.

'I don't know what I feel like eating. I don't know when I want to eat. Sometimes I black out when I'm at the supermarket and I just end up with the same stuff in my basket. It's just a shitty routine I can't get out of at the moment.'

Coyte sets herself tough challenges, I say. 'Oh yeah,' she says, with the hint of a smile. 'I go all out.'

# The Grade Cricketer
## SERIOUS FUN
DECEMBER 2015

As Australia take the field at the Melbourne Cricket Ground today, he'll be looking on with a vague sense of what might have been, and an acuter sense of what isn't.

It could have been him out there, you see. He played juniors and rep cricket against a few of the Aussie guys. He's seen a couple up of blokes up close. One of them once looked in his direction with a hint of recognition, then condescendingly called him 'champ'. He consoled himself with the thought that he plays the highest standard of amateur cricket in the world. For he is The Grade Cricketer.

None of the foregoing is quite true, except in slightly soured spirit. The Grade Cricketer is instead a three-year-old Twitter handle and a month-old book by three disarmingly cheerful young men from Sydney, 30-year-old Sam Perry, 30-year-old Dave Edwards and 29-year-old Ian Higgins. It concerns the cricket, seldom described, just below first-class level, where 'young blokes morph from polite teenagers to arrogant pricks in the space of a season.'

*@gradecricketer* has 42,000 followers, including Test cricketers from Kerry O'Keeffe to Ed Cowan, while *The Grade Cricketer* (Melbourne Books) has won testimonials from personalities as diverse as Big Brother's Ryan Fitzgerald and Booker Prizewinner Thomas Kenneally ('The finest tribute to a sport since Nick Hornby's *Fever Pitch* and the best cricket book in yonks').

Most any cricketer can identify with the hopeless addictedness of such reflections as: 'I couldn't tell you what colour my girlfriend's eyes are but I'll never forget that one glorious cover drive I hit in 2006.'

Nor is it entirely a joking matter, for the authors also cast an eye on the mores of the young, insecure Australian sporting male. 'We're not academic experts,' says Perry. 'But we've tried in a clumsy way to make broader sociological commentary on Australian men. And it does strike us that the cricket club has been left behind as the world has moved on.'

Of this world, Perry, Edwards and Higgins have firsthand experience. They started together in the mid-1990s as junior cricketers at the venerable Gordon District CC, home base through history to such names as Victor Trumper, Charlie Macartney, Bert Oldfield and Adam Gilchrist. Higgins is still there captaining the Third XI, after six years in the Seconds never quite cracking the Firsts.

Both Edwards and Perry crossed paths again at North Sydney CC, then moved to Melbourne where they hovered in the middle grades of Prahran and St Kilda respectively before a combination of injury and adulthood took their toll.

Each by now worked on the fringes of media, in sales and communications; and wrote a group blog, *The Public Apology*. And in September 2012, Perry chanced on their subject.

To mark the first cricket pre-season of which he had not been part since childhood, Perry dashed off a 1500-word instructional guide to 'How to Make It in Grade Cricket' which identified the central importance of looking the part — on the field, in the nets, in the sheds, in the showers.

'If you've batted for over forty-five minutes, and have a modicum of sweat about you, definitely call for new gloves,' was a typical recommendation. 'In essence, this will demonstrate to your team that you are committed enough to have multiple sets of gloves, which therefore means you are *good at the game*.'

To the trio's surprise, the piece was widely circulated. Appreciative comments were forthcoming from likes of former Test opener Justin Langer and one-day international player Brett Geeves.

Emboldened, Perry began tweeting in the persona of a cricketer 'unemployed, pushing 30, and barely clinging to my spot in 5th grade' yet somehow unable to give the game up.

After nine months, Edwards and Higgins started pitching in, and the character began developing a kind of back story complementing his sardonic advices and rueful self-reflections.

On Twitter, TGC has a demanding father: 'Dad never told me he loved me but he did say "nice shot" once, so there's that.'

His friendships are few and strained: 'I'll miss my best mate's wedding if I think I can score a fifty against the bottom placed side in 4th grade'. His possessions are few and shabby: 'My car smells like pad-sweat, grass stains and wasted youth'.

The persona, as Perry observes, 'breaks the rules of Twitter' in its instability. Some tweets are young and arrogant: 'Oh, you're new at this club? Allow me to bestow a demeaning nickname upon you in order to cement my fledgling alpha dog status.'

Others are older and sadder if none the wiser. TGC's personal life has trended from the flaccid ('I shine the ball suspiciously close to my groin because I haven't had sex in 7 months and I yearn for the touch of our tea lady') to the downright shriveled ('As a boy, I honed my signature hoping one day I'd be asked to autograph a mini bat. Doesn't have the same impact on child support cheques.')

The persona of the book, the 'autobiography of a failed cricketer', was a different matter. Warwick Todd and Dave Podmore had been done. The wannabee alpha male had to become a beta man.

All the collaborators really knew as they sat down one day with a Melbourne University CC second grade match in the background, for atmospheric purposes, was how the book would end: 'Maybe I will go round again next season.' But that decision had to be convincingly arrived at.

In this they've largely succeeded. TGC between covers cuts a more sympathetic figure. He is still basically selfish, often morose, physically self-conscious, desperate to be taken seriously. But he has a droll perspective on his lonely younger self: 'I dreamt of one day meeting a girl that liked cricket. Mainly, I just wanted somebody to give me throwdowns.'

The younger cricketers with whom TGC now competes he regards with chagrin and pathos: 'There's nothing that makes me feel more alive than sledging a 15-year-old all day and getting into my 1991 Nissan Pulsar and driving to my parents' house. Absolutely nothing.'

TGC describes the institution of the evening 'circuit' — alcohol-fuelled bonding with female enticements — in anthropological detail. Bad sex and bad cricket prove to have a good deal in common: 'A few minutes of bumbling foreplay ensued. This was no different to the way I usually start all my innings: scratchy at the start and never really "in".'

But he also starts a real relationship with a girl in a book club whose easy-going normality causes him to question his own 'delicate equilibrium': 'If I got out twice during a net session, it's take me days to get over it. Likewise, if I smashed the lst ball of my net 120 metres, I'd dine out on that for weeks. Fucking *weeks*.'

*The Grade Cricketer*, then, offers the redemption @thegradecricketer is afraid to seek, which reflects the authors' themselves achieving a detachment from youthful ambition.

Perry was a very earnest young cricketer. 'I didn't take a gap year because I was sure I'd play for Australia,' he admits. 'I never felt in grade cricket that there was much sense of enjoying the game for the game's sake. I felt that everyone was competing very hard to be as high up in that pyramid as possible, as part of this feudal system.'

Edwards was serious enough that he can't quite get over how his world expanded when he stopped playing: 'I was suddenly able to go to brunch on a Saturday with my girlfriend. I'd never done that. Smashed avocado and feta...I mean, I'd never even *heard* of that dish.'

Higgins is sort of in recovery. 'Writing this book has been a healthy experience,' he says. 'I enjoy cricket from a different perspective, because I'm outside and playing the sport with my mates. Whereas before, it was because I loved the battle and I was trying to be as good as I could possibly be.'

Higgins senses that grade cricket culture is now in a phase of accelerated change. 'It's certainly a lot different to when I started, probably for the better,' he says. 'There was a lot more drinking then because I think there were a lot more older guys playing.'

'I reckon about eighty per cent of grade cricketers now give it away when they finish Uni, around 22 or 23, and start work — when they realise that getting to training and giving up the whole of Saturday is hard.

'Even the circuit is different. I'm the oldest in my team by six or so years, and my guys are going to twenty-firsts and house parties rather than coming back to the clubrooms and heading out as a group.'

Some parts of cricket, of course, remain unaltered, such as the ritual of Boxing Day, to which *The Grade Cricket* pays tribute in its dedication: 'For all those who ever dreamed that one day they'd play for Australia.' But given that only eleven fulfill that dream every Boxing Day, the 'autobiography of a failed cricketer' seems the ideal reading accompaniment.

# PART 2

## Matches and Despatches

# Australia in South Africa 2014
# FAST MEN, SLOW LANE
MARCH 2014

When the Australians arrived at SuperSport Park a week ahead of the
First Test, the field was an expanse of uninterrupted green, the square
indistinguishable from the surrounds.

My esteemed colleague Peter Lalor circulated a Twitpic of what
resembled a cow meadow, anointing it 'Deck of Death II' — reviving a meme
he originated in Perth last year which set the interwebs humming.

Graeme Smith won the toss, sent Australia in and threw the newie
to Dale Steyn, six foot of flint, fortitude and fast twitch fibres. And, well, you
know what happened next, don't you?

Steyn and also Morne Morkel were unwell, but even at their best
would have struggled to penetrate. In the first hour balls were coming
through to the keeper on the second bounce; Australia batted almost nine
hours in all. The pitch responded only to Mitchell Johnson's methods, about
15kmh faster than anybody else's.

So it goes, in Test cricket, now often as not. A pitch can come on as
green as St Patrick, then leave bowlers feeling in need of St Jude — patron saint
of lost causes. For against the modern paceman, multiple forces are ranged.
Administrators keep mandating flat and often slow pitches, and programming
hurried tours full of enervating back-to-back Tests. Broadcasters crave simply
a warm rain of sixes. Batsmen are better protected than riot police, and better
armed too, with bats that should require licensing as assault weapons.

And yet, and yet — what we'll recall of the three superb Tests in South
Africa this month will be the brutal insurgencies of pace bowling, and not only

Johnson's. Indeed, it was the faintly unpromising conditions that made for such a rich spectacle. This was a tour de fast, in which every aspect and dimension of the skill was revealed. There was vivid attack and asphyxiating defence; old ball and new ball alike were made to swerve, veer and wobble; there was raw pace on an uneven wicket, reverse swing on a moribund wicket, life-threatening bounce on a benign wicket.

At the denouement, from Ryan Harris, there was almost superhuman strength. Expected to bowl only ten overs in the fourth innings at Newlands, out of deference to his dodgy knees and aching hips, he continued, on crash through-or-crash principles for nearly twenty-five. So long has Harris lived with sensations that his next Test might be his last that they seem to have become liberating rather than inhibiting.

In this sense, the series encapsulated a little remarked shift in the patterns of the game, of fast bowlers meeting demands for greater resourcefulness and versatility in the face of homogenising influences.

Back in the day, bowling's division of labour was simple: the grassy pitch and new ball were for the seamers, the bare surface and old ball for the spinner. But safety-first curation, encouraged by international oversight and domestic economic concerns, have steadily eliminated outliers. The onomatopoeic WACA is hosting its last Test; once home of the 'green mamba', Kingsmead has lately been kinder to slow bowlers than fast.

'Gone are the days of the greentop,' chuntered James Anderson in the October edition of *The Cricketer*. 'Not even the first day does anything any more. The frustrating thing as a seamer is seeing a bit of grass two days out, then you get to the day of the game and it's gone.'

Fewer are the pitches, too, that verifiably crumble, meaning more work to be shared round at the back end of innings, when the chief variation is in movement up and down rather than side to side.

That's necessitated new variations: reverse swing, cross seam, wobble seam, changes of pace, changes of angle. Such is the concentration on 'preparing' the old ball nowadays, that it's by no means uncommon for pace to be more effective after over 40 than before; the softer, more ragged sphere makes scoring harder too.

No longer is the pitch the only factor underfoot either. By affecting the condition of the ball, an abrasive square or a lush outfield can be just as influential.

For all his complaints, Anderson has been a trend setter in adaptation to those new realities. Originally the archetypal purveyor of orthodox swing, he still pays least for his wickets at home (27.8) but next least in India (29.8). On England's most recent tour there, MS Dhoni called him 'the major difference' between the sides.

Still more remarkable is Dale Steyn, to whom dry pitches seem to come as naturally as selfies to Shane Warne: Steyn takes wickets in India more cheaply (20.39) than at home (21.37), and far more cheaply than in England (31.65).

For fast bowlers the far side of 30, of course, there's a physical imperative. Better to be equipped to probe away with an old ball at 135kmh than always to rely on busting a boiler with a new ball at 145kmh.

Economic considerations come into it as well. Back in the day, the subcontinent was a hardship posting for pacemen: where bounce was so minimal and shine so short-lived, there was no disgrace in ineffectiveness. But India especially has become a place to do well because, as Willie Sutton said when asked why he robbed banks, 'that's where the money is.'

Whatever the case, cricket's a better, richer, more various game for fast bowling's new possibilities, which is why the distinction between polishing and 'preparing' the ball has come to seem so arbitrary, even archaic.

The tip-for-tat bleats of batsmen; the paranoia around sweetie sucking and trouser zips; the new rigmarole around umpires adjudicating on excessive bouncing of the ball: this is cricket at its pettiest. The same censurers have turned a blind eye to the revolution in bat making that is every bit as much about television's interests as cricket.

So perhaps everyone should take a chill pill, assuming these aren't on banned substance list, and enjoy skills that are adding a new layer of intrigue to cricket and helping restore the equilibrium of bat and ball. After all, even if we find Deck of Death III, it will probably be disappointment anyway.

# Australia v India, Melbourne, 2014
# MR SMITH GOES TO MELBOURNE

## DECEMBER 2014

Cricketers demonstrate toughness in a variety of ways: physical courage, mental resilience, self-motivation, self-sacrifice. Yesterday at the MCG, Steve Smith demonstrated it by what he did not do. Grimly, pragmatically, Smith closed out the Border-Gavaskar Trophy by giving India not the whiff of a glimmer of a jot of a semblance of a hope of victory.

In assuming the captaincy *pro tem* three weeks ago, Smith promised he had 'no intention of changing any plans of anything'. Perhaps he was having a bit of a lend: turns out that he is not a Michael Clarke *manqué* but his own man. For those still in thrall to Clarke's grand funk field settings, it was odd; and, actually, oddly impressive.

It wasn't only armchair captains, harking back to the palmy days of Steve Waugh's 400-runs-a-day-or-your-money-back machine, who arrived expecting a bit of a thrash and an early declaration. So, apparently, did the visitors. After three balls, a gentle mist descended, and Shaun Marsh and Ryan Harris jogged off. The Indians watched, scanned the skies, looked quizzically at the umpires, paused about halfway to the boundary, then followed about 90 seconds later.

Play resumed after a half-hour hiatus, whereupon Marsh and Harris added 17 in 51 deliveries before a second rain interruption. At this, the visitors turned as one for the dressing room, then traipsed off in twos and threes. By now the message was clear: there would be no generous invitations issued, no kid-lined gauntlets thrown down.

Dhoni kept waiting. It is his natural state. He makes Alastair Cook look like General Patton. He set fields without slips and posted sweepers to the cover boundary; he had two men back for hook shots nobody was playing; he declined to take the new ball, compelling his perspiring quicks to carry on with the old one for nearly 100 overs.

Which made you wonder. Wasn't it India who needed to win this Test to stay in the series? Wasn't it India who therefore needed wickets? Depending on Australia to indulge them, they brought nothing else to the contest when this did not eventuate; they could have made a more meaningful contribution to proceedings had they voted for their favourite pizza topping on Channel 9.

You could follow Smith's reasoning too. The outfield was quick, the pitch in excellent nick, one of those drop-ins that refuse to deteriorate under the influence of anything short of dynamite: the sun-spot discolourations were neither deep nor overly dusty, the reverse swing subdued, the turn slow.

Hitherto this summer, India had scored at 3.7 runs per over, playing their strokes in every circumstance. Even given the opportunity to seek safety at Adelaide Oval, India had continued attacking — and given away eight wickets in a session.

Test cricket, above all things, involves forcing your opponents to play against their natural instincts. To approach 386 in 70 overs when the closure was made at lunch, then, India had to bat in a fashion for which in two and a half Tests they had shown no aptitude. And for a while showing no aptitude is what they continued to do.

Dhawan, anxious to close the bat-pad gap that Harris prised open in Adelaide, erred the other way; Vijay succumbed unluckily to seam, Rahul haplessly to awe. Virat Kohli faced a situation ill suited to his natural flair and brazen exhibitionism. He hooked awkwardly, pedantically down, as if taking a carpet-beater to a rug. He nearly ran himself out ball watching. He walked a full length of the pitch for the reassurance of some glove love with his partner.

An earlier declaration would have afforded Smith more time; but as it was, he could attack without inhibition, with support in the cordon, where most wickets in the game had fallen, and around the bat. Eventually, Kohli settled in again with Ajinkya Rahane, but without the freedom and fluency of the first innings; both gave chances, as Dhoni did later.

Ryan Harris and Mitchell Johnson bowled with skill and tenacity; the rest plugged away with little encouragement; the Test was decided in the final session of the last day, which is as it should be. Four wickets remained when the final handshakes were exchanged. But the declaration's timing was a smidgen or two away from a nicety.

Michael Clarke would probably have been bolder. Michael Clarke *was* bolder, at the Oval last year. But that Test was posthumous, and the declaration one of his worst captaincy calls, a vanity project that put Australia within a few lux of a 0-4 defeat. This Test was well and truly alive, and only Smith's second in charge — even if he already seems part of at least a little era of his own.

Least convincing of all were those on social media, and anti-social media as well, who claimed to detect some grievous blow to cricket in Smith not gambling all in pursuit of victory. Test cricket will not pass away because a Test match has been drawn — and if it did, it would hardly have been worth saving anyway.

In any event, Smith's caution showed respect for the format, recognizing that while Test matches are important to win, they are important not to lose, and not lightly gambled on. And while the Border-Gavaskar Trophy might be a World Cup warm-up for MS Dhoni, Smith approached his deliberations like it was a prize worthy of those it was named for.

There will be criticism for Smith in the aftermath, and he will know it. But that will make him tougher still...

# World Cup 2015
# BAZ STAKES HIS CLAIM
## MARCH 2015

*'I want to win a tournament, the World Cup. Why not?'*

Five years ago, when he was simply New Zealand's keeper, Brendon McCullum published a little instructional book, *Inside Twenty20* — a cheerful, straight-talking read mainly about his introduction to the Indian Premier League.

One of the straightest talkings was about money. McCullum described returning home from captaining Kolkata Knight Riders in IPL2 and agonising over whether to sign a contract with New Zealand Cricket or becoming a full-time T20 troubadour.

McCullum, he confessed, came 'bloody close' to the latter. 'In what other industry would you be expected to take options that cost you hundreds of thousands of dollars?' he grumbled.

In opting for the former, McCullum said in his book, he was going to need incentives. The World Cup? The way he couched it was in the expectation of incredulity. But, well, even the World Cup ends up being just XI versus XI on a given day — and one team must win, right?

Five years on, McCullum is the man of the hour, even if he barely needs as long as that to turn a game, having added a 15-ball one-day half-century to a portfolio of recent distinctions ranging from a 74-ball Test hundred to a 559-ball Test triple hundred. Can New Zealand win against Australia at Eden Park today? Can they win the final at the MCG four weeks hence? *Why not?*

To the outside observer, McCullum always looked like a leader —

the batting panache, the bulging physique, the abrasive surfaces. Even when simply crouched behind the stumps, he could be seen adjusting and tidying field settings, motioning a man a few metres here or there.

Yet he took a strangely zig-zagging route to his personal summit. When Ric Charlesworth was New Zealand Cricket's high-performance manager between 2005 and 2007 and set up a leadership group, McCullum missed out to Hamish Marshall. He gained the vice-captaincy then lost it five years ago to Ross Taylor.

When NZC interviewed McCullum and Taylor for the task of succeeding Daniel Vettori in June 2011, McCullum missed out again. He took undisputed control eighteen months later only after the controversial advocacy of newly-appointed coach Mike Hesson, another Dunedinite, which for a period alienated Taylor and tainted Hesson.

'A little bit rough,' was the description Stephen Fleming gave of the young McCullum last week: 'He always talked about leadership and captaincy, but he was always viewed as if he would have to smooth the edges a little bit.' And measured against suave Fleming, studious Vettori and reticent Taylor, McCullum might well have looked an outside-the-square appointment.

Ironically, McCullum may have been a beneficiary of New Zealand's decline. Two years ago, New Zealand ranked eighth, ninth and eighth in Test, one-day and T20 international cricket respectively. Had they been, say, fifth or sixth, a mandate for change might not have been so readily obtainable. But the decisive influence on McCullum has been IPL, where he scored the very first century — an incandescent 158 from 73 deliveries in the inaugural match in April 2008 for the Kolkata Knight Riders against Royal Challengers Bangalore.

New Zealand Cricket had many reasons to fear the rise of T20.

Its players were among those chiefly targeted by the agents of the Indian Cricket League (which antagonised the Board of Control for Cricket in India). Always stretched to meet the payment expectations of its players, it was essentially forced to take the pragmatic course of facilitating its players' IPL ambitions, amid some controversy, even scorn.

Yet it's proven a fruitful accommodation. For McCullum's flinty poise over the last two years, in his comfort with big occasions, zeal for experimentation and air of worldliness, you can give at least some credit to his IPL experiences. Ten years ago, he was a 23-year-old keeper from South Dunedin. Now he's a millionaire many times over who's represented three IPL franchises, two Big Bash teams and two counties, and counts Ricky Ponting and Sourav Ganguly as friends. If that's possible...well, why *can't* New Zealand win a World Cup?

New Zealand's reputation or profile in international cricket has always been for 'punching above its weight' — plucky underdogs doing the best they have with limited resources and playing pool etc. I doubt McCullum is in sympathy with that cliché; his bowling coach Shane Bond certainly isn't. Bond's 2010 autobiography, one of the more interesting recent volumes in the genre, concludes with a tough-minded chapter about cricket in his country that impatiently dismisses 'hard-working', 'always-competitive' New Zealand cricket as an enfeebling myth.

On the contrary, Bond argues, New Zealand has consistently produced players of immense talent; they have simply, in the main, never pushed themselves hard enough. 'It's not because our players are lazy,' he says. 'It is just because they've never been taught how hard you have to work to become great until they find themselves playing among the greats.'

McCullum, I suspect, has challenged New Zealand to think along similar lines. He has been a dedicated improver of his own cricket: a dasher who built a defence capable of batting thirteen hours in a Test; a keeper who become an outstanding fielder; and, if Fleming is to be believed, a smoother of his own rough edges, just as his captaincy counterpart today [Michael Clarke] has self-consciously roughed a few of his smooth ones. These are inspirational qualities.

There remains a frontier to ford. New Zealand meet Australia on ideal terms at Eden Park today, with a full strength line-up unchanged in four matches. To seize the World Cup they must win in Melbourne, and the Black Caps on the road have prevailed at only ten of their last thirty starts.

But their captain looks on the world with a confident authority. It has been good to him, rewarding of his talent, welcoming of his personality. In an era changing so fast and unrecognizably, the realm of the possible is only a burst of boundaries or a scattering of stumps away. The world can change in an hour. Why not indeed?

# World Cup 2015
# **BLEED BLUE**
## MARCH 2015

In Mike Marqusee's endlessly perceptive travelogue of the 1996 World Cup, *War Minus the Shooting*, he describes a skirmish between cricket authorities and cricketers over the logos they could wear. It was, he says, 'not over either the aesthetics or morality of advertising, but over control of the most prime of prime sites, cricketers' bodies', and the subsuming of 'individuals into corporate identities.'

Marqusee died this week, aged 61, one of the game's most trenchant and protean writers. But how little his writing has dated, I reflected a few hours later on my way to the MCG with an invitation in my pocket headed 'Bleed Blue.'

No, Beyond Blue had not merged with the Blood Bank: the event heralded the launch of the Indian cricket team's new one-day international uniform.

Actually, I'm underselling it. We are talking Nike. We are talking Team India. We are talking Star India, their naming rights sponsor, and stars Indian, such as MS Dhoni and Virat Kohli. In other words, the branding of a branded brand of brands: on that 'most prime of prime sites', there are now multiple, overlapping, clamorous claims.

The launch represented a continuation of one of the Board of Control for Cricket in India's original big deals: Nike bid successfully to be apparel supplier in December 2005, forking out around $50 million for its initial four-year term.

The dealmaker in the first place was a fast-rising BCCI vice-president,

Lalit Modi, the Indian Premier League still a twinkle in his eye. Now, of course, he is the BCCI's most implacable enemy, having revealed himself a month ago as bankrolling a legal action that has bound the former employer hand and foot for almost a year, to the extent that it has been unable to hold elections. Cricket, as they say, is a funny game.

But hey, on Thursday at the G, we were here to learn about uniforms. We even had a host, Alan Wilkins, flown in for the occasion. Nice bloke, Alan. Trundled away for Glamorgan in the 1970s, before commencing a broadcasting career in South Africa and India. Had something very important to tell us, which he commenced reading from very small cards. The uniform was blue.

And how he told us. In so many ways. Thought you'd seen blue? Think again. In the annals of blue, this was the ne plus ultra. Team India told blue what to do and where to go. Team India owned blue's ass. If blue was a country, Team India had invaded and subjugated it. If blue was a religion, Team India was its Godhead. I'm exaggerating, but you get my drift.

Then the other takeaway: the uniforms were made from polyester recovered from plastic bottles. How many plastic bottles? If you were there on Thursday, you will never forget. Thirty-three. Not thirty-two. Not thirty-four. Thirty-three.

Actually, I looked this up, and they seem to have been making clothing from PET bottles since the early 1990s. So it was like the old Lucky Strike ad: 'They're toasted.' Everyone's cigarettes were toasted, but Lucky Strike was the first to say so. Not only that but, when I checked, the last Nike ODI kit for Team India was also made from recycled polyester; it also had 'laser ventilation holes' and a 'breathable engineered knit'; and, of course, it was blue, too. Hmmm. Might be struggling for news angles here.

OK, so maybe the players would say something: presently, Wilkins introduced eight, Dhoni, Kohli, Ravi Ashwin, Ajinkya Rahane, Shikhar

Dhawan, Ravi Jadeja, Rohit Sharma and Umesh Yadav, for a 'press conference.' Some serious talent this: added up, they were paid well over $US10 million in the last IPL. And here they were, lined up like schoolboys — the world's most expensive schoolboys. Not so much Just Do It as Just Do As You're Told.

You don't often get simply to look at cricketers. You're usually concentrating on what they're doing or, sometimes, saying. Here they had chiefly to stand, and not look bored. They did it better than I would under the circumstances.

Alan Wilkins asked some toe-curlingly tedious questions, with relation to the blueness and to the bottles. And funnily enough, even in this environment of utter banality, the players' individuality could not quite be effaced: Dhoni looked as he often does in press conferences, half-amused; Kohli stood there like an action figure, or a superhero sans cape; at one point, Rohit puffed out his cheeks and looked at the sky. It may never happen again, but Rohit and I were at this stage of exactly one mind.

Personally, I like Ashwin: he's thoughtful, competitive, carries himself well. I noticed that he has that little tic of lifting the shirt off his shoulder even in repose. At a present conference in Brisbane, he referred to Steve Smith as 'Smudger', and wanting to get him to 'nick off': there was a pleasing familiarity and colloquial regard about it. Now he was asked, poor chap, about the bottles. Yes, he obediently agreed, it was 'socially responsible.'

Actually, Ashwin seems like the kind of guy who might know what this means. But my guess is I'll never really know, so rigid is the *cordon sanitaire* round this current Indian team. Certainly, nothing was to be allowed to obscure this corporate message, uniform being very much the operative word: Rohit, Dhawan, Jadeja and Umesh remained studiously silent.

Until, after ten minutes, all were excused. One man from Indian television hurried forward with his microphone and was brushed aside, foolishly literal about the promised 'press conference', which had, of course, been an advertisement all along. Mind you, when I scoured the interwebs later, there it was being reported as 'news' right across India. Blue. Thirty-three bottles. Job done.

And, well, it was kind of instructive. I was reminded again of the chapter in *War Minus the Shooting* where Marqusee recounts the cola wars, Coke versus Pepsi, of the 1996 World Cup. 'Thus cricket populism was made to serve the interests of the elite,' Marqusee concludes. 'The elan and individualism of sub-continental cricket stars became the human mask for a faceless multinational.' Five World Cups on, we hardly even notice.

# World Cup 2015
# LEFTIES TO THE FORE
## MARCH 2015

Left-handers, it is usually estimated, comprise about a tenth of the world's population. You'd hardly believe it watching this World Cup.

Yesterday afternoon at Adelaide Oval, the new ball was taken for Australia by Mitchell Starc. He was relieved by Mitchell Johnson. From the opposite end came James Faulkner. When Michael Clarke rolled his arm over for practice, it looked less like simulation than symmetry.

For his part, Misbah-ul-Haq held back Pakistan's equivalents, Wahab Riaz and Rahat Ali. He had cause to lament the absence of Mohammed Irfan, leaving in his resources a suitably sized hole.

For the Cup's last quarter-final today, meanwhile, New Zealand will choose its XI to oppose the West Indies from a squad containing three speedy bowlers, Trent Boult, Corey Anderson and Mitchell McLenaghan, also sliding in from the left. Overs of spin will be provided, as ever, by Dan Vettori.

Such incidences have tended to make sameness elsewhere stand out: in their last two games, the West Indies have had nothing except right-handed slows to break the monotony of their right-handed medium pace. England have already followed a similarly uniform route to its logical conclusion.

Here, then, is a new variation on a familiar theme. At various times in the last few years, the rise of left-handedness has been a cricket talking point, if almost invariably in terms of the visible abundance and statistical success of left-handed batsmen — ten of the sixteen specialist batsmen Australia have debuted in the last decade, for example, being of that ilk.

There's been much less interest in or acknowledgement of the specifics of left-arm bowling. Probably the game's benchmark textbook, Bob Woolmer's *The Art and Science of Cricket* (2008), devotes it one paragraph in 654 pages.

Open any instructional text, in fact, and you'll see virtually nothing but right-handed grips and actions — as subtly discriminatory as those seats in lecture theatres with built-in desks on the right. That, though, might be changing — the attention anyway, rather than the seats.

The mirth when Peter Moores seemed to hug his 'data' like a security blanket after England's defeat by Bangladesh in Adelaide was misplaced. Oceans of data are washing round this World Cup, into which a lot of coaches are delving in search of advantages, pitfalls and patterns generally.

The statistics have arguably been more than usually salient, partly because certain accustomed variables have not been a factor: the matches have been played in only two countries, within a fixed time period and involved fixed squads.

We the punters, of course, glimpse the merest fraction of such analysis — in, for example, those magnifications of a batsman's 'strong zones' and 'weak zone' where the broadcaster links telltale replays the way gossip websites serve up celebrity wardrobe malfunctions and sideboobs. But the success of bowlers coming from the left, who've accounted for nearly half the four-wicket bags of the tournament, has been so obviously disproportionate as to register with the lay fan.

Left-arm pace bowlers have been the stand-out category, giving away runs at less than five an over, claiming wickets at just over 20 runs apiece. They have met the need for early breakthroughs, now accentuated by the new/old style of batting acceleration involving the preservation of wickets until the 35th over.

They have also become their captains' preferred instruments

in batting powerplays, being more a quarter more economical than and almost twice as penetrative as right-arm pace bowlers in the same scenarios. Differences are narrower in the final ten overs but in the same favour.

Why might left-arm pace have become such a disruptive innovation in this era otherwise so commodious to batsmen? Part of it is to do with the range of geometric propositions the skill offers — witness yesterday, for example, the difference in trajectories seen between Starc bouncing a 150kmh bouncer from over the wicket to right-handed Sarfraz Ahmed, and Johnson whizzing one across left-handed Haris Sohail from round the wicket.

Maximum power of strokeplay requires a sound platform and a strong shape — to confound these, it's reasoned, the best possibilities lie in variety. A lot of bowling captaincy, too, is now about trying to corral activity within areas occupied by your artificially rationed outfielders, and thwarting those blows, straight and to leg, that tend to carry furthest. A left-armer here can come into his own. His standard fullish delivery canted to off-stump is, for example, difficult to hit outside the cover and point region; the left-armer's bouncer can also be awkward to fetch.

Anyway, such theorising has useful comparisons. Almost a quarter of the pitchers in Major League Baseball are left-handed, such efficacy usually being ascribed to their angle coming over the inside rather than the outside the plate and against the natural pull-hit of most right-handed batters.

It has its precedents too. The star of the last World Cup final down under was a left-arm quick, Wasim Akram — perhaps the finest of all. The most effective bowlers in the last World Cup final, Zaheer Khan and Yuvraj Singh, were likewise left-handed. Even the associate members invested in variety ahead of this event, the UAE bringing Manjula Guruge, Afghanistan including Swapoor Zadran.

Others groped for the formula in advance without finding the elements. A year ago, England flirted a year ago with Essex's Tymal Mills before deeming him too wild. Then they gave ten ODIs to Nottinghamshire's Harry Gurney before finding him not quite sharp enough. And bad bowling doesn't matter from which direction it's coming, as South Africa discovered when they deployed Wayne Parnell at the MCG against India, only for him to bowl ten overs of filth.

The most lateral choice was perhaps Boult, previously considered a five-day specialist. At the start of the year, Boult had played only ten one-day internationals to go with his thirty Tests. It was then intuited, rightly, that he could be as penetrative with the twin new white balls as he was with the single red.

Down the track lies a challenge to such selection calls. If your best Test bowlers become your best ODI bowlers and thereby, perhaps, the most sought after for T20 tournaments as well, when will they rest and recover? Perhaps they'll start to feel like an oppressed minority. Mind you, left handers will already have some experience of that.

# World Cup Final 2015
# BOILOVER
## MARCH 2015

All through the forty-minute dinner break at the Melbourne Cricket Ground last night, New Zealand went through their impressively disciplined paces on the outfield.

Bowlers ran in hard, practising their variations, visualising their desired outcomes. Fielders tackled vigorous drills. Senior players consorted. Backroom staff milled about. Plans were laid.

It was purposeful, persistent, professional, and also sadly symbolic — to be at their best, New Zealand needed Australia not to be there. For the hosts were cheerfully chowing down, comfortably on top, ready to rumble again.

The Australians' fast bowling had already wreaked havoc; their batting had merely to administer the coup de grace. It was at times an austere finale to an often spectacular World Cup, but there was a sense in which that was not entirely unbefitting: the winners' was a forty-five-day campaign not a one-night stand, and involved subduing their doubts and dilemmas as much as besting the competition.

At one stage in this forty-nine match epic, Michael Clarke's team went a fortnight without playing a game, a hiatus into which could have been squeezed an entire Champions Trophy.

Brendon McCullum's team, meanwhile, were carrying all before them, and had secured three comfortable victories by the time they hosted, and beat, their co-hosts in Auckland.

Australia then hewed the harder route through the finals, the bouncy wicket at Adelaide Oval and the slow wicket at Sydney not quite negating their home advantage but certainly evening the contest. In each game, they were stretched and forced to bounce back.

At the same time, New Zealand were treating the West Indies like the Harlem Globetrotters treated the Washington Generals. Help from the elements in their exhilarating semi-final against South Africa suggested the blessings of providence.

Quibbles with Australia's capabilities were not far to seek: their openers were a hit-and-miss coupling; they lacked a specialist spinner; their senior all-rounder was, involuntarily, a temporary absentee; their captain finally, voluntarily, foreshadowed a permanent exit.

With each match, nonetheless, could be measured a kind of deepening purpose, expanding effectiveness. With every over of India's innings at the SCG on Thursday night, their outcricket seemed to tighten and sharpen, until it finally slammed shut like an iron maiden. And while New Zealand had won golden opinions through their unbeaten run, it was also hard to imagine them playing better.

So to the final, which at once appeared qualitatively different to that which had gone before. The crowd was a vivid coral reef of colour. The outfield stretched from horizon to horizon, a space of uncompromisingly Australian dimensions, a space Clarke controlled with the lightest of touches, so that the fielders seemed to exert a kind of magnetic influence on the ball.

New Zealand never found a tempo to suit them once McCullum, having taken his team a step forward by winning the toss, took them two back by succumbing to Starc in the first over. It seemed almost too soon for the crowd, still reaching for their drums and vuvuzelas, with the flame machines still warm.

The New Zealanders sank into introspection bordering on grief. Maxwell's first ball was half-tracker. Guptill picked out point. Maxwell's second ball was straight at off-stump. Guptill, straining to hit a gap, simply missed it. When Williamson failed to pick Johnson's slower cutter, Plans A, B and C lay in tatters, and D demanded digging in.

Again, New Zealand's efforts hinged on the wiry, unassuming Elliott, who accumulated prudently without ever threatening to reprise his Eden Park heroics. At one stage he reverse swept with the back of his bat, as though striving to find a trick the Australians had not seen. Yet every time New Zealand threatened to insinuate themselves into the match, Clarke found a way to hold them back and spoil their fun, like a vigilant bouncer at a velvet rope.

Bowlers were turned over constantly: fifteen changes in forty-five overs, Maxwell bowling his six overs in three spells. Back and back they came, a relentless relay: Starc's pinpoint yorkers, Johnson's buzzsaw bouncers, Hazlewood's vertical seam; best of all, on this occasion, player-of-the-final James Faulkner with his indiarubber arms and puffball change-ups. Six weeks earlier, Mitchell Marsh had devastated England on this same arena; now he was a supernumerary, a statement of Australian cricketing riches.

Maxwell then claimed the last wicket with a rasping short-range throw at the bowlers' stumps from short mid-wicket on the mere suspicion of a vagrant non-striker — a suspicion which proved well-founded. Five overs went to waste, not that the visitors were best placed to use them anyway.

Finch perished early in Australia's reply, Warner needlessly. But although the ball nibbled around, the swing did not linger, and nor did McCullum's attacking configurations. At two for 68, Smith inside edged Henry into his pad and the ball menaced the stumps, nudging without breaking them. A few overs later, Clarke thick edged over slip and flailed just wide of gully. New Zealand heads shook and rueful smiles were shared; the rumble of an Australian juggernaut could be heard.

For Australia's captain departing one-day cricket, the scenario was perfect: little hurry, negligible pressure, much attention, no tomorrow. He played strokes crisp and powerful, peachy and meaty, as the terraces twinkled with photographic flashes.

It was fitting, too, that Smith should hit the winning runs shortly after 9pm, at the climax of a season of chain-batting few could have forseen. Barely six months ago, Clarke was urging that Smith's progress not be rushed, but there has been no holding him back. A tide has come in his affairs to carry Australia forward. By Thursday, footballers will own this arena again. Last night it had only eleven proprietors.

# England v Australia, Cardiff, First Test, Day 1, 2015
## GAUNTLET THROWN DOWN

JULY 2015

'England 0 points' and 'Australia 0 points' shows the lo-fi scoreboard at Sophia Gardens, as if at the outset of a game of rugby. Yet certain points have already been made, even at this commencement of the long Ashes haul.

For the Australians, the preliminaries of the series have revolved around two fine cricketers just either side of the long goodbye. The obvious one was Brad Haddin, who had the opportunity to reduce England to four for 43 with both their captain and vice-captain gone, to expose Ben Stokes under circumstances that would have tested his commitment to all-out attack, but who dropped Joe Root to his right, first wrongfooted, then diving awkwardly.

Asked when it dawned on him that it was time to give the game away, Haddin's predecessor Adam Gilchrist cited a catch he missed in his final Test proffered by VVS Laxman — Gilchrist said the idea of retirement came to him 'somewhere between the ball hitting my gloves and the ground'.

Whether the same occurred to 37-year-old Haddin, only he can know. Yet it was a catch in his prime of which he'd have made short work. It also continued his chequered form at home last summer, which mixed the brilliant and the insecure — he had earlier made a difficult catch to dismiss Alastair Cook look easy.

Already it may have given the Australians a jolt. Before the game, supporters were loyally backing Haddin to carry on years yet — Gilchrist's predecessor Ian Healy pronounced him, 'in good shape with the gloves, really good shape'. But Josh Hazlewood's well-meaning comments at stumps — 'Hadds usually takes more than he drops, so hopefully he can improve and catch the next one' — sounded a little like the captain of a club third XI discussing his choice of a part-time keeper at selection night.

The other key Australian was, less obviously, Ryan Harris. When you saw the effect of his absence, in fact, you understood why such strenuous and expensive efforts were made to get him onto an English Test field one last time.

This was the kind of pitch and sort of scenario calling for that relentless Harrisment of the top-of-off that characterised Australia's bowling through 2013-14. Instead, balls were sprayed wide of off and speared down leg, four clumps of four byes passing the non-plussed Haddin. Short stuff sat up on the slow surface, imploring the punishment meted out.

Joe Root, who fell to Harris five times in eight Tests of the last Ashes cycle, enjoyed the absence of Harris as well as the mercy of Haddin. Two years ago, he made merry at Lord's then progressively less merry as the Australians probed away at fuller lengths and down tighter lines. At times he looked weighed down by expectation and responsibility as much as by actual accuracy.

Part of Root's hot streak since has been a shrugging off of that dull care. Twenty balls after being dropped on 0, he was 32. He took advantage when rain dampened the ball; he tucked in when the part-timers operated; his bat drops down in defence now only as a last resort once all attacking options have been reviewed and deferred. The highlights were drives threaded to the left of cover then of mid-on. The first brought up Root's hundred; the second seemed to gather pace as it rolled toward the straight boundary.

Root's partner in a partnership of 153, Gary Ballance, is perhaps where Root was two years ago. His back foot cross step bunkers him in the crease like a soldier taking cover in a foxhole, while his preliminary backlift draws intricate signals in the air. He is grooved for the cut, which he was he was in position to play so early off Johnson that he could almost have played the shot twice; when the ball is full, his pads present inviting targets, and his defensive shots are barely more than twitches.

The Australians pitched it up to him early in search of late movement; they banged it in later, aware that he eschews the pull. A livelier surface than this would test him more sternly. Yet in favour of Ballance's method is that it is *his*; he knows it, and it suits him like a comfy pullover. His captain, who rebooted his game in mid-career only to have to deboot it later, is a reminder that in technique the perfect can be the enemy of the good.

At four for 43, England could well have been bowled out for 200; at four for 280, they distantly glimpsed 500. While his final figures flattered him, Mitchell Starc did well to restore order in stages, in and around a tender ankle that briefly took him from the field: his is a growingly useful knack of scattering wicket-taking diamonds even among dross. Mitchell Johnson lived to fight another day — not in Cardiff if he has any say in it, one suspects. England would have settled for 430 at the outset; with the prospect of bowling last, they will have eyed with interest some inconsistencies of bounce as well.

If the scoreboard is understated at Sophia Gardens, there is plenty else to detain the eye. With every passing game, the visual clutter at international cricket grounds grows. The Aussie cableknit has now been marred by a red airline logo that looks like a stab wound in the breast; there are no longer drinks breaks but 'hydration breaks' spruiking a spring water brand; you will see fewer zebras, symbol of the Ashes sponsor, in the savannah.

Yet the 'We Are England Cricket' corporate message repeating from the big screen sounds more like an introduction than an affirmation: 'Hello. We are England Cricket. And who might you be, little chap?' 'Cymru,' comes the reply, and what feels a little like an away Test for both sides rolls on.

# England v Australia, Cardiff, First Test, 2015

# A SHOCK TO THE SYSTEM

JULY 2015

Swing was always envisaged as a crucial factor in the Ashes. So it has proved: the swing in fortunes. Future fans may struggle to make sense of it all: three Ashes series so close together involving such swerving trends.

Every time you look up this summer, the press box televisions seem to be showing highlights of the glorious Ashes summer of a decade ago, a drama improbably well-cast and finely-scripted, and also long-awaited, for England were regaining the urn after sixteen long years.

Sixteen years! No wonder people began to believe in the replacement of an Ashes cycle by an Ashes conveyor belt. There is, of course, a legislated advantage in Ashes incumbency, in that the holder need only draw a series to retain the trophy. Yet the last thing the rivalry seems inclined to throw up at the moment is anything as mean as a stalemate.

Eight of Australia's eleven at Cardiff were common to the team that humiliated England just eighteen months ago; Mitchell Starc's injury at the time prevented him being a ninth. But Michael Clarke's team were a pale shadow of the all-conquering ensemble who received the thanks of a grateful nation on a stage by Sydney Opera House in January last year. Has the fat lady now sung for them?

Certainly, the 169-run defeat raises the possibility among the Australians of both complacency and hubris. 'If we continue to play the way we have been playing over the last 12-18 months,' said Steve Smith of England on leaving Australia, 'I don't think that they'll come close to us to be honest.'

New English attitude? Brad Haddin and Shane Watson were dismissive of it on the eve of the series: to them, the Pom had resumed his posture as Australia's natural supplicant.

This is actually the optimistic reading of Australia's performance: that they were a bit arrogant, a bit lazy, and will now switch to afterburners and surge off through the sound barrier. But there are hints of deeper changes, that also go beyond the obvious shifts in conditions and home advantage.

For there *was* a new English attitude on show in Cardiff. Alastair Cook was serene and purposeful, Joe Root spry and spunky, the discipline relentless but not inflexible, the tactics systematic but supple.

They looked like a group having fun too. Each morning, for example, the whole squad, including support staff, took to the outfield for a vigorous game of football — the kind, of course, that when a Rory McIlroy gets injured always seems to fraught with risk, but was on this occasion for a lot of roughhouse fun, cheerful nutmegging and netting of goals past one another. When Moeen Ali nodded in one day, you thought for a moment he was going to pull his shirt over his head.

The Australians, by contrast, were barely seen, and little heard too. Has there been a less obviously jagged Australian performance in the field these last five years? Perhaps all those Simon Heffer columns have had their effect. Mitchell Starc shooshed Ben Stokes on the first day, but his teammates seemed to take it on board. The usual Australian ringleaders, Brad Haddin and David Warner, were conspicuously inconspicuous in Cardiff — Haddin's reasons for brooding were obvious, Warner's enigmatic.

Perhaps an explanation lies in the nature of the last thirty months as a period of unexampled big cricket in Australia: three Ashes series, two Border-

Gavaskar Trophies, a World Test Championship showdown with South Africa, a Champions Trophy and a World Cup.

These are the big occasions for which players hang on. Between times there has been little breathing space, and some players have filled this anyway with Indian Premier League contracts. How easy it must be under the circumstances to think: 'Well, just one more, eh? I'm still good enough, aren't I?' To quote Sugar Ray Robinson: 'You always say: "I'll quit when I start to slide". Then one morning you wake up and you've slid.'

These are also the big occasions when selectors cleave to known quantities. Australia made its most venturesome change at its lowest point, swapping coaches on the brink of the 2013 Ashes. But while failure gives a mandate for change, success breeds conservatism and continuity.

About three years ago, Australia's selectors resiled from their previous policies by stating that performance was now the only currency, and that age was no bar. There were exceptions to this: Shane Watson's 59-Test career is arguably the longest-running potential-based selection experiment in Australian history. But the recognition of Chris Rogers, the restoration of Brad Haddin, the rebuilding of Ryan Harris and even the ongoing primacy of Michael Clarke were the basis of a solid Australian renewal. The question the Ashes of 2015 is now set to answer is whether this renewal became at some point a reoldal, and whether a policy sensible for a time ended up being carried through to a fault.

It won't be as simple as this. It never is. Let's not forget that none of this would be up for consideration had Brad Haddin held onto the chance offered by Root on Wednesday: England would then have been four for 43 on course a first innings in the region of 200; their vice-captain would then have been dismissed by four of the last ten Test deliveries he had received for precisely one run. No kidding — look it up.

In English cricket's favourite bedtime story of 2005, of course, Australia won the First Test only to lose the series. But what back then took sixteen years to happen now seems possible within sixteen months, if not sixteen minutes...

# England v Australia, Cardiff, First Test, 2015
## THE CAPTAIN AT BAY
JULY 2015

In the afterword to Michael Clarke's diary of the Ashes of 2013, his wife Kyly provides a vivid cameo of the morning after the Fourth Test at Chester-le-Street, of 'sitting across from Michael at breakfast', seeing 'the disappointment in his eyes', and knowing that her husband hated losing 'more than anything'.

Sunday breakfast hardly bears thinking about. Sophia Gardens had hosted a Test to ruin any losing captain's morning intercourse. Few Australian teams can have played so far below the sum of their collective talents. On the eve of the Test, the Clarkes had announced Kyly's expecting their first child. Dad now has four Tests to prevent his heir being born into a world in which England hold the Ashes.

For Clarke, the Ashes have never loomed larger. He has retired from one-day and T20 international cricket; he has largely forgone the Indian Premier League; he has yet to represent his new Big Bash League franchise. He bridges Australian cricket's generations, from the high summers of Shaneness to today's myriad Mitches. Yet he has a record to redress, having been on the losing end in four of six Ashes series.

At the same time, he appears ever more a man apart, still setting his leg gullies and short mid-wickets, but from a remove, inscrutable at slip behind his opaque, space-age shades. Off the field, he gives the impression of a man rather worn down. At the pre-match press conferences in Cardiff, his tone was cold and mechanical. He disposed of the questions as perfunctorily as a net of throwdowns, with an 'ah look' here, a 'no doubt' there, a 'to be honest' every other sentence, and the automatic response to any question about the composition of the team: 'Well, I'm not a selector...'

He was a selector once, of course, and it's arguable that for the first two years of his captaincy Clarke was the most powerful figure in Australian cricket — indisputably its leading player, most marketable personality, and most authoritative voice, with a coach, Mickey Arthur, seeking to  march in lockstep with him. Rightly or wrongly, the perception was that Clarke, because of his closeness to Arthur, enjoyed essentially two votes at the selection table.

That ended just over two years ago, with Australia's ruinous campaigns in the Border-Gavaskar and Champions Trophies, and the sudden change of coaches: Arthur was succeeded on the selection panel by Darren Lehmann, and Clarke by no-one. For all sorts of well-rehearsed reasons, it's arguable that Clarke should never have held selection responsibilities in the first place. But authority, once held, can be hard to get used to the lack of — just ask any former politician. Clarke has always said that he stepped down of his own volition. But some volitions are more volitionary than others.

Last summer in Australia, Clarke played an inspirational and uniting role in the mourning of Phillip Hughes. Millions watched his deeply moving eulogy. But this has tended to obscure in memory the very real tensions about Clarke's various injuries going into the summer, and the protracted wrangling afterwards around his availability in the World Cup. As is his wont, Shane Warne brought these to a head in February with accusations that Australia's selectors had 'tried to break' the captain by imposing a deadline on his fitness, and hints that Lehmann's remit were 'something that Australian cricket has to look at.'

Strenuous denials of any rift ensued, and it's true that Warne these days rather acts his role in Australian cricket — that of The Shane, built on the same outsize proportions as The Hoff and The Donald. But Clarke and Warne, roommates ten years ago on what was Clarke's first Ashes tour and Warne's last, are assuredly tight — almost, at times, alter egos. Certainly, Clarke will have welcomed Warne's 597th placing in Las Vegas's World Series of Poker, expediting his flight to London. 'I don't think I've ever come out of a conversation with Warnie where I don't have a smile on my face and am walking a bit taller, ready to face whoever or whatever,' Clarke has said.

At the same time, Australia's strange ennui at Cardiff seemed to be about more than the better execution, shot selection, bowling discipline and catching Clarke has prescribed as cure. In 2013-14, Australia were energised with the bat and in the field by the sight of English batsmen dancing to the tune of Ryan Harris and Mitchell Johnson. Reinforced by various verbal asperities, it lent their cricket a relentless, minatory edge.

In Cardiff, there was no blue touchpaper. There was no Harris, conditions averse to Johnson, and thus less of a climate of intimidation. Such funky fields as Clarke set looked like gestures rather than serious strategems; Brad Haddin and David Warner, usually so locquacious, were palpably subdued. Australia needed something else: that precious sense of cohesion and enthusiasm that is built off the field rather than on, and expresses itself within games as perseverance and resilience. They needed that something else, in fact, that England had.

Is it something Clarke can now build? It has not, perhaps, been his strong suit, intuitive and quick-witted as he has appears while ringing on-field changes. But if Warne is right, and that in the Australian cricket team 'the captain is in charge', then it is to Clarke that the team must now turn for its inspiration. We won't come to know Clarke as a husband in succeeding weeks, but we will learn something of him as a man.

# Shane Watson
# INTERNAL EXILE

JULY 2015

One had always imagined the end of Shane Watson would be accompanied by something like Richard Nixon's famous 'last press conference' after the failure of his 1962 gubernatorial campaign in California: 'But as I leave you I want you to know — just think how much you're going to be missing. You won't have Watto to kick around any more.'

There wasn't anything of the sort, of course. It proved more like one of his more protracted reviews, with a long wait to establish the eminently forseeable: a leak here, a tweet there, a veiled reference, a muffled conjecture, and finally the decision, to a chorus of virtual approval.

In theory, Watson could be back for the Edgbaston Test in a fortnight; in practice, it is difficult to imagine him working his passage back, if only because his opportunities to impress in the meantime will be confined to a tour match at Derby, and because a selectorial bullet bitten cannot readily be unbitten.

At thirty-four, too, failures have more obvious contexts. In truth, Watson has been breasting the bar of the Last Chance Saloon since his replacement Mitchell Marsh's emergence last year in the UAE — Australia's one unqualified gain of that unhappy tour.

Watson was then in the familiar position of being *hors de combat*, having sustained an injury while in the process of recovering from a different injury. In years to come, in fact, students of the game may struggle to make sense of a career of fifty-nine Tests played and fifty-six Tests missed.

During the Australian summer, Watson reappeared at number three, the place into which he first slotted at the Oval in 2013, arriving there almost by default, as it was the last place left in the order following the inclusion of James Faulkner at the expense of Usman Khawaja.

Like Watson's shirts, which always seemed to stretch a little too tightly across his iron man's chest, the role of first-wicket-down was never a wholly comfortable fit. But, then, neither did any of the others, except, for a period, opening the batting, a role he also came to occupy by accident on the previous Ashes tour.

Resuming the patterns of a lifetime, Watson squandered a series of beginnings, and during the World Cup was left out of a game at the WACA — a dry run for yesterday's events.

'Experience' was the explanation for his recall; the same factor now works against him. England have plenty of experience of Watson, and lately sense it favours them.

Watson's omission leaves Australia looking suddenly a little light on: at Lord's a middle order of Marsh, Adam Voges and Brad Haddin's proxy Peter Nevill, Australia's numbers five, six and seven will be occupied by players with seven Tests' behind them in toto. But against that have been weighed Watson's all-round averages since the start of last year, an elliptical 27.5 with the bat and 52.3 with the ball.

Nixon's farewell famously proved no such thing. Watson's, more muted, might well stick.

# England v Australia, Second Test, Lord's, Day 1, 2015
# BUCK'S DAY
JULY 2015

Where is the next Chris Rogers coming from? So goes an Australian cricket question being asked by precisely nobody, even though an answer will need to be found before all that long.

And make no mistake: the answer is elusive. There used to be lots of Chris Rogerses. You know the type: hard little men with deadpan defensive bats who used the pace of the ball to work it into gaps, who became objects of respect if not affection, and who were likely if anything to be taken for granted.

Nowadays they are far thinner on the ground; they may even be a discontinued line. What coach would now encourage a young player to follow in Rogers' footsteps? What agent would go looking for a Rogers to represent? What Indian Premier or Big Bash League franchise would be clamouring for a broad-batted Bucky of their very own?

Rogers is a long-form batting specialist in an age of wannabee multidimensional, multi-format players, like a typographer who when everyone else is revelling in Comic Sans and Phoreus Cherokee sticks resolutely to Times New Roman, and maybe Helvetica when he feels a bit daring.

His Australian summers have become like nobody else's. He plays his Test matches in steady succession. Then when the technicolour extravaganza of the BBL sweeps the nation during the holiday season, he slips back into the sepia tones of weekend club cricket.

Yesterday, however, was the kind of day for which he was selected, and almost for which he was devised: a big Test match, and at his county home ground of Lord's, where he now averages almost 60 in first-class cricket. For Australia he was the equivalent of the guy in the office who knows how to put the toner in the photocopier and where they keep the nice biscuits.

This was his eighth century under the gaze of Father Time, for whom during a flash of candour in Cardiff he suggested an affinity: 'I'm old, I can feel it. Days in the field are hard work and even just being in this environment is fairly draining.'

It was England for whom the environment was draining yesterday instead: they have now bowled 246 of the last 316 overs in the series, with, one fancies, a good many more to come, depending on Michael Clarke's humours.

Australia skated away early, on a pitch flat and bare, and an outfield as frictionless as a roller rink. Warner emerged from his Cardiff introspection to hit seven colourful boundaries before the red mist descended and he sought a third four from Moeen Ali's first over.

Rogers' misadventures were involuntary — of the occupational sort for an opening batsman, sometimes survived, sometimes not. An ambitious drive at Anderson's third ball flew at just above head height between second and third slip. Root and Bell hesitated, and might have had it at the backs of their minds the rest of the day.

Thereafter, Rogers proceeded in his minimalist manner, backlift a jerk, follow-through a shudder: there can hardly be a batsman in the game whose bat moves through fewer degrees in the course of a stroke. He is occasionally more animated in the act of letting a ball go, which he is inclined to do with a jump and a whirl to one side; he can look intense merely in the act of stopping at the non-striker's end and staring hard at the ground.

With Steve Smith, meanwhile, something like normal service resumed after the untimely interruption at Cardiff. He neither pushed his luck, nor reined himself in. He was content to leave English pace in the wide channel they favoured in the First Test; he remained prepared to use his feet against English spin.

After lunch, he and Rogers reappeared early. Sensitive to protocol, they paused by the boundary line playing shadow strokes until the umpires had come down the steps and the English fielders had begun fanning out. The impression was of batsmen barely able to await the beckoning feast.

Delectation followed tea, when their differences enhanced England's difficulties in containing them — the lack of pace encouraged Smith's sorties down the wicket as it favoured Rogers' pet cut. Thirty-three overs yielded 146 untroubled runs. A wicket looked no likelier than a Rogers reverse-sweep.

After Smith had reached his hundred with a pull shot and a primal scream, Rogers did the same with an economical punch, a fist pump, and a brief but meaningful communion with the turf. It is a pitch of a kind he would probably like to roll up and re-lay in his backyard — frankly, it is also fit to cover a bowler's grave.

The end of Rogers' late-blooming Test career is now in sight — he has, of course, explicitly foreshadowed it, having had the end in sight almost from the instant of his call up two years ago. He has spoken of returning to county cricket in England to round his career out, to add a few more to his total of seventy-three first-class centuries, and to maintain an average that quivers around 50. Rogers' popularity in these parts was evinced in the round of handshakes he exchanged with the home team as they left the field at stumps.

Australian cricket's altered priorities and benchmarks are summed up by the record of Rogers' understudy on this tour, Shaun Marsh, who has spread fifteen first-class hundreds across fifteen years and averages 38.8. When an answer seems out of reach, of course, one possible solution is to change the question.

## England v Australia, Second Test, Lord's, 2015, Day 3
# AN INNINGS FROM COOK

JULY 2015

The apparel oft proclaims the batsman, but not always. Alastair Cook is a case in point.

Watch him lead England onto the field in his whiter-than-white uniform, or leaning nonchalantly on his bat at the non-striker's end, and he cuts a figure of seeming elegance: slim, erect, dignified, the type to look good on an old-timey cigarette card, or inspire passages by R. C. Robertson-Glasgow or E. V. Lucas.

The impression lasts for as long as it takes him to settle over his bat. Cook is a left-hander: that's a plus. But he's a left-hander who makes John Edrich look like David Gower. He holds the bat low, crouches lower. It is a stance verging on a squat. As the bowler approaches, his back foot veers across the stumps and his bat gestures expansively towards third man. As the bowler releases...well, usually, not all that much happens.

At Lord's on Saturday, England needed not all that much to happen a very great deal — a task that called for their expert in the field. About 9.30am, England's 30-year-old captain was to be seen walking across the sward from the pavilion to the nursery. He bore on his back a heavy-looking bag — how long before cricketers have caddies? It was not a bad symbol of his day's burden: 21 not out in England's four for 85, 481 runs in arrears of Australia's first innings.

Cook appeared, it must be said, disarmingly relaxed. He chatted amiably with Jos Buttler, by his side. He stopped near the square for a bit of banter with the Test Match Special crew, and left an exchange with his old mucka Graeme Swann beaming broadly. He returned after his hit-up with a measured, meditative tread, the same pace at which he might take guard, survey a field, or walk up to a partner between overs. You might almost say he takes life at the pace of a Test match — not languidly, or haltingly, but not hastily either.

An hour later he was settling in with the same air of deliberation, methodical in his movements, houseproud around the crease, setting himself to score in his safe zones — off the pads, with a horizontal bat behind point, with a vertical bat down the ground.

Cover drive? In eighty years time, *The Sun* may reproduce a picture of Cook playing a cover drive. The editor will want to be sure the public interest is served by such a publication; readers will be well advised to consider the context of the stroke. The cover drive may have been a joke. Cook may not have fully understood the significance of the cover drive, or he may have been put up to a cover drive by his uncle, a notorious cover drive sympathiser. Because, frankly, any such publication will be a gross distortion. Perhaps no top-flight batsmen in history has so abjured a cardinal batting stroke. Cook's general abstaining is such a statement of self-discipline that it amounts to a shot in its own right: an anti-drive; a cover-refusal.

In the general scheme of Cook's career, this innings was a fluent affair. The conditions for batting were verifiably superb. Cook met them. He nailed his pull; he clicked with his cut; he once hit Nathan Lyon in the air down the ground, perhaps just to show he could do it.

Shortly after he gave his only chance, at backward square leg on 63, Cook glanced, on-drove and cover drove to the fence. This last was not, of course, a classic cover drive — more a flexion of the wrists in the direction of the cover point boundary. But it happened, and the timing was additionally sweet for the stroke's sheer shock value.

The core competence of Cook's batting is the leave, which is a wave, almost a flourish, belying the discipline it expresses round off stump. When he defends, by contrast, it is with an almost overpowering inertia. The bat emits the sound of a gentle door knock; occasionally that of splintering plywood. This is harder than it looks. Such is the percussive force of modern bats, it is almost non-scoring strokes that require the greater act of will. On Friday, Mitchell Marsh dropped a defensive bat on his first ball, and it fairly pelted for four: a cover drive from Wally Hammond could have reached the boundary no more directly. On Saturday, Cook's defensive shots were falling at his feet like dud grenades, disarmed bombs. To the very full delivery, he essentially placed the bat in the blockhole waiting to be struck, so dead it was almost lying in state. The ball dribbled a few metres before rolling to a stop, looking suddenly as if it was made of lead.

At Cook pace, the deliveries and minutes continued passing. His score grew too, although this was a secondary consideration: with Cook, especially on days like these, occupation precedes everything. Finally, when he had batted eight minutes short of a full day, and was also four runs shy of a twenty-eighth Test century, he pushed forward, shaping again to drive toward cover, perchance to go through it. Instead the delivery from Mitchell Marsh went through his defences, via bat and pad. The cover drive: Cook went down on one knee to curse that fickle jade.

Then he rose, stood tall, and moved off at his own pace, a figure again serene and good-looking — until next time. With his rival's declaration on the brink of lunch on Sunday, his vigil effectively resumed. For England's captain, this has been a very long match indeed.

# England v Australia, Third Test, Birmingham, Day 1, 2015
# LEARNED HELPLESSNESS

JULY 2015

The first day at Edgbaston was what Australians jokingly think of as an English summer's day: intermittent rain, little yielding gloom, the need for jumpers on the field and anoraks off it, beer the warmest feature. Except that this soon became no joking matter.

'Give us English conditions', the England team have implored groundsmen all summer long. These were as much God's work, overhead to go with underfoot. Australia's batsmen, meanwhile, trusted too much to providence. God's preference, of course, is for helping those who help themselves.

Not surprisingly, Edgbaston was stalked through the morning by memories of the almighty's last friendly visitation here, ten years ago, when He mischievously placed a cricket ball in the path of Glenn McGrath's ankle. The video screens played highlights; the match programme and newspapers basked in nostalgia; Ricky Ponting and Shane Warne were warming the commentary seats, recalling the morning when Warne was the agnostic among believers in Ponting's decision to send England in on winning the toss.

The pitch was slightly paler than the stretch of camouflage brown revealed by the withdrawal of the covers on Tuesday, but not much. Closely mown as it was, it promised seam movement; it also promised to be better for a day or two exposed to the elements. While Alastair Cook gave it no more than a glance before play, Clarke lingered on the square with Warne, whose sunglasses seemed an undue precaution. Steve Smith appeared with bat and gloves to take up his stance at each end, then walk it each way, prodding furtively; coach Darren Lehmann and chairman of selectors Rod Marsh also paid respectful visits.

Clarke had spoken airily a couple of days earlier about sending England in. Perhaps the thought occurred to him again. Eventually, when the coin fell to his advantage, he did the sensible thing and batted. But sensible is as sensible does. When Anderson's first ball passed Chris Rogers' hesitant edge, it was clear that we were not in for another Lord's. The bowling looked envenomed, the batsmen at least temporarily at bay; deliveries were still ascending as they reached the wicketkeeper, the Hollies Stand rising with it. It was a proper, old-fashioned new ball strafing: more deliveries beat the bat in the first half hour than on the whole first day of the Second Test. But Australia, frankly, batted as poorly as for years.

At 188cm, James Anderson was the smallest of the seven pacemen to enlist the conditions yesterday, giving away as much as half a head to the likes of Steve Finn (201cm), Stuart Broad (196cm), Josh Hazlewood (196cm), Mitchell Johnson (190cm), Mitchell Marsh (193cm), and Mitchell Starc (197cm). He is a reminder that fast bowling is about sinew as well as muscle. His physique is limber, his tread light, his action all about hydraulics — the relations of the front arm to the back arm, the front leg to the stumps, the fingers to the seam. At his best the parts move in exquisite harmony, like one of those superb industrial revolution engines, all steam and brass and grease. Four breaks kept him fresh, as well as interrupting the rhythm and concentration of his quarry.

Yet while unwelcoming, the conditions were far from inimical to batting, as Chris Rogers showed: endlessly vigilant around off stump, exhaustingly finicky about the sightscreens, he was prepared to do it hard so that others might find it easier. Otherwise the Australians were chronically indecisive. Three batsmen fell letting the ball go: Voges and Starc too late, Nevill too soon. Two batsmen fell not letting it go: Smith on a fourth stump line, Mitchell Marsh on something like a sixth. This was not so much falling between two stools as making a dive for the setee and knocking over the sideboard.

Smith's dismissal, of course, removed the pivot on which Australia has swivelled this last year. It exposed, in the eighth over, a captain whose old ambivalence about batting at number four has quietly returned. Clarke faced ten deliveries. Four he defended, two he edged, one he left, and three he simply missed — the third of these by a long way as it hit off stump low down. If it was not the short ball again that again proved Clarke's weakness, it was perhaps the possibility of the short ball setting him slightly on his heels.

Here was another turn of the wheel. The bowler was Steve Finn, last seen in Ashes cricket being bullied by Brad Haddin at Trent Bridge; now he was bowling exuberantly fast again, while Haddin, his weathered cap a contrast with his bright orange reserves bib, relayed gloves to batsmen, and later helmets to fielders. Above all, Haddin was not coming in at 82 for five, the kind of scenario where his presence was so talismanic for Australia just over eighteen months ago. Whether he would have made a difference is a moot point, although his advocates will be free to speculate accordingly.

Later the clock turned back, when Ian Bell took Starc's sixth over for three boundaries, including a glide to third man, reminiscent of his lighter-than-light touch two years ago. There could hardly be a player more familiar with Edgbaston gloom — at home he probably dims the lights and sleeps in a sleeveless pullover. When stumps were decreed after a final squall at 6.45pm, the home team had nearly achieved parity. A quarter hour later, the deserted terraces were bathed in the loveliest sunlight of the day — how very, very English.

# Australia in England 2015
# A TOUR TOO FAR?

JULY 2015

A story is told of a conversation in an Australia dressing room in the early 1980s, when a few players debated the right time to hang up the boots. Some thought you should go with a little left in the tank; others opined that you were a long time retired.

Overhearing this for a while, Rodney Hogg is reputed to have butted in. "You blokes don't know what you're talking about," he said. "How often does a player get the opportunity to quit on their own terms? Ninety-nine per cent of the time the selectors drop you and that's it."

The conversation ended there, because everyone had to acknowledge this fundamental truth. The game rolls forward remorselessly, and only the very blessed control their destiny by going out, as it is said, "while they still say why, rather than why not?"

When they do, it is actually deemed somewhat unusual. When Mike Hussey called it quits in December 2012, colleagues pleaded with him to reconsider. What was he thinking? He was playing well, had good cricket left. Hussey was ready; it was others who weren't.

All this is by way of considering the position of Michael Clarke. What awaits Australia's captain? At Edgbaston, he suffered what ranks as among his poorest games in charge. He has surely never endured a poorer match of equivalent significance. Clarke failed twice with the bat, which can happen in the best-managed careers — that's Test cricket. But a hesitancy has crept into his batting in the past year. He is rivalling Jesse James in trigger movements.

The statistics are not definitive but they are powerfully indicative. His Test average here slipped below 50 for the first time in more than three years. No top-four batsman who has played more than a handful of Tests has a poorer record over the past 12 months — an unwanted title of which Clarke relieved Ian Bell during the game.

Clarke's decision to bat first on Wednesday will not follow him around like Ricky Ponting's to bowl first here ten years ago, but maybe because we are more forgiving of hewings to convention than of deviations from orthodoxy. Thereafter he was doomed to playing catch-up captaincy, and did his honest best. But the stardust he scattered over Australia's efforts in 2013-14 was missing. He dropped a crucial slip catch early in England's chase, then quietly withdrew from the cordon to stand at mid-off. Steve Smith stood in his usual spot. It might almost have been a bloodless coup.

It wasn't, of course. The Ashes remain in dispute. Talk of Clarke's replacement is confined to the extremes of former players' punditry and the more febrile reaches of social media. All the same, the purpose he expressed on his retirement from one-day international cricket in March, that this gave him "the best chance of prolonging his Test career", now sounds more like a wish.

Clarke is hardly alone facing such challenges. For all their professional empowerment, modern players are not always best equipped to weigh futures. "They hold on because they like the money, don't they?" one sometimes hears it said, and this may contain a grain of truth, but I doubt it is the whole story.

So much of a player's day-to-day decision-making is now outsourced to coaches, managers and agents that calls only they can make must grow disproportionately harder. The enclave of the team, too, is a poor environment for unflinching self-appraisal: rather is it a refuge, a provider of a feedback loop of positivity, because this, it is thought, is most conducive to success.

Players get attached and so, nowadays, do their families. Australia's touring party swelled at one point on this tour to nearly a hundred once all the wives and children of players and support staff were included. Here may lie a source of the discontent in Australian ranks rumoured around the decision to omit Brad Haddin from the Edgbaston Test: it betrays the uneasy fit of this thrown-together community with the inherently despotic nature of cricket teams.

Clarke in this scenario is an intriguing figure, for it is not actually clear who in this Australia team forms part of his inner circle. His deepest affinity is with an outsider: Shane Warne. But Warne has been more in the nature of an advocate, not to mention a kind of lucky charm.

Warne was also an ambivalent retiree. He curtailed his Test career quickly in December 2006, only to be drawn back to the fray by T20, and did not officially retire from all formats until two years ago — the living embodiment of form being temporary, class permanent, and legend indestructible.

The other example Clarke will have in mind is that of his predecessor, Ricky Ponting. In his autobiography, Ponting described his retirement decision two and a half years ago as arising from a deterioration not so much in his physical faculties as in his mental state. "It wasn't a decline in my reflexes or my eyesight or my fitness that stopped me scoring runs in Test cricket. It was the pressure that got me," he wrote.

Perhaps that is why Clarke was anxious last night to reiterate a continued enthusiasm for his job, and for the hard work he has always found integral to success. "For me," he said, "it's about the preparation." But another Test like this one and he might have to widen the scope of those preparations.

# England v Australia, Fourth Test, Trent Bridge, 2015, Day 1
## HELL ON GRASS
AUGUST 2015

With 20 minutes to go to lunch at Trent Bridge, Darren Lehmann walked purposefully towards the middle, bat in his gloved hands. He strode the length of the pitch on which the Australia team he coaches had just been bowled out for 60, scanning it intently. He stood at the crease and looked towards the pavilion, played a lugubrious shadow block and a rueful shadow leave.

As he wended his way off, it was tempting to eavesdrop on his thoughts. Was he about to make a comeback? After all, apparently form is temporary, class is permanent. But perhaps he waxed more philosophical — here was one of those days that dramatises Lehmann's plight. For games of international cricket nowadays, players have never been better prepared. They are fitter, and stronger, they train harder, eat better, know more about their oppositions, conditions and challenges generally. Yet it is still the case that at 11am each morning they go out on their own.

For the game does not hinge on how diligently players have worked or how assiduously they have war-gamed; it is determined by their capacity to reproduce skills under pressure. And seldom can an Australia team have experienced such a collective skills seizure as on the first day at Trent Bridge.

Every batsman would have known what to do. Chris Rogers has made 38 centuries in England. This is Steven Smith's fourth visit to this country in six years. This was Adam Voges's 20th first-class match on this very ground. Shaun Marsh was coming off consecutive hundreds and Michael Clarke has been, by his own account, working like a veritable Stakhanovite.

Conditions overhead and underfoot were conducive to seam movement. For batsmen, that entails lots of discretion around off stump, playing from alongside the ball so as best to afford it free passage, rather than trapped behind it. Yet within half an hour, all these technical commandments had been violated — not once, but serially.

Batsmen turned chest-on rather than side-on. Batsmen chased what they needn't have. Instead of hard heads and soft hands, there were hard hands and soft heads. It was "batting with intent" in the same sense that Jonestown was Kool-Aid drinking with intent.

Clarke's shot was most abject and culpable of all — a wild drive at an all-day sucker of a ball for a batsman desperate to feel the pleasing kiss of willow on leather. Australia's captain had almost been bowled by his second ball and caught from his ninth. Remember when we used to talk of Australia's "aura"? Clarke's is collapsing, vortex-like. His wicket is ceasing to be a scalp, becoming a souvenir.

Was it the pitch? It looked before play to be drumming on minds. The respective camps presented a study. Cook offered the surface only a perfunctory nod on his way back from the nets. England enjoyed their kickabout and adjourned.

Clarke looked pensive, careworn, brooding perhaps on the similarity to conditions when he won the toss and batted at Edgbaston, perhaps trying to remember those old meteorological nostrums ("Grey sky at morning, captain's warning"; "Rain before seven, choose another XI"). Long-headed Brad Haddin joined him. Smith, Nathan Lyon and Shane Watson looked in. Voges imparted local knowledge as a former captain of

Nottinghamshire. Clarke conversed longest with Rod Marsh, the chairman of selectors . . . then proceeded to lose the toss.

The Australians looked up now and saw Stuart Broad — not James Anderson, their nemesis two years ago, but Broad, their nuisance. Broad galls the visiting team. He throws down markers, picks up gauntlets. He chats freely about the Aussie batsmen's weaknesses, about the peculiarities of English cricket balls. He features in an advertising campaign for an Australian wine company sponsoring the England team, playing up to his reputation. It is pretty funny; more than that, it is on Broad's part a gesture of cheeky confidence.

Eighteen months ago, Brisbane's *Courier-Mail* famously refused to use Broad's name in their match descriptions, referring to him instead as an "England medium-pacer". Their front page today will need to be an entirely blank sheet, which may not be wholly inappropriate — a spell of eight for 15 needs as little elaboration as the Gettysburg Address.

Yet Broad did need help, and got it, from six slips — not four slips and two gullys but six proper slips, like a chevron of razor wire that nothing escaped. Ben Stokes made one miraculous snare. Otherwise it was made to look as natural as a practice drill.

Perhaps this was a reflection of the efficacy of good coaching. On their jolly to Spain at the end of June, England's new coach, Trevor Bayliss, made slip-catching all but his solitary focus. Although they paid for a drop at Lord's, England since have missed precious little. When England batted, Cook's edge bisected Clarke and Smith, as painful to both as a poke in the eye.

Lehmann by now was looking on from his team's balcony — subdued and serious, weighing up plans and plots, while knowing that 60 is not so much a total to defend as to apologise for. Batting, bowling, fielding and conditioning coaches, management and administrative staff came and went. Shane Warne, Glenn McGrath, Ian Healy and Michael Slater were in the commentary boxes; Allan Border was in the crowd. What names, what talents, what legends. And nothing to be done about what was happening on the field by any of them.

# England v Australia, Fourth Test, Trent Bridge, 2015, Day 2

# THE CAPTAIN ON THE BRINK

AUGUST 2015

For a split second after tea yesterday, Michael Clarke must have thought that he lived again. The ball he had skewered to slip had bounced in, out, in and out of Alastair Cook's hands, and now hung in the air slightly out of his rival's reach. When you are as out of form as Clarke at the moment — and "out of form" hardly does it justice, for it is a state beyond form, nearly beyond hope — you can convince yourself that the sunny uplands are just a chink of light away. You need to miss that one you've been nicking. You need a few tasty half-volleys. The second chance offered by an unpunished error is best of all — not quite getting away with murder, but maybe like the clean getaway from a burglary.

As Clarke looked behind him, however, the chink of light disappeared. Slips these days are ever alert to rebounds, so fast do edges fly. Ian Bell had hovered in attendance on his captain and interposed beneath the falling ball.

Clarke walked towards the old pavilion, up the steps from where his predecessor Ricky Ponting harangued Duncan Fletcher ten years ago — the point at which England sensed Australia's spirit broken. Clarke walked straight, head down, face blank, until he had receded to vanishing point, rather like his own career.

England has never really seen Clarke at his best. He probably peaked between his second and third Ashes tours, when he gushed runs like a geyser.

By the time he led Australia back here two years ago, the good days were more occasional, less predictable, if still impressive: he remained a batsman of charm and timing in days increasingly defined by big bats and bulging biceps.

Yet the final fading has come quickly. Clarke attracted a good ball yesterday. But it had taken only an ordinary ball to dispose of him the day before, at the time when his team needed him most. He spoke afterwards of wishing to hit the delivery in question to kingdom come. Yet that was the 31st ball of the match, Australia were already four wickets down, and he could barely reach it — this was the reasoning of a novice.

The threadier the pulse of Clarke's batting too, the paler has grown his captaincy. It would be hard to dispute that the two are related, the energy required to restore the former being unavailable to rejuvenate the latter. At Edgbaston, the team's general unease seemed to localise in the discontent about Brad Haddin's omission, while Clarke was busy fending off questions about retirement with invocations of his work rate.

To be fair, it is not like there was very much Clarke was able to do yesterday except repeat the gruff instruction of Brian "Tonker" Taylor, of Essex — "Same batting order, better batting" — and hope that cricket would even out. After all, on the first day, everything had been nicked, and everything had gone to hand, and such a perfect storm could only be followed by more isolated squalls and showers.

For a time, the inches did favour the visiting team, while the gasps and sighs formed in English mouths. In the last over before lunch, Broad passed Warner's outside edge four times in virtually identical fashion: it was like watching photocopies drop on to a tray.

When Warner did get a nick off Broad after the break, Cook could not quite hold on. Warner immediately celebrated by pilfering four, four and six from Finn's first over: a forthright drive, a sly glance and a jubilant hook when a long hop sat up at waist height. Australia's openers took barely 20 overs to surge past 100, a time in which Geoff Boycott might have unfurled a leg glance — that's modern Test cricket for you. Warner's second six, another hook, landed ten rows back off a leading edge. Cricket bats — bloody hell.

In mid-afternoon, the cricket was drifting into normality — a rare interlude this summer. Cook turned to his fifth bowler — the fifth bowler of which Australia deprived themselves at the selection table — and it paid off. For England, Ben Stokes looms not only as a talent but a talisman — a beamish, buoyant, barnstorming presence, exuding energy and possibility, an all-rounder in the way of an Ian Botham, rather than a Shane Watson. Yesterday he grabbed the game as though administering it a bone- crushing handshake, arrowing the ball into off stump, swinging it at lively pace and following through with a swagger.

For the key wicket Stokes also caught Steve Smith, who since Lord's has made 26 runs in 57 balls, four of which have dismissed him. Cricket can take perverse directions. One of the stronger arguments in favour of Clarke's continued tenure has become the failures of his deputy, still trying to nail down No 3, still straining to reconcile natural instincts with the responsibility of protecting a vulnerable middle order.

For again there was about the Australia batting that air of the golfer in P G Wodehouse who "missed short putts because of the uproar of butterflies in the adjoining meadow", and Clarke did not relieve it in 45 tentative minutes. He was beaten thrice. He defended diffidently, left doggedly, worked a few off the pads, nicked a boundary.

Then Mark Wood bowled him a full ball at his deceptively skiddy pace on a fourth stump line. Michael Clarke outside off stump: what could go wrong? It's seldom that the game simply lets you go. It likes to mess with you a bit first.

# Michael Clarke retires
# THE ONLY CALL
AUGUST 2015

Did he fall? Would he have been pushed? Does it matter? Whatever the case, it's surely better for all concerned that Michael Clarke agonistes is over.

There's often something unedifying about the final rites of a fine sporting career. After a while a great athlete answers all the questions we have of them and leaves us with one: when will they retire?

The question becomes like a drumbeat, on their nerves, and on ours. The denials begin to jar, the expressions of public support to cloy, the discussions of the timespan to concern the end rather than the totality.

Just five days ago, in an unbidden and unequivocal column in Sydney's *Daily Telegraph*, Clarke committed himself to carrying on as Australian captain for the forseeable future: "People are talking about how I'm going to retire after this series. Well, they don't know me...I'm 34 not 37 and I want to keep playing for Australia beyond this series."

Between the ages of 34 years and 123 days and 34 and 128 days, we are left to conclude, what Clarke knew about himself changed. Clarke said yesterday that the column had been motivated by a desire to send a "positive message" to team-mates — that the last few days had crystallised his thoughts. It leaves us to ask what is the message in his retirement, and what reliance can be placed on his statements in future? That in making his announcement he first of all "spoke exclusively" to Channel 9 added further to the air of stage management that accompanied quite a deal of his cricket. Were we witnessing the end of his cricket career or the beginning of his broadcasting career?

That said, the fourth Test at Trent Bridge would have been clarifying for anyone. They formalised Clarke's transition from a shadow of his former self to a silhouette — not just an absence, but a taker up of room. The selectors sought to lighten his lot in this game by swapping Marshes — specialist batsman Shaun for all-rounder Mitch. The move was an abject failure. Shaun soaked up all of ten deliveries as Clarke's cover at number four; Mitch's absence then left Clarke short-handed with the ball, even as his English counterpart Ben Stokes was laying Australia's batting waste.

After Edgbaston, Clarke candidly described his team as "playing with ten" on account of his underperformance; it was here more like nine and a half. The stroke that Clarke played to the 31st ball of the match, meanwhile, sent a message to his dressing room as negative as could be. The weather was to clear; the pitch would flatten out; batting after lunch had to be Australia's objective, and Clarke had to know it.

Instead his stroke reeked of nothing but defeat: it said that the conditions were insuperable; it said that he as senior batsman had no answer; what hope everyone else? Ricky Ponting's batting had lost its way and its shape by the end, but never did it exude such defeatism.

How will Clarke be remembered? He was a skilful and dashing batsman, mainly self-made, in an era that tended towards overcoaching; he held injuries at bay by sheer willpower and dedication; he had wavering relations with the Australian public. "I've never been comfortable with fame and I never will be," he once said. He was comfortable with wealth, and these days, of course, the two go glamorous-hand-in-brandname-glove. But that arguably made him a more interesting and contemporary figure. So what if he wasn't Bill Woodfull?

Clarke led Australia to a World Cup, to an Ashes whitewash, to captures of the Border-Gavaskar and Frank Worrell Trophies; he briefly had his hands on the World Test Championship mace. But under him Australia's away record flatlined, and he also played in five losing Ashes series, even as Ian Bell correspondingly participated in five triumphs. This hardly seems a fair reflection of their abilities, but from it can be inferred a tapering in Australian cricket since the collapse of its two-decade dynasty, understandable but now measurable.

That is not Clarke's fault. He has maintained, in the main, sky-high standards; had every player during his watch maintained the same utter commitment to technical improvement and physical fitness, the Ashes would not now be in England's custody. But they are. For cricket is never about one man. Because men all come and go.

# Cook v Clarke
## HEAD TO HEAD
AUGUST 2015

On the eve of the Ashes of 2015, *Cricinfo*'s excellent George Dobell aired a thought-provoking idea about Alastair Cook, that he was a better leader than captain, seen to better advantage off the field than on.

It set me to wondering whether the distinction might apply oppositely to Michael Clarke, that he might eventually be considered a better captain than leader: on the field a wonderful intuitive cricket intelligence, at the crease a superb sight in full flow, but also a man apart, with limited means to inspire once his performances attenuated.

A couple of months on, the distinction isn't entirely crisp: Cook has established himself a pleasingly quick-witted tactician this summer; nor could Clarke be faulted in the setting of a professional example or the maintenance of a public demeanour. But faced by similar scenarios during these Ashes — that of restoring the confidence of teams that had been heavily beaten — Cook succeeded where Clarke failed. And to a great degree the skills involved in such situations are those of a leader.

Coach Trevor Bayliss used an interesting word to describe the discussion in which England players were involved after Lord's: 'honest.' Honesty can be hard to come by in sport, for legitimate reasons: too much realism can discourage and inhibit. But a culture that allows the admission of mistakes in order to set them right is a robust culture, and it's only right to credit Cook with it.

Cook is as Cook does. Captaining and opening the batting is

an onerous twin burden, but does substantiate one as a character — it is literally leading from the front, setting the tone and in some degree sacrificing the self.

More English captains have opened the batting than those who batted consistently at five and six, perhaps because players find it natural to follow someone morally whom they also follow numerically. When teammates look at Cook, as they look at a Hutton, Gooch, Atherton or Strauss, they see a comrade bearing a brunt on their behalf. It engages their sympathies, lightens their own loads.

Cook has not, in fact, had the rewards for batting he has deserved in this series, but his contributions have been vital. Not only was he England's best amid the ruins of Lord's, but he lasted a crucial hour and a quarter at Edgbaston and two awkward hours at Trent Bridge in building bases for Joe Root.

In appraising his development as a captain, meanwhile, Cook on Saturday presented it not in terms of aggression, innovation or proactivity; he described it as a kind of personal education, as he came to an accommodation with what he now understood to be 'stubbornness', 'relaxed a bit more' and 'opened my ears to a number of people' — Brendon McCullum possibly not least of all.

Cook, we sometimes forget, is thirty. How mature and self-knowing is the average 30-year-old male? He has spent his whole life within a game and a system, being paid a lot of money for certain narrow specialist skills. What kind of values might such a cloistered, privileged upbringing be expected to instill?

Cook's, though, are obviously sound and considered, and he professed in the aftermath of Trent Bridge to being 'proud I have managed to stay true to a lot of my principles as a bloke and as a player' — notice that the 'bloke' came first.

Michael Clarke bears a great many similarities to Cook. They were chosen young, have been inclined by nature to Test cricket, have never tired of the routines of training and touring. Their mutual regard is unfeigned, arising not only from parallel experiences but from recognizing something of themselves in the other.

But Clarke is four years Cook's senior — quite a difference in the terms of a sporting career, where primes are so relatively brief. Nor does he seem to have introspected in the same fashion as Cook. Over his career, in a way, he grew ever more like himself: more driven, more self-directed, more self-demanding, especially after handing in his selectors' epaulettes two years ago. And as ever more of Clarke's time and energy was dedicated to overcoming physical infirmities and finally to deteriorating form, one fancies that ever less was available to his team.

His dedication could not be faulted. But, then, nor could an anchorite's. And it's possible that Clarke's personal austerity this summer has shaded his own team's ambitions. Certainly while English players have been talking of expressing themselves and showing off their talents, their counterparts have fallen back on those joyless cliches about 'work rate' and 'work ethic', as though toiling in a coal mine.

On the field, Clarke has looked an ever more isolated figure. Instead of the splendid Brad Haddin at his elbow in the cordon, he has ended up flanked by newbies Nevill and Voges, and his heir apparent Smith. For spells of the Third and Fourth Test, in fact, he went to mid-off, as though he no longer quite fitted in.

There was then something poignant about the scene of the captain's final decision, taken in a hotel bar with wife Kyly and Shane Warne, Clarke's roommate on his first Ashes tour a decade earlier. He seems to have consulted nobody in his own team or management — wasn't there anybody to whom he was close enough?

At the last Clarke *did* demonstrate the qualities of a leader: he held himself accountable, and conducted himself with dignity. Some tougher times in Australian cricket now impend, which may require more leadership than captaincy.

# The Ashes 2014–15
# BIG PRODUCTION NUMBER
SEPTEMBER 2015

In the last two years, Ashes cricket has resembled not so much a cricket series as a blockbuster franchise. A saga's sweep. Big production values. Characters you love to hate, whether David Warner, Stuart Broad or Giles Clarke, all in a wacky, self-contained world watched by a fanatically loyal fan base although maybe disturbingly few beyond that.

The attrition rate alone has been Westerosian: Graeme Swann, Jonathan Trott, Matt Prior, Kevin Pietersen, Monty Panesar, Tim Bresnan and Chris Tremlett; Michael Clarke, Chris Rogers, Ryan Harris, quite possibly Brad Haddin, Shane Watson and Adam Voges. That's before you work your way down to the likes of Ed Cowan, Jackson Bird, George Bailey, Michael Carberry, Simon Kerrigan, Boyd Rankin, Scott Borthwick and maybe Adam Lyth too. Don't forget the coaches either, and the ambitions of Mickey Arthur, Peter Moores, Alistair de Winter, Ashley Giles and above all Andy Flower swallowed up along the way. To the survivors at the Oval should almost be distributed 'Still Standing' T-shirts.

Where it's most resembled Game of Ashes have been the increasingly wild extremities, which posterity will have a devil of a job making sense of. Since England's original 14-run squeak at Trent Bridge in 2013, the margins have conveyed the carnage: 347 runs, 74 runs, 381 runs, 218 runs, 150 runs, eight wickets, 281 runs, 169 runs, 405 runs, eight wickets, an innings and 178 runs. Ascendants belonged to England, then Australia, and finally to England and Australia in turn. Australia won more Tests — seven to six. But of the Ashes, England started and finished as hosts and holders.

In this sense, the real winner has been not so much either side as the quaint, old-fashioned notion of home ground advantage — passing strange in this world of hyperprofessional preparation and huge caravans of support staff and WAGs that turn a touring party into a plush cocoon away from home. Maybe that is part of the issue, so much effort being devoted to making players cosy and confident these days that a kind of learned helplessness in adversity is the result. Certainly there's something telling about the highest scorer across the three series being not either of the current rivals for batting's blue riband, Steve Smith and Joe Root, but have-bat-will-travel Chris Rogers (1310 at 48.52), the soul of self-sufficiency. Whatever the case, it's becoming another issue for administrators, who in order to provide a telegenic contest and to burnish their own team's success obviously require visiting sides to fall *just* short of victory.

The outstanding bowler across the epic trilogy, meanwhile, has been Stuart Broad, with 64 wickets at 25.26 — not always brilliant, but never consecutively indifferent, which by modern standards makes him the acme of consistency. And if 2013-14 was a compelling exhibition of pace bowling at the pressure points of a batting line-up's nervous system, 2015 has made a good case for simple accuracy as a disruptive strategy. How the Australian attack was improved at the Oval by Peter Siddle, a bowler who generates pitch maps that resemble bunches of grapes rather than the aftermath of a game of paintball. It's not that the visitors were indisciplined so much as calling on a combination of a methods less stable, less reliable. There is a reason why few attacks have ever featured two fast, slingy left-handers.

Has selection been crucial? Often it is overestimated. Selectors make convenient scapegoats for the shortcomings of a country's talent and resources, and everyone is wise after the event. But the large number of players whose careers have been finished by failures across these last two years suggests that, on both sides, there has been a reluctance to engineer change pre-emptively. As players grow more expansive, are selectors growing more conservative, less pro-active?

Ashes cricket is big cricket, and seems to demand big occasion players, rich in experience and honours. Into the last two years has also fallen a World Cup, a World T20, and Pataudi and Border-Gavaskar Trophies, seeming to call for the reassurance of track records and known quantities. Yet some decidedly grey XIs have been put into the field by both countries, who have then played every bit as nervously as bunches of novices. Australia has come off the worse in comparison, compulsory change now descending like a guillotine: seldom has a Test against Bangladesh held such interest as the one that Steve Smith's team will commence in Chittagong on 9 October. This being so, Australia has had rather more cause to defend the quality of its deliberations in the last few weeks. Pat Howard, Australia's general manager high-performance, seemed on Saturday to dispute that selectorial effectiveness can ever be evaluated: 'If you go down to each individual decision everyone has a view but you can't ever go and argue the other side because you never know if you would have been better or worse without the other person.' It sounded a little like one of Donald Rumsfeld's epistemological musings. Nobody thinks selectors have it easy. They also need, from time to time, to examine their own practices and prejudices.

Many challenges await; such is the rate of change in cricket at present, many challenges that aren't yet even recognised as such. That's the consolation of a good franchise, of course, always throwing up new plots, new opportunities. And of the Ashes, they're already planning the sequel. Lots and lots of sequels.

# Test cricket at night
# WHY NOT?

OCTOBER 2015

Test cricket at night? The wonder is surely not that it is in the offing, but that it has taken so long, nearly four decades since Kerry Packer trailblazed one-day cricket after dark at VFL Park and the Sydney Cricket Ground, and in the process pioneered a premium television product.

It's all been a bit hard for the game's administrators — or, rather, easier just to let things slide, to play Test matches not because they value the format but because it puts them nearest the ICC exchequer. Innovators? Yeah, we had one of those fellers once. He's holed up in London now and we don't like to talk about him...

There is a tendency these days to ask the question will Test cricket survive? But who wants to watch a game merely survive? To endure it must prosper. And that, in many parts of the world, it is far from doing.

Playing at night is no panacea. The export opportunities are limited. In England, for example, floodlights are less effective in mid-summer and nights too cold in late summer. Dew in Asia is a problem. But grounds in the Gulf would be a great deal more hospitable in the evening than in the infernal heat of the day.

In any event, it's encouraging to see a willingness to experiment where Test cricket is strong. Innovation is too little too late too often, which then stymies new ideas, and wealthy Australia is in a position to provide leadership.

Will it work? That is another question. In one sense, of course, it already has. It has stimulated interest, freshened perceptions. The Sheffield Shield, in which the format is being trialled, has seldom enjoyed such attention. Newspapers and websites are full of pictures of scuffed pink balls, their surfaces resembling those of Jovian moons.

The players are more guarded, and not without good reason. The ball is the still point in a relentlessly evolving game. Save for developing a white variant, its dimensions and materials have barely changed in 200 years. In harmony with white clothing on a green expanse, it is integral to Test cricket's palate. By comparison — and this is purely a personal opinion — the pink ball looks as yet a bit naff.

There's a sense, too, in which such a fundamental change is at odds with what not just players but fans, broadcasters and sponsors have grown used to over the last twenty years, which is greater uniformity of conditions — of playing regulations, of playing surfaces, of over rates, of preparatory regimes, of professional standards.

The pink ball, from what little we have seen, is sensitive, capricious. When new, it can swing very sharply. When old, it softens and discolours markedly. Even when it is in mint condition, batsmen struggle to discern the seam. In contact with an abrasive square, it trends towards very limited visibility. Cricket Australia's precaution has been to schedule the first night Test at Adelaide Oval, rather than at the Gabba or the WACA — they took the additional measure last week of decreeing a pitch for the Shield match with an extra thatch of grass.

CA's purpose in staging night Test cricket is nakedly commercial — and, of course, that's the nature of the beast. But a curious irony of the pink ball might be cricket more volatile, less homogenised, and also less even — insofar as when you do things might be almost as much a factor as how well you do them.

Back in the day — way back in the day — cricket was more like this. Before pitches were covered, conditions within a game were far more inclined to fluctuate. Teams would declare early. Teams would delay their best batsmen coming in. Teams included specialists for adverse conditions.

Moves to standardise Test cricket only really began after World War II. Till then all Australian Test matches had been played to a finish and all English Test matches limited to three days — a remarkable quantum of difference, almost equivalent to that between one-day international and T20 cricket.

Despite the impacts of the last twenty years, too, variety remains stubbornly ingrained in the game by the absence of a standard ball and of a uniform playing area. Nor, thanks to the Board of Control for Cricket in India, is Test cricket umpired the same the world over.

So you could consider night Test cricket a return to former customs — and it is, after all, the year of *Back to the Future*.

Yet there is another aspect to the to-and-fro over the pink ball that's worth remarking on. The Test is being played for $1 million in prize money. This fact has been widely aired in the last week or so, with the implicit notion of: 'Look at these prima donnas. What are they complaining about? For that coin they should be prepared to play a Test match with rulers and rolled-up socks...' On Thursday, CA's CEO James Sutherland stated gruffly that players needed to 'understand that it's happening' and 'just need to focus on what's ahead.'

Both parties want to be wary of what spin doctors now call 'the optics' of this. The perception that CA overrides objections with money, and that the players allow reservations to be overridden then air them anyway, might not be felt to cast either of them in favourable light.

For what it's worth, the last week or so has seemed to me healthy and robust. The pink ball has been used to less than universal satisfaction. Players have been asked about it, and given straight answers to straight questions. Their observations have in the main been constructive. I would rather that than the mouthing of corporate pieties.

If any group has kept Test cricket relevant in the last decade, it is the players by their continued belief in the format as definitive of excellence. Their views matter. And on the day-to-day practicalities of cricket their expertise should be regarded as indispensable. If night Test cricket succeeds, it will be in large measure their doing.

# New Zealand in Australia 2015
# FREQUENT FLIERS
### NOVEMBER 2015

It is difficult to talk about cricket schedules. They simply are. It is not like there's ever a range of better or worse options to choose from. If you're a player, or a journalist, or even simply a fan, 'The Schedule' simply turns up one day, and you might as well remonstrate with a cuneiform tablet.

Schedules are complicated to organise too. They must suit both parties. They must strike a balance between off-field profit and on-field equity. They must meet the wants and needs of the public. They must reflect the available facilities. Be that as it may, schedules at the moment reflect nothing so faithfully as the short-termism and self-interest that has enveloped the cricket world in the last decade, and it's worth trying to understand why.

Consider the schedule under which New Zealand agreed to tour Australia this summer. There have been worse arrangements this year: Bangladesh hosting South Africa at the peak of the monsoons in July which resulted in play on only four of the ten scheduled days may be the stand-out candidate here. But it's still an alsation's breakfast.

It started with a Prime Ministers' XI game — the earliest that venerable fixture has been held since the fixture's 1951 inception. The following morning, the Black Caps began a two-day second-class fixture against a thrown-together Cricket Australia XI in which eight batsmen retired out. This was followed by four sessions on the now-infamous goat track at Blacktown.

And, errr, that's it — on to the Gabba where, amazing to say, batsmen who had not played a Test since May struggled to adapt to pace and bounce. Tuesday the teams flew 3600km crossing three time zones to Perth for the Test that began yesterday. Ever done that flight? It's Australian civil aviation's version of extreme rendition.

Oh, and in a week's time New Zealand will prepare for the Adelaide Test by playing a two-day game against a WA XI — whoever they may be — *in Perth*. That's because there were no floodlit venues available in Adelaide for a pink ball try out.

Coaches and players hold a certain amount of responsibility for 'it'll-be-all-right-on-the-night' schedules like this, grounded as they are in that philosophy of Duncan Fletcher's about it being better for a team to be 'undercooked' than 'overcooked.'

Such schedules reflect an anxiety around fatigue, which it is true sets in quickly on the modern train-play-travel treadmill. A vogue word at the moment, for example, is player 'loads', rather than anything so quaint as 'games' or 'overs'. 'Loads' are to be 'managed'. Loads are to be 'adjusted'. Thus the dreck of two-day cricket, barely more than a centre wicket training, because of the inconvenience about first-class matches that they must actually be played rather than manipulated.

But how well are these arrangements working? Correlation may not be causation, but perhaps you've noticed how difficult away Tests are becoming to win against anything but abjectly poor opposition.

In Brisbane last week, the Black Caps chased the Test from ball one. Two bowlers broke down. Three others looked as though they wouldn't have minded doing so. In Mohali last week, South Africa, ostensibly the world's number one Test team, were overwhelmed twice in barely 100 overs on a pitch which was no worse than averagely bad.

Their lead-in had been as sketchy as New Zealand's here: three one-day internationals, and a leisurely two-dayer. Hashim Amla — he of the epic concentration and yogic calm — left a straight ball that hit off stump.

If the idea of preparation for anything is to approximate the challenges and stresses you will shortly experience, then it is pretty obvious how contemporary conventions fall short. For this is not simply a matter of 'acclimatising', to pitches, heat, light or even 'loads'. It is about intensity, scrutiny, duration, consequentiality. With the best will in the world, it is difficult to see how playing lo-fi matches against muck-up XIs in empty grounds over two days gets anyone in the right frame of mind for big occasions over five days against quality oppositions in the full modern media blare.

But we should not stop here in considering modern schedules, because all players and coaches really do is fall in with the finite resources and time at their disposal, rationalising as they go, with occasional use of the catch-all phrase 'not ideal' through gritted teeth when it gets too ridiculous.

Because international cricket's calendar is in a sorry state. It has been since the Indian Premier League and Champions League started gouging hunks out of it eight years ago, and especially since the shameless shakedown of the International Cricket Council by boards of India, England and Australia in February last year.

This made the arrangements for all tours 'bilateral' — a soothing word because it suggests some form of negotiation takes place, when everyone knows that the large basically dictate to the small.

In this world, tour matches stand friendless. They cannot win sponsors; they do not interest broadcasters. They are an actual cost for an unquantifiable benefit, an encumbrance also to increasingly crowded domestic schedules. The trend is in the other direction. Back before the ICC's Future Tours Programme became something to make paper aeroplanes from, it imposed a set of reasonably sensible protocols: a tour could be no shorter than two Tests and three one-day internationals; there were specified hiatuses between Tests and limitations on the number of short-form games within fixed periods, and so on.

To the Big Three's world of the bilateral 'FTP Agreement', none of these protections, which existed for the game as well as for the players, apply. There is not even a standard 'FTP Agreement'. Yet the process is self-defeating. If touring teams are not given the opportunity to produce their best cricket, if Test matches are prepared for in so perfunctory a way, then the format will generate more one-sided, sub-standard cricket.

Speaking of which, the West Indies arrive in a week for perhaps the least-awaited tour in modern memory, having just been beaten off the park by a weak Sri Lanka. Three of their players have played Tests in Australia before. Yet their preparation for a three-match series, including a Boxing Day Test, will be a solitary game against a CA XI at Allan Border Field. That's not a schedule. That's preparing to write your PhD by dashing off a limerick on a table napkin. And unfortunately that's twenty-first century international cricket.

# Australia v New Zealand, Third Test, Adelaide Oval, 2015
# THE BOYS LIGHT UP
## NOVEMBER 2015

The word 'test' can be variously interpreted, as a competition between rivals, or the evaluation of an inherent quality against an external standard. In the case of the Third Test at Adelaide Oval, both apply, and for once the former is of secondary importance to the latter.

Australia versus New Zealand? It's third versus fifth on a rankings ladder of, these days, realistically seven. Even if New Zealand equalise the series, Australia will maintain custody of the Trans-Tasman Trophy. A few of the players on show make it a tasty prospect, but as a contest it might be thought of paramount importance.

The real trial is of the plasticity of the Test match format. At stake is even more than the telegenia of the whiteclad cricket evening, the visibility of the pink ball and the versatility of the players. For the first time in memory, followers are being encouraged to think of the five-day format as amenable to innovation in ways similar to other variants (whose playing conditions are, of course, tinkered with almost obsessively, amid complete indifference).

With other propositions it has brought in its train — four-day Tests, a revived World Championship, the scrapping of the toss and of the draw, even a franchise structure — the prospect of night Test cricket has also opened up the possibility of a realistic appraisal of the state of Test cricket all over the world.

Up till now the International Cricket Council has had little to say about the paltry crowds and somnolent mood of rather too much Test cricket round the world. Its only active measure has been the Test Match Fund, a smooth-the-dying-pillow initiative to make last year's Big Three takeover vaguely more palateable, handing back in loose change what the Board of Control for Cricket in India, Cricket Australia and the England Cricket Board were extracting in bankrolls.

A few years ago, when it was pushing the World Test Championship under CEO Haroon Lorgat, the ICC had a London-based agency develop a concept marketing campaign for Test cricket. Well, why not? After all, every other damn thing is marketed to the last atom.

But the campaign perished with the championship, and the format has gone on being sold, as former *SportsBusiness International* editor Richard Gillis has put it, like broccoli or medicine: 'Get this down. It's good for you.' This isn't showing respect for the format. It's simply neglect, and characteristic of an organization bereft of common purpose — for which CA, sad to say, bears a degree of responsibility.

It's a shame, too, because actively trying to sell Test cricket could have been a challenging and clarifying exercise. By comparison with most institutions devised in the nineteenth century, it's going pretty well. But there's no doubt that the format is at odds with a lot of conventional thinking about sport.

It has resisted standardization, restriction, mechanization, overcommercialisation. It retains a host of ceremonies, courtesies, protocols, and agreed restraints: by convention, for example, it continues to be played in white beneath national caps regarded as off limits to brands and logos.

Test cricket does not package easily. Matches can end in two days, fail to conclude in five. On the contrary, the format savours of more leisured days than ours, for consuming a contest in its entirety is beyond all but a tiny minority.

Conditions exert huge influence. No game sweats its surface so much

— then, paradoxically, leaves choice of innings to be sorted by the toss of a coin. Long duration lends weather a disproportionate impact, whether cloud cover or enervating heat.

Test cricket pits players against each other, and also the systems and structures that foster and prepare them. It lacks equalizing mechanisms, and does not conduce to upsets. Weaknesses are harder to mask; opposition strengths are more difficult to suppress. In the long run, the better team prevails.

At the same time, it is also the form of the game most free. You can bat for days, bowl indefinitely, set your field wherever you please, without reference to circles or playing conditions. You get two goes, often in very distinct scenarios.

Opportunities await different temperaments and techniques. And you're welcome for what you can do, not how you look: body types as different as those of David Warner, Hashim Amla, Rangana Herath and Stuart Broad are on show.

A virtue of the night Test cricket concept is that while varying some these essences, it leaves them basically intact. In due course, some may be up for negotiation, for change has a way of begetting further change, but not yet. What we have in the interim is an opportunity to obtain clarity on what is integral to the five-day format, and what might advantageously be varied. But make no mistake. As Mike Atherton observed this week: 'A game with no live audience has no future.' We're at what you might call a Lampedusean moment: things will have to change if they're going to stay the same.

A serious conversation about Test cricket, of course, would range far more widely. It would involve posing hard-to-answer questions about distended schedules, doctored pitches, unequal power relations between boards, inequality of rewards between players, the ideal coexistence of all cricket's forms, the duty that countries owe one another for the welfare of the game. In the bigger scheme of things, the pink ball is a relatively minor issue compared to the crystal ball of cricket's future.

But nor should the conversation only be about what's wrong with the game; it should involve us affirming and acclaiming what is great, fascinating, epic, unique. That's a test for us all.

# The Decline of the West Indies
## SMOKE IN BABYLON
DECEMBER 2015

They all play basketball now. Or football. Or T20. Sad isn't it? They should set up some academies. They should pick some kids and get Viv in to talk to them. Yeah, wasn't he great? Did you see that film? Cool huh?

For a long time, it seems, people have been having the same sort of conversations about cricket in the West Indies, ending for the last five years with a reference to Stevan Riley's colourful 2010 documentary *Fire in Babylon* about the team in their 1980s pomp.

The film has served as an entertaining distraction from a direction of cricket in the Caribbean that can now be obscure to nobody — certainly not those who've watched proceedings at Bellerive Oval these last two days. A meeting of the West Indies Cricket Board tonight will address a recommendation by CARICOM (the Caribbean Community and Common Market) for its immediate dissolution. How long before the same measure is advocated for the team?

In the last twelve years, opponents have scored 43 per cent more runs per wicket than the West Indies. West Indies' away record in that time has been one win against thirty-seven defeats. A year ago they did not even get that far, players walking out of a tour of India before the three Tests were played in a contractual dispute with the WICB, leaving behind a damages bill of tens of millions.

The West Indies used to be baaaaaaad. Now they're simply bad. And in international cricket, bad easily gets worse, there being no equalising mechanisms, such as draft picks, salary caps or a transfer market, to arrest a subsidence. On the contrary. In June, the International Cricket Council held their annual conference formalising measures to channel more money to the Board of Control for Cricket in India, Cricket Australia and the England Cricket Board...*in Barbados*. From time to time it is said that 'cricket needs a strong West Indies.' Cricket sure has a funny way of showing it.

The fact is that the West Indies has always been vulnerable. It draws on a population less than six million, on nations with a gross domestic product a twelfth the size of Australia's, an eightieth the size of India's. Its political, economic and geographic fragmentation leave little basis for consensus organisation and only a tiny group of Pan-Caribbean corporate enterprises as potential sponsors; its time zone is little help in broadcasting into India. All that's happening now is that these abiding disadvantages are biting. It's amazing really they were staved off so long.

The rise of Caribbean cricket began in the 1950s, after the West Indies first won in England, and players began following the prewar trail blazed by Learie Constantine and George Headley to league clubs in the north of England. Over the next decade or so, every West Indian player of note basically subsidised their playing Test cricket by playing as a league professional: Worrell, Weekes, Walcott, Gilchrist, Hall, Griffith, Sobers, Smith, Ramadhin, Valentine, Butcher, Lloyd, Kanhai. They were the cricket equivalent of remittance workers. They also learned to handle pressure — the pressure of being the man expected to win games each week, of knowing that their performances would determine the generosity of the spectators' benefactions. As Worrell said in his autobiography: 'The league professional has a tremendous burden to shoulder and it is a good thing for any cricketer who aspires to international fame to learn how to shoulder tremendous burdens.'

When England's counties abolished their residential qualification for foreign cricketers in 1968, West Indians became prized recruits. In the next twenty-five years, forty-five West Indian players appeared in county cricket, almost half of these playing more than a hundred first-class matches. Again the experience of regular competition in unfamiliar conditions amid high expectations enhanced standards. 'It instilled tremendous confidence in me,' wrote Viv Richards, actually recruited by Somerset before he had played Test cricket, in his autobiography. 'Slowly I became a better cricketer.'

The third finishing school of West Indian cricketers, briefer but more intense and lucrative, was Kerry Packer's World Series Cricket, in which eighteen players participated, including the backbone of their great side for the next decade and a half: not only the captains Lloyd and Richards, but their irrepressible opening partnership of Greenidge and Haynes, and the pace phalanx of Roberts, Holding, Garner and Croft.

So *Fire in Babylon*'s appealing tale of a cricket pride rooted in racial awakening is really only part of the story. What you had, really, was a very talented and superbly athletic generation of cricketers hungrily making the best of growing professional opportunities. Into the bargain there was the resistless spread of the one-day international, to which their brand of cricket was well-suited.

The rewards, however, spread neither deeply nor widely. That's why governance and infrastructure remained in a state of arrested development. That's why West Indian cricketers signed up eagerly to play rebel tours in South Africa, despite the iniquities of apartheid. That's why as that lauded generation retired and other teams improved, West Indies began very clearly to falter.

What's completed that process has been the collapse of the

monopsony basis of international cricket, where national boards enjoyed unchallenged precedence as employers. Ten years ago, West Indies' top players were snagged in a rare Caribbean corporate battle involving rival telcos. The WICB had done a sponsorship deal with Digicel. The leading players had been signed up as individuals by Digicel's rival Cable & Wireless. When the WICB left them out, those players had no choice but to accept the lay of the land.

No wonder, then, that West Indian players were first in line when the Indian Premier League hove into view. Previous generations had always tended to earn their money elsewhere. The rewards were now so discrepant that there was hardly a choice to make. On top of that their cricket's biggest benefactor, Allen Stanford, turned out to be a crook.

What's paradoxically surprising is how predictable the last five years have been. After all, West Indian cricket had been a miracle so long, had found a way of accomplishing so much with so little. But in Test and ODI cricket at least, the little appears to have run out. Now, to borrow a line about the West Indies from the Caribbean's Nobel laureate Derek Walcott, 'there is too much nothing here.'

# The rise of the Big Bash League
## COMPETING ATTRACTIONS
JANUARY 2015

In Sydney last week it rained. It rained and rained. Seldom has a Test match field looked so desolate as the Sydney Cricket Ground, which seemed enshrouded by its own personal cloud, dense and inky, as Australian and West Indian players huddled out of sight for all but 150 overs.

It rained elsewhere too. Mainly sixes, and also money, as the fifth season of Cricket Australia's Twenty20 franchise tournament, the Big Bash League (BBL), surged into a third eventful week, starting with a world record crowd for a domestic game of the shortest form: 80,000 on a balmy Saturday evening at the Melbourne Cricket Ground for the game between ready-made "crosstown rivals", the Stars and the Renegades.

Not only did more than a million watch at home, but more than 400,000 had already tuned in for the curtain-raiser: a Women's Big Bash League game showcasing the distaff versions of the same clubs. A silly-season social-media storm then made a hashtag hero of a ten-year-old boy eating a whole watermelon in range of the camera — "Watermelon Boy" has now attracted six million Google hits.

The news wasn't all good. One of the Stars' sponsors collapsed; *soi-disant* Universe Boss Chris Gayle attempted a corny flirtation with a nonplussed female reporter and was heavily fined after issuing a no-apology apology. The cricket, meanwhile, fluctuated between the exhilarating and the pretty mundane. Yet somehow this was all grist to the BBL's mighty mill, mixing the dramatic and the confected, the funny and the inane, and this summer well and truly overshadowing the deeds of Australia's Test team. After all, 250 sixes bashed into 300,000 paying spectators can't be wrong.

The participants, not surprisingly, love it. Most of the time Australia's domestic cricketers could walk unrecognised down a main street. Three months ago, South Australia's young captain, Travis Head, plundered 202 from 120 balls in the interstate 50-over competition, the Matador Cup, in front of a scattering of spectators on a suburban oval in Sydney. On new year's night he blazed 101 not out from 53 for the Adelaide Strikers against the Sydney Sixers in front of 46,389 fans and a huge television audience including Andy Murray, who tweeted his approval ("Unbelievable performance...great entertainment").

Also loving it is the Ten Network, which bought the rights for five years in June 2013 for A$100 million, and which covers it with the right mix of jocularity and geekiness, Ricky Ponting having become far and away Australia's best commentator. Normally Ten is a ratings laggard. But perhaps precisely for this reason, it has spared no effort at pumping the BBL up, and also turning the BBL into a billboard for its other programming wares. Nobody is in any doubt what its cricket commentators think of Ten's forthcoming reboot of *The X-Files*.

Yet the real stars are the fans. In one respect it is a tribute to the deep and abiding Australian love of cricket. Make the game accessible, regular and cheap, it seems, and the public will turn up and tune in almost irrespective of who is playing — certainly the television audiences fluctuate remarkably little, suggestive of people following the event rather than events per se. In another respect, the BBL reflects a public desire to be part of a success, forming, as it were, a virtuous circle: fans come because of the publicity and form part of the publicity themselves. At the MCG on Wednesday night, the game between the Stars and Hurricanes being a fizzer, the cameras searched the crowd restlessly in search of spectators to dance, wave, cheer, kiss or otherwise have fun on cue. Watermelon Boy was earnestly interviewed, recounting his various media engagements. BBL has become the party everyone wants to say they've been to.

Quite what it means in the medium to long term is anybody's guess — that's the nature of the animal spirits of the marketplace. But the contrast with Australian Test matches is acute. That Steve Smith's team are strong at home is a mixed blessing. Australia have not lost a Test in their own backyard for over three years, which gratifies the partisan fan but provides little tang of genuine competition.

The stir around the inaugural day-night Test in Adelaide in November dissipated quickly with the arrival of a West Indies team barely of first-class standard, who departed the SCG having barely left a footprint let alone won a game.

Interestingly, if England eclipse South Africa on their tour, Australia will be within sight of the No 1 ranking in Test cricket that they have held only fleetingly since 2009. Yet you would be hard pressed finding anybody in these parts fretting over such minutiae. At next summer's height, Australia will be hosting Pakistan: a fine team but hardly a great drawcard down under. The chief near-term beneficiary is women's cricket, whose inaugural WBBL has experienced the halo effect of the male version's success. Nine of its 59 games, clustered mainly around weekends with free admission, have been televised, to growing audiences. People who have heard of Meg Lanning and Ellyse Perry are at least getting the opportunity to watch them, and coming away impressed.

Cricket Australia has basically paid to get the WBBL to air, to popularise the women's game, attract a new audience and potentially, down the track, to sell the rights. In this context it is anxious to look progressive and enlightened. When l'affaire Gayle erupted this week, James Sutherland, the CA chief executive, issued a stern rebuke: "I don't think at the end of all this Chris will be under any illusions as to what we think of it. Anyone that sees the humour in that is misunderstanding it and somewhat delusional about the situation. It's not a nightclub."

There is risk, too. For all the BBL's success, international cricket is still what keeps the lights on at Cricket Australia. Domestic cricket has a long way to go to match it. There is talk of more day-night Test cricket, including for the Ashes in 2017-18. But the game could look quite different by then. It already looks different from three weeks ago.

# New Zealand v Australia, Second Test, Hagley Oval, 2016
# MACE DREAMS
MARCH 2016

On Wednesday in Christchurch, Australia's cricket team went number one. In what, it wasn't immediately clear.

There they all were, Steve Smith's boys, arms round shoulders, wreathed in smiles, index fingers cocked in the time-honoured gesture of athletes who've finished top of their league.

Yet the two trophies they were pictured with had nothing to do with this accomplishment: they were the Trans-Tasman Trophy, which Australia has held so long James Sutherland probably keeps his cufflinks in it, and something from the series sponsor which looked like a section of wall.

The ICC Test Championship is actually symbolised by a mace because, well…nobody knows, really. Maybe there was a special on maces fifteen years ago when the championship was first presented. See page 138 of Steve Waugh's *Ashes Diary 2001* for a poignant photographic memento of the first captain to accept it, flanked by Shane Warne and Adam Gilchrist: it's so long ago now that they are smiling at the same time.

Smith's team had to let their fingers do the talking this week because the symbol of their supremacy was nowhere about. When you clicked on the Test Championship table on the ICC website, in fact, it continued showing India enmaced by a solitary point. A championship without a trophy with an out-of-date ladder? Here was an opportunity to have the Test Championship actually mean something, to at least reiterate its visual identity, and instead there was a kind of absentation ceremony, effectively with a note to Smith: 'IOU one mace.' That there was no ceremonial handover, and that there's actually never been an established protocol for the presentation of the mace, arguably tells all you need to know about the Test Championship's sunken profile.

The curious thing is that Test cricket means a helluva lot at ICC. Why? Because it's the basis of their split of the moolah, the ten 'full members' eligible to play Test cricket getting to make off with the bulk of monies raised from selling rights to the World Cup and World T20. At the same time, those full members base their Test interchanges on ever-less-secure bilateral relationships, to the extent that one of them, Zimbabwe, has not actually played a Test since November 2014. There's some serious prize money, $US1 million, for whoever is top of the Championship table every 1 April. But otherwise victory or defeat in a Test match has little more significance than it does in a football friendly.

In January 2014 the full members squibbed an opportunity to invest their exchanges with a deeper context, by abandoning plans for a four-team World Test Championship play-off that had been scheduled for 2017. They can put a man on the moon, as they say, but the ICC could not find 'a workable format' — that is, frankly, one that guaranteed India playing, preferably winning, and thereby maximising revenues. Call it the lesson of the 2007 World Cup, cruelled by India's premature exit: uncertainty is glorious up to the point where it might impact on broadcast cash. Back into the schedule came the previously-maligned Champions Trophy, because India had won it, thereby enhancing its commercial value.

Anyway, two years, three chiefs and one cynical scam by its three biggest full members later, the ICC is having another crack. Late last year, chief executive David Richardson announced a period of consultation with all members about enhancing 'contexts and meaning' in bilateral cricket, including a 'Test league.'

Richardson himself has mooted, for the purposes of debate, Test cricket in two divisions of six, playing two-Test series over a three-year home-and-away cycle. It has some points in its favour, in that it would guarantee a minimum amount of cricket for all, unlike the present non-system, underpinned only by the vestigial Future Tours Programme: in 2015, England played seven Tests at home and seven away, Bangladesh five at home and zero away.

The risks are also manifest. Test cricket is barely bankable for Sri Lanka and West Indies now; in a second division it might be untenable. But the present laissez-faire helps nobody, and Australia is as guilty as anyone in contributing to it. Having backed Bangladesh's promotion to full member status sixteen years ago, for example, we have hosted them for a grand total of two Tests, held way back in 2003.

The ideal is elusive. A cultural challenge is that the tradition of Test matches being played in a series is at odds with cricket's crammed and changeable calendar, and also with the modern genre of the one-off, knock-out final. A financial challenge is the existing fragmentation of television rights for bilateral cricket, which in ideal world would be pooled, but which in their uneven, often bedraggled state remind us how far we are from an ideal world.

At least the debate is being had. At the recent meeting of the chief executives' committee at ICC in Dubai, which brings together the seniormost executive officer from each full member, Richardson opened the floor for responses to a question: why do we play Test cricket? The replies, apparently, were varied. Some spoke of the players' commitment to the format — that it was clear they still regarded Test cricket as paramount.

Others went, well, yeah, why *do* we play, given that all its does is cost us money?

Worrisome? Maybe. Yet cricket shouldn't shrink from existential conversations like this. Test cricket is complex, subtle, demanding, confounding, expensive, prolonged. It does not readily reconcile with any of the entertainment values prevalent in modern sport. And yet...

A bleak summer for Test cricket finished strongly at Hagley Oval. The Second Test contained more thrust and parry than The Three Musketeers. Nor was it an example of a 'niche product' or a 'boutique fixture', to cite a couple of recent condescensions to Test cricket. It had the sweep, the scope, the characters, the stories, the setting and occasion of which epic drama is built.

It lingered in the eye and in the mind, which may be difficult to monetise, but does not mean it lacks value. On the contrary, people who watched that game will remember it always — for those whose introduction to cricket it was, it might be the basis of stark raving fandom. At the end it, of course, a mace-shaped hole. But, surely, possibilities.

# Test cricket's future
## C'MON AUSSIE
### NOVEMBER 2016

If every Test match series these days seems somehow a sort of referendum on the format's future — Texit, perhaps — then the signs lately have been pleasantly positive.

Through our winter, international cricket has warmed the cockles. Sober judges pronounced England v Pakistan one of the best of all series, full of skill, dash and nerve — Pakistan have been to 2016 what New Zealand were to 2015, a transformed team thrilling a nation. Who knew that a press-up could be such a motif of unity and vigour, as it became when Misbah ul-Haq's tight-knit team celebrated their July victory at Lord's?

Sri Lanka and South Africa, in the meantime, defied forebodings about their medium-term prospects with victories of stunning comprehensiveness over Australia. Has a less prepossessing figure loomed so large over a Test series as Rangana Herath during the Warne-Muralidharan Trophy, or a star more super than AB de Villiers been so little missed as in the Proteas' recent one-day whitewash?

When India seized Test cricket's number one ranking recently, the games were notable for healthy crowds at Kanpur and noisy crowds in Calcutta, animatedly orchestrated by Virat Kohli, who amplified this with a post-match sales pitch: 'A challenging situation in Test cricket is the most exciting thing a viewer can see, and for a player playing to feel. You can sense that energy, which no other format can provide for you.'

Nobody who saw the Test match that ended in Chittagong on Monday with England pipping Bangladesh by 22 runs would have differed.

So tight were the margins of advantage throughout that the game did not so much fluctuate as vibrate. Stuart Broad, about to play his 100th Test, placed it in his best five — 'a fantastic game to play in', with 'two countries going hell for leather at each other with a lot of passion', which is 'what Test cricket is about.'

Is it? For Australia, unfortunately, not so much. As the First Test begins in Perth on Thursday, it's going on two years since we hosted a five-day match of truly memorable quality. For a long time, this country has preened itself as a pacesetter in the longest format, last year's day-night Test an exhibit of our self-praising commitment. But in content as distinct from packaging, we're in danger of slipping off the pace.

Test cricket was last the main attraction in the summer of 2013-14, coinciding with the prime of Mitchell Johnson; 2014-15 showcased the one-day international, 2015-16 domestic T20. There have been upticks of interest since, coinciding with brief custodies of the International Cricket Council's Test mace, after visits to South Africa in 2014, and to New Zealand earlier this year. Otherwise there has emerged a disturbing pattern of monotony at home, calamity abroad. On our increasingly moribund pitches, we remain smugly unassailable. Elsewhere, Australia's performances have been downright neurotic: to hosts India, Pakistan and Sri Lanka since 2013, we have played nine, lost nine.

One wonders, in fact, whether these parallel phenomena are related — that we travel so wretchedly because we are so cossetted at home; that we have become so accustomed to dispatching underprepared and out-of-season visitors as to develop a kind of brittle complacency that dissolves at the first sign of resistance.

Whatever the case, the results should embarrass us, beyond simply the ignominy of surrendering the Ashes. 'The sub-continent' is not an exotic, faraway location fragrant with spices; it is where cricket lives. In hindsight, crying off from last year's Bangladesh tour, from which an injured David Warner would have been missing, may have been a blessing.

We are seeing signs and hearing noises of how Australia intends addressing this. They are not encouraging. Indeed, they are symptomatic of an inward-looking culture reverting to stale habits and shrinking from criticism.

In South Africa, for example, Steve Smith complained that his team had recently 'lacked a fair bit of energy in the field' which 'cost us at times'. He foreshadowed a return to 'the old Australian way of puffing your chest out and making your presence felt'. When Matthew Wade and David Warner started strutting round during the ODIs, they seemed to have received the memo.

Alas, 'puffing your chest out and making your presence felt' while you're being absolutely smoked just looks juvenile — there's swagger, and there's posturing, and opponents and fans aren't so dim that they can't tell the difference. If 'energy' is so integral to Steve Smith's thinking, then he should be investing in renewables.

Australians want to take pride in their Test team, to feel a stake in it, to link it with XIs of yore, to see membership of it as cricketers' paramount aim. And at the moment I'm not sure they do. They observe the team's steady marginalisation by the face-painted funfair of the Big Bash League. They hear former members grinding axes, current management's waffling self-justifications. They are confused by the comings and goings, the sprawling schedules, the shouty marketeers — last week, Cricket Australia momentously foreshadowed 'fan initiatives' ahead of the Brisbane Test featuring 'Test ambassador' Stephanie Rice? Cricket 'fan initiatives' featuring a retired swimmer: gee, who wouldn't want to be a part of those?

Would you not like to hear an Australian Test cricketer dedicating their team, perhaps in the spirit of Misbah, Kohli and Broad above, or even Brendon McCullum during last year's Cowdrey Lecture, to the greater good of cricket, to universal principles of sportsmanship, and to honouring the 140 years of Test match tradition, rather than falling back on the gimcrack cliches of energy, positive body language and 'we-know-there's-a-line-you-can't-cross-and-frankly-we'll-set-it-where-we-want-got-a-problem-with-that-buddy?' Just a hint or two of the value of representing the nation, of respect for the opposition, of a wish for Test cricket to prosper.

That's not all it will take, of course. Test cricket needs pitches with possibilities: heaven help us if Perth serves up an autobahn like last year's. Test cricket needs commentary showing it to best advantage: not the garrulous prattle that has for years gone unchecked. But ultimately it is teams and their leaders that excite and engage us. There's hope around, if you care to look, from Lord's to Galle, from Calcutta to Chittagong, and it's time Smith's Australians built on it. Who knows? They might even find it inspiring.

# The WACA
## LAST ORDERS

NOVEMBER 2016

Two days in, the First Test can already point to a winner of sorts: the venue. The pitch's bounce and carry has excited the bowlers. The outfield has been fast. The sun has shone and the stands have teemed.

Yet pleasure is seasoned with regret: the WACA Ground may be staging its last Test of significance. By the time the Ashes come to Perth next summer, administrators hope that the Perth Stadium, now rising over Burswood, will be in action, with its vastly greater capacity and multiple purposes.

It may make the deadline; it may not. Whatever the case, a way of watching cricket is passing. It is intended that the West Australian Cricket Association's traditional home will revert to a mix of training facility and boutique stadium.

The move has had critics: in a new autobiography, former WACA president Dennis Lillee, who fought a losing battle for the ground where a stand bears his name, pushes off the sightscreen in raining bouncers on former colleagues, calling the Perth Stadium a money pit, and worse. In general, though, the WACA Ground is slipping quietly into twilight, culminating what has really been a thirty-year fade.

Through its seventies and eighties heyday, the WACA's microclimate was unique in the world: the world famous speed and bounce offered by its Harvey Waroona soil, the brutality of the heat relieved by the ministrations of the Fremantle Doctor.

WACA may have been an acronym, but it was also cricket's great onomatopoeia: here was where batsman were whacked and whacked back. Literary critic Barry Andrews melded it into the title of his classic survey of sporting Australianisms: 'Tugging Four Bits Off the Deck at the WACA.'

It impressed outsiders too. In Patrick Eagar's 1982-83 Ashes pictorial *Summer of Speed* (1983), the section on the Perth Test concludes with a photograph of patrons clustered round the pitch after the drawing of stumps.

Such intimacy is unthinkable today, of course: you'd be gang tackled by a cadre in dark glasses and fluoro vests if you got anywhere near a square. But on Eagar's image there is neither disorder nor nuisance. The tone is reverential. Nobody is talking. Every eye is on the surface, mute testament to its reputation; some push furtively at the dark cracks; most wish merely to pay homage.

Arguably the WACA's zenith was 1986-7 when, having become Australia's third floodlit cricket ground, it hosted a Test and a seven-match one-day international quadrangular to coincide with the America's Cup defence at Fremantle. 'The fireworks which illuminated the sky after the final might have been lighting the future path of Australian cricket,' reported *Wisden*.

Alas, spasms of austerity after the 1987 sharemarket crash meant that the regeneration was never quite completed. Football came, then went when Subiaco Oval was equipped with lights. Other sports were courted unsuccessfully. Debts worsened, deals soured.

A comprehensive refurbishment was mooted just before the Global Financial Crisis, then delayed, debated, disputed and at last abandoned. In 2014-15, forty-four years after the hard-won first, there was no Perth Test. Nobody seemed to care much.

Yet through all this the WACA's folkloric character has endued. Even as the pitch was toned down, the *mise-en-scène* remained spectacular: the brilliant light beneath the expanse of the azure blue skies, lately complemented by the massed ranks of flaming orange for Big Bash League games, colour coding the crowd's parochialism.

The caravan park quality of its amenities, the snaggle-toothed smile of its architecture, the Spartan shortage of shade and homespun improvisation of barbed wired parapets balanced by the old-fashioned hospitality of grassy slopes and a 60-year-old scoreboard — all these have lent the WACA a frontier feel in a game growingly short of such sensations.

Although the press box seemed so cramped and antique that it should almost have had inkwells, for a time there was the splendid innovation of open air press tents, with fridges to cool libations and laptops alike. And there was a lively symbolism when Ricky Ponting held his farewell press conference in a gym, exercise equipment pushed up against the walls.

In due course, this rough-and-readiness became arguments for the WACA's phasing out. When Cricket Australia's CEO James Sutherland was asked last year about the loss to cricket's pageant, he tossed off lines you could parse at length: 'The big picture I think comes back to the fact that cricket's not played for the cricketers; international cricket's played for the fans.'

Yet this is not really a 'fact', still less is it a 'big picture'. On the contrary, it is a reductive appraisal of 'the fans', as though they care at bottom only about their comfort and convenience, when if these were all that mattered then spectators would hardly budge from their couches.

Live sport has traditionally been about totality of experience, the hope of excitement and romance, the risk of disappointment and annoyance. Yet administrators plough on in their determination to limit the variety of potential experiences, to homogenise, pasteurise and bowdlerise, all the better to monetise. Still, at least the boss remembered to call them 'fans' this time rather than 'consumers'...

For the fading of the WACA is on one level about practicalities, the heft of Australian rules, the anachronism of the 'cricket ground', the burdens of infrastructure and the economic advantages of monotonous discs with vertiginous stands. But it also concerns the fate of cricket in a consumption culture and of sport annexed by an entertainment industry.

The WACA has an integrated wicket block; Perth Stadium will have drop-in pitches. The WACA has wind; Perth Stadium will have wifi. The WACA neighbours a trotting track, Gloucester Park; Perth Stadium will cluster with a casino, Crown Perth. The WACA is a name with a powerful local connection; Perth Stadium will be a 'brand', cosily rubbing shoulders with the likes of BHP Billiton and Chevron. At risk is another of those transitions in sport leaving us measurably richer, unmeasurably poorer.

This Test is giving us a renewed appreciation of the WACA. But maybe the appreciation won't be complete until the experience of watching cricket there is only a memory.

# MAXWELL ON THE MAT

DECEMBER 2016

It is turning into a season full of unintended consequences. Australia's cricketers reclaimed the Chappell-Hadlee Trophy last week, while putting the spotlight on their twelfth man.

Not since Gary Pratt has a substitute fielder brought such attention on themselves as Glenn Maxwell, although the latter's visibility owed nothing to events on the field. Maxwell took a catch occasioning somewhat muted celebration, and otherwise carried drinks and towels like his own set of stocks.

Maxwell's non-selection was not directly related to press conference comments eight days ago expressing frustration about batting down the list for Victoria, behind his wicketkeeper-captain Matthew Wade. But it was easy to infer that he was serving penance for...well, what was it, exactly? Offering a straight answer to a straight question? Those free speech warriors are never around when you need them...

But let's leave this aside momentarily, and also whether Maxwell's comments were right, wrong or mischievously amplified. My colleague Will Swanton performed a valuable service on Wednesday by quoting the remarks in their entirety, enabling readers to satisfy themselves on the question of context.

In the first instance, interludes such as l'affaire Maxwell convey how primly shockable we have become, in this era of institutionalised conformism and emollient half-truths, about the idea of an athlete sharing what has been on their mind.

There's pious talk about 'team unity', although what's being appealed for is simply the comforting public pretence of unity, and 'letting your bat do the talking', which perhaps brings closer the day a player sends a bat to a press conference in their place. This might on occasion be more informative.

Few have noted that most of Cricket Australia's policies in domestic cricket over the last few years have been dedicated to reducing it from a proper competition to a forum in which players duke it out for the delectation of national selectors — in the context of which Maxwell's grievance, that it is failing to provide him satisfactory opportunities, actually makes some sense.

Yet the significant dimension of CA's position on this spat is that, at least publicly, it has been hands-off. The official view is that Maxwell's comments did not breach article 2.2.3 of their code of conduct — 'public or media comment that is detrimental to the interests of cricket' — and that any response has been 'a matter for the players.'

The penalty was levied on Maxwell not by CA but by the 'player leadership group', consisting of captain Steve Smith, vice-captain David Warner, Mitchell Starc and Josh Hazelwood.

This group, introduced three years ago by coach Darren Lehmann, had hitherto confined itself to semi-serious issues of day-to-day discipline: its last public role was fining a worse-for-wear Chris Rogers for arriving late and wearing sunglasses to Ashes celebrations in January 2014.

One might suggest that CA signified approval of the penalty in its divulging by Smith in his column on Cricket Australia's website ('Steve Smith exclusive: Why we fined Maxwell') — lotsa clicks for that content.

But let's say, for the purpose of argument, that Smith, Warner, Starc and Hazelwood took it unbidden into their heads to penalise Maxwell for, as the captain put it, being 'very disrespectful' of Matthew

Wade: 'In this team we talk about respect and respecting everybody involved in the game, from teammates, to the opposition, our fantastic fans and the media' etc etc.

Now 'player leadership groups' in cricket mainly reflect instincts to ape other sports and give everyone a title: Churchill could inspire an empire against Nazism, yet somehow eleven cricketers need leadership from a nominated group. In general, fortunately, they're pretty harmless, mainly an opportunity for the cool kids to hang together.

But when they start issuing public judgements, meteing out undisclosed fines and revealing their handiwork by means of 'exclusives' on their employers' website, they assume a somewhat different status. They become a visible part of the disciplinary process that's nonetheless opaque and uncomfortably unilateral.

Some things, in fact, it would be useful to know. What code was followed? What charge was laid? What scale of penalty was referred to? What evidence was led? Was the press conference transcript read to ensure that Maxwell's remarks had been satisfactorily represented in media reports? Was Maxwell allowed a plea in mitigation, or offered alternative means of making amends? Did he have support/representation? Does he have a right of appeal?

Because combine this verdict with his coach's public scolding, the instant opinings of ex-players who naturally never nursed a personal ambition in their lives, and visual enactment of Maxwell's pariahhood in his exclusion from the XIs in Sydney and Canberra, and it's hard to recall an Australian cricketer more humiliatingly penalised since Homeworkgate. That the scenario involved David Warner, once so indulged that it cost Lehmann's predecessor his job, and Matthew Wade, not perhaps the first cricketer who comes to mind in the context of 'respect', adds thick layers of irony.

Of course, there's a logic at work here that's comprehensible, even laudable. In an ideal world, players *would* have more say over the behavioural standards they are required to observe. And funnily enough, like a lot of ideas in cricket, it's older than it seems — although it was, back in the day, tried and found wanting.

The Australian Cricket Board's original 'code of behaviour', adopted in July 1980 and credited to Greg Chappell with the example of golf in mind, involved a jury, as it were, of peers. The experiment lasted eighteen months, an indirect victim of the Perth confrontation between Dennis Lillee and Javed Miandad, when Australian players docked their great teammate only $200 and issued a statement deploring Miandad's provocations.

The board, confirmed in a long-held suspicion that players' judgements of one another would be personally coloured, steadily moved to a more centralised model involving independent commissioners.

Yet similar reservations might be entertained here. Maxwell's punishment does not savour of disinterested discipline in the interests of the whole; it smacks of a captain who's spent months in an echo chamber of macho bullshit about the necessity of his taking charge and being tough.

Along wanders a peripheral squad member naively forgetting that pressers are for talking about 'good areas' and 'executing our plans', and presents Smith with an opportunity to publicly flesh out his captain's credentials. Add to this that Maxwell's comments involved a player, Wade, whose selection Smith is known to have pushed for and an unkind eye might see it as less about creed and more about clique.

Let's be charitable. Every captain must find their own way. And toughness *is* necessary. But so is wisdom and insight — the capacity to bring out the best in different characters, rather than the dogmatic insistence on absolute uniformity of character. On the field Smith has had a superb week. He might want to direct his efforts to having us concentrate on that.

# Alastair Cook Stands Down
# LAST OF THE SLOWHICANS
FEBURARY 2017

There is a whiff of Ashes in the air. As of last week we know that, barring calamity, it will be Joe Root joining Steve Smith at the coin toss at the Gabba some 285 days hence — and if other uncertainties await removal, this captaincy head-to-head has seemed inevitable for nigh on two years.

Perhaps as much attention will fall, meanwhile, on the batsman who, all things being equal, will face the first ball for England: Alastair Cook, paying a fourth visit to the land where he averages nearly 50 from fifteen Tests

Cook's resignation last week brought generous, well-earned bouquets. Yet in voluntarily scaling down his role to that of Test specialist, his decision also reflected Test cricket's scaled-down significance. Cricketers are always passing through. Few have, like Cook, experienced watching themselves become almost anachronistic. If Misbah ul-Haq remains nominally Pakistan's Test captain, the rest of those who hold that role for their countries are now multi-format players in a world where it is almost de rigueur.

Cook, who only weeks ago was named captain of the International Cricket Council's Test Team of the Year, was the last of the Slowhicans, having since his debut faced 51 per cent more deliveries than any other player in the world. He tried and failed to buck that status by assimilating one-day cricket, but his strike rate of 77 savoured of more leisured times, and he reverted permanently to whites two years ago; he had played the last of four T20 internationals more than six years before that.

Cook returned his captain's commission after his usual quiet fashion and sober deliberation, and there were personal factors at work: last year he flew to Chittagong to lead England just 18 hours after becoming a father for the second time. He was also accepting the inevitable, that his carefully honed artisanal skills were a worsening fit with the modern game's mass market priorities.

Remarkably, despite his 30 Test hundreds and veteran's status, Cook is still only 32 years old. He may add significantly to his 11,057 Test runs, closing the gap on Tendulkar's far-off record. That is also not inevitable. Last weekend's deliberations at the ICC in Dubai portend fewer Tests more perfunctorily played, for the sake of economic efficiency. And if a 'Test series' can be one match, as the ICC is oxymoronically suggesting, some will wonder: why play any more?

For the player who wishes to make a speciality of the long-form, or whose methods lead simply to their typecasting, this implies futures of more sporadic activity. From the example of Cook, one might infer that opening batsmen will be disproportionately effected, their tasks now varying so much depending on duration.

To bat in the top three in Test cricket has historically implied robust technique and stoic temperament; to bat in the top three in the game's other variants today is, really, to get the best seats in the house, when the ball is hard and the field (compulsorily) up.

David Warner can do both — there often seems little he cannot. But what careers will be led by the two other probable starters in Brisbane, Australia's Matt Renshaw and England's Haseeb Hameed — both 20, built to last, who might yet adapt to T20, but who have so far not played a single game of it at domestic level?

There are also parallels between Cook and his counterpart during the last Ashes. Michael Clarke was a superior one-day cricketer to Cook, if not perhaps by as much as might be imagined, with a strike rate of 79; at T20 he was never able to accelerate much beyond a run a ball, which these days seems little hastier than a slow-motion replay.

Test cricket, where he scored 28 hundreds, was Clarke's metier; confronted by incapacitating injury, he fought characterfully to prolong his career, before giving it away with great reluctance.

Such reluctance, in fact, that a year ago Clarke made a well-publicised comeback at grade level, excitedly spruiking his services for T20: 'There's BBL next summer, I'd love to be a part of that, IPL, county cricket...

'All I know is, I'll never say never to anything. I'll start with Western Suburbs and we will see where it takes me. For now, my focus is definitely the shorter format of the game.'

The demography of T20 has proved broader than was once forseen. Value has been detected in experience and presence — nothing in the BBL was so exhilarating as Mitchell Johnson exhaling dragon fire for the Scorchers. Recalibrating a game built around Test match durations for T20 priorities has proven far harder, and it was beyond Clarke. His comeback made it no further than two games for the Kowloon Cantons in the Hong Kong T20 Blitz last June, before he settled for the commentary box and for revealing his marriage secrets (not, fortunately, at the same time).

This was probably a sensible decision. The greatest disappointment of the BBL these last two years, for example, has been Kumar Sangakkara, compiler of 63 international hundreds over a storied career.

In 2015-16, Ricky Ponting tipped Sangakkara to be the BBL's highest scorer. Yet, now in his 40th year, he has sometimes resembled a vintage motoring enthusiast driving his Hispano-Suiza or Stutz Bearcat in the World Formula One, the game zooming past him.

Will there be no Cooks, Clarkes and Sangakkaras in future? One should never rule anything out in cricket. But even if there do arise batsmen of old-fashioned obduracy, inclined to construct innings across days, they may find the stage too small to become stars.

A subtle feature of Cook's marginalization was its abetting by his own employers. The England and Wales Cricket Board has been pushing for four-day Test matches for the last two years. Last September, it overhauled its central contract system to 'recognise the increased focus of the shorter format and the importance that we place on this'.

No particular hurry attends Root's appointment as Cook's successor because England does not play its next Test until 6 July. In some degree, Eoin Morgan, England's ODI and T20I captain, has already grown into the more relevant leader.

The Ashes? It is already an outlier; the game's direction is bound to make it more so. And Alastair Cook? Imagine, in a decade or two, trying to explain to the young that there were once batsmen like him.

# India v Australia, First Test, Pune, Day 1
# RUNS ON THE BOARD
FEBRUARY 2017

The injunction to control the controllables in sport comes with the implication that the uncontrollables are best ignored. Sometimes they cannot be; sometimes there is no avoiding them.

For almost two hours before lunch yesterday at MCA Pune International Cricket Stadium, Mat Renshaw looked like he had digested only the most wholesome influences of his touring experiences. He had left judiciously, defended decisively, with a long forward press. He had coped coolly with Ravi Ashwin, profitably employed the lofted on-drive as his release shot against Ravi Jadeja. As lean and angular as Bill Lawry, he revealed a head prefect's boyish features when he shed his helmet.

India, however, throws up unique challenges. It is, after all, a land with more mobile phones than toilets. And when Renshaw had sudden need of the scarcer of these, he started backpedalling faster than a conservative panjandrum from Milo Yiannopolous.

This did not endear him to the bleed-green-and-gold brigade, maybe even to his captain, drawn into the tripartite negotiations with the umpires. But it was also a lesson of sorts. This is the tour of lurking, unforseeable danger. Batsmen will look settled in, until they aren't. 400 will appear like a good total, until it isn't. Sessions will drift by as if in a dream, then overs unfold like gory hallucinations. That's India.

It happened that just before Renshaw's unscheduled pit stop, Australia had met with its first crash, Umesh Yadav coaxing David Warner into playing down a fifth stump line with an ambivalent bat.

As Renshaw scampered up the steps, Australia abruptly had two scoreless batsmen at the crease, and for the next fifteen minutes what had been a picturesque landscape of batsmanship grew more like a washed-out still life. Steve Smith and Shaun Marsh scratched about under the attention of newly excited crowd and a seemingly more hostile sun.

Australia had made the best of the day's first uncontrollable at least. Smith was so ecstatic on winning the toss that when asked for his 'combination' by Ravi Shastri could offer no more than, well, two fast bowlers, some batters...errrr...a few other guys...eleven basically...but, y'know, phew.

Virat Kohli appeared sanguine, as though India would be happy to take their turn at the crease in the dark and under water. But after a wicketless ninety minutes, India's captain was assuming a stance that is his equivalent of Allan Border's old 'teapot' of annoyance; in Kohli's case, his eyes narrow, his arms fold tightly across his chest and he tilts slightly backwards at the waist. Kohli had cause to tilt tightly, for Jayant Yadav, included ahead of Bhuvneshwar Kumar here, had managed to bowl Warner round his legs with a no ball — and a Jayant one at that.

The SG ball, fast shedding its lacquer, was doing little untoward, while the openers were showing an impressive preparedness to concede inches in order to gain feet — stretching wide of off stump with bat ahead of pad to the left-armers to stave off lbw; playing down the line of off stump to the off-spinners, countenancing defeat of the outside edge in order to protect the inside.

Of the two teams, India were at this stage arguably the less patient, expending both reviews by 12.30pm. With five left-handers to pick over, Ashwin and Jadeja looked determined to live up to their billing as numbers one and two on the ICC Test rankings, and to offer Pune something by which to remember its inaugural Test. Australia made them wait.

In the afternoon, however, momentum took another of those Newton's Cradle shifts, when Smith and Peter Handscomb went from calmly established to dejectedly dismissed within five deliveries. Smith departed with a helmet slap — cricket's equivalent of the facepalm. Renshaw reappeared, a little wiser, and perhaps a little lighter. Australian fans were experiencing sensations akin to his in the morning.

The 30 runs Renshaw added were Australia's most fluent of the day. He reached the boundaries of backward square leg, mid-wicket, mid-on with strokes of youthful conviction. He was unhurried, found gaps, worked singles, protected his off stump, but pushed no wider. He was obliged to play the Ashwin delivery that dismissed him; he can take some comfort from being worked over by a master.

Australia was blessed thereafter that Mitchell Starc had one of those days where his 360-degree batting arcs make solid connection. Under the circumstances, the temptation of the mid-wicket boundary was worth giving into. Having scored at 2.5 an over from the first new ball, Australia took 4.5 an over from the second.

The assurance with which he did rather belied Australia's dark glances at the pitch over the days preceding the Test. It is as dry as the state of Maharastra during its recent election; succeeding days will reveal how hard it is beneath.

Having gone nineteen Tests without tasting defeat, Kohli will be confident. But there is no doubt that batting last here will be worthy of his mettle, and uncontrollables impact on even such as he.

## India v Australia, First Test, Pune, Day 2
# EARLY WARNEING SIGNS
FEBRUARY 2017

The night before this first Test, Shane Warne was holding court amid an Indian audience in a Pune hotel when he was asked about Virat Kohli. Warne smiled, made a gesture of assent, and spoke admiringly of Kohli for a full minute: the best in the business, the star of the show.

Mind you, Warne added, Kohli *was* inclined to go a bit hard at deliveries pushed wide, wasn't he? If Warne was out there now — and part of him has never quite left the middle — then he would challenge Kohli on a fifth or even sixth stump line, where India's captain was inclined to chase the ball with an angled and open blade.

Cue 10.45am local time on the Test's second day. Kohli descends the white-washed staircase from the home dressing room amid universal acclaim, almost as though he is not about to bat but to host the Oscars.

Stepping onto the playing surface, Kohli does not stride or strut. Rather does he saunter, reminiscent of R. C. Robertson-Glasgow's description of the English amateur Cyril Walters approaching the crease "like a free man, one going out to a hard but agreeable task". No wonder, really. For 30 months he has been lousy with runs — has almost had more than he has known what to do with, and could conceivably have donated a surplus to charity. More beckon.

There is little ceremony or ostentation about Kohli taking guard: as usual, he can hardly wait to get started. He holds his bat from harm as the first ball from Mitchell Starc zooms along a fourth stump line. Starc's left-armer's angle will always tend to tempt a batsman wider, but the second ball floats wider still, deviating about a foot from its basic flight path in the last half of its journey. Kohli is unconcerned by this movement, impatient to make contact, to go about his business of being best.

With the benefit of a little time to acclimatise, Kohli's second ball might next have been seen bouncing back half way from the boundary boards at deep backward point. Instead, Pete Handscomb has just time for the half-formed thought that he must hold onto this heaven-sent offering: bending his knees, he watches it all the way into his midriff, as does Kohli, eyewitness to his self-destruction.

Maharashtra Cricket Association International Cricket Stadium is a ground as atmospheric as his name, but what little Kohli's arrival has introduced now escapes until the ground feels depressurised. Except perhaps the Australian huddle, towards which Starc runs as though into the arms of a long lost family.

Of Warne the pundit, the rest of the day is a little less flattering. Steve O'Keefe's low-slung round-arms and minimalist variations do not appeal to him; in that same hotel gathering, Warne had scattered stardust over the junior leggie Mitchell Swepson. But it is O'Keefe who, having opened the bowling with Starc, commences after lunch to widen the breach in India's batting until it gapes.

Twenty-four deliveries can go by in these parts without time seeming to pass at all. Now they encompass six wickets for O'Keefe, and the home dressing room might as well have a revolving door: India, having looked a tad impatient on the first day, are as panicky and adrift in the conditions as some touring teams have been over the years.

Smith is moving fields as if drawing on divine inspiration. Nathan Lyon is bowling his best spell in Asia since Delhi in 2013, at speeds comparable to Ravi Ashwin, at the expense of his drift but with an enchancement of his threat to the stumps.

It is not a raging turner of the kind folkloric in the sub-continent. If anything it is the ball travelling straight on and tunneling through that is causing gravest consternation. Nothing goes along the ground or menaces the clavicle. Batting should be possible, yet the batters are almost aphasic. The gregarious O'Keefe grows ever more nonchalant about his wickets. As he has Umesh Yadav caught to secure Australia a 145-run lead, he hitches his trousers, exchanges a few high fives, and saunters off almost as casually as Kohli had arrived before lunch.

In hindsight, the day can be said to have turned on that Kohli walk and that Kohli wicket. It is as if the hosts have simply never factored in the possibility of his failure, or taken at face value all the tributes they have paid themselves about home ground advantage, improved athleticism and bench strength. They are, today, all duck and no dinner.

Out the back of the media area, Warne can be seen smiling with Michael Clarke. Like their radio colleague Simon Katich, Australian coach Darren Lehmann and visiting Cricket Australia director Michael Kasprowicz, they were playing when Australia last won a Test in India 12½ years ago; they have been in all likelihood been watching the next, on a day to reward and defy everyone's best guesses.

# India v Australia, First Test, Pune, Day 3
# MISSION POSSIBLE
## FEBRUARY 2017

To the third ball of the third day of this First Test, Steve Smith played forward and guided it behind point for an easy single. At first glance anyway.

Before one knew it, he had turned and begun pelting back. Jayant Yadav did his best to trap and release swiftly, and a direct hit would have been opportune. But Australia's captain was quicker still, and his dive perfectly executed — so perfectly that he almost picked himself in the same motion, wearing a bit of Pune dust as do-it-yourself desert camouflage.

The clock had barely nudged 9.30am, his team was comfortably positioned, and a day stretched out ahead. Yet Smith had started the allocated overs as he meant to finish them, by winning every trick, however trifling. There was no risk of Australia being the dog that caught the car and didn't know what to do with it. The quarry was to be shaken till its teeth rattled.

So it went. Less than five and a half hours later, stump in one hand, other arm round David Warner, Smith was leading his team off MCA Stadium in what used to be called India file, but so thoroughly have his team assimilated local conditions might almost be deemed an Australian walk. His first break here was luck: winning the toss. All the rest have been pluck, preparation, perseverance and finely-honed skill.

At the tail of the line, as if to make the moment last, trailed unlikely man-of-the-match Steve O'Keefe: not young, not flash, absent discernable X-factor, finding a home away. His was not a bold charge or frontal assault; it was more like a denial-of-service attack, launched from all angles.

For those with long memories, O'Keefe's mirror six-fors paralleled Bhagwat Chandrasekhar's in Melbourne forty years ago. Australia and India have shared a rich cricket history, and O'Keefe makes a wonderfully improbable addition to its lists.

'4502 days': the length of time since Australia's last Test win here tripped from Smith's tongue as he and O'Keefe took their media turns soon after. The adaptability Australia has shown in Pune suggests that the next will not take so long.

Credit was spread throughout this Australian side, but each individual owed something to Smith, and his 109 was an expression of cumulative purpose as much as an individual feat. Third-innings hundreds can be casual canters: this was a monument of self-control. Even Smith's wriggly mannerisms, which used to make him look like someone who'd had ice dropped down the back of his shirt, now conform to a sort-of check list: helmet, gloves, pad flaps, box pat, bat tap, knee bend, bring it. When he leans on his bat, legs-crossed, at the non-strikers' end, he might almost be any other player.

Except that he's not. The next highest score in this match was 68, made on the first day. As he passed that minor milestone yesterday, Australia's captain came down the pitch at Jadeja, and slapped a delivery nine inches outside off stump in the air between mid-on and mid-wicket. There is not even a name for this shot. It should be a Smith. He had been dismissed playing a version of this strike on the first day; once bitten, never shy.

Some have quibbled that Smith's century cannot be judged as among the best, or even his best, on the grounds that he enjoyed several lives. But a dropped catch isn't so much a flaw as an event; it mars only a surface purity rather than substance. It's arguable, too, that a few of the chances went begging because of the sheer gold-platedness of Smith's wicket.

The Englishman Joe Hardstaff once said that every time he thought of Bradman his feet felt tired; mention of Smith must cause at least a little anticipatory tenderness among players in these parts too. Against this opposition, he has scored hundreds in five consecutive Tests and averages nearly 90.

At Galle and Colombo last year, having himself referred to the heinousness of the offence, Smith was twice bowled by Rangana Herath as the ball passed by his inside edge. Here, until he played across Jadeja, it was hard to recall a similar instance. And although deliveries often caressed his outside edge, if anything they deepened his defiance, and a play-and-miss is no use to a bowling side if it sows no doubt.

As for Smith, so for his team. The analysts totted up no fewer than fifty outside edges beaten during Australia's second innings. Yet one seldom felt the imminence of a wicket. Beat me all you like, each Australian seemed to say: I'm still standing.

India did not present such a united front. Before their second innings had been in progress 25 minutes, they had lost both openers and squandered both reviews: a BCCI campaign for the repeal of the DRS, perhaps, starts here. Smith's counterpart Virat Kohli then provided a symbol of India's veering expectations. On the first day he had waved his bat like a cutlass; now, committing too early to a leave, he kept it sheathed. As the Australians celebrated the loss of Kohli's off stump, he paused in apparent supplication.

His teammates proceeded to lose seven for 30 to go with their 7 for 11 the day before, and 'soft' hardly begins to describe some of the dismissals: they were soft like a Pillsbury Dough Boy full of Cool Whip. Towards the end, the Australian effort was infinitesimally marred by an overthrow. Smith looked ever so slightly peeved. He wants to win it, win it all.

# India v Australia, First Test, Pune
# COUP D'ETAT
## FEBRUARY 2017

In years to come, my recollections of the Pune Test will be in terms of a toilet. Although not in a Matt Renshaw way.

Bear with me on this. In the malodorous gents on the northern side of MCA Stadium, beneath the media area, there were three cubicles. Of the last of these, the installers had made a bit of a hash, screwing the lock with its "vacant/occupied" dial to the inside of the door with the result that the user could not close it. As is standard in these parts, a solution had been improvised: a bolt on the front of the door. This meant that it could be closed only from outside — the purpose of privacy was thereby lost.

I won't elaborate on the interior of the gents more generally as you may be reading this at breakfast.

Anyway, as information steadily emerged about the 11th-hour intervention of the Board of Control for Cricket in India in the preparation of the Pune pitch, this lavatory cubicle developed an ever stronger resemblance to the home side's predicament. Aiming to shut the visitors out, they actually left the door ajar; and while the Indians were busy within, Australia swiftly locked the door behind them.

In their comments during and after the game, captain Virat Kohli, coach Anil Kumble and opener Murali Vijay conspicuously played the pitch down. "I don't think it was any different from the turners that we played in the past," said Kohli. "We just didn't play good cricket."

Superficially, this was a manful refusal to blame conditions for his team's deficiencies; at a deeper level, it smacked of deflection. Whatever the case, it has turned into an omnishambles. Various local newspapers, notably *The Indian Express*, have blamed "team management", abetted by BCCI officials, for the decision to shave the pitch and withhold water for the three days before the game. The International Cricket Council's match referee, Chris Broad, has subsequently graded the pitch "poor" under a new four-point criteria penalising surfaces for "excessive" seam movement, turn and uneven bounce.

The irony is that the popular conspiracy theory before the match was that the pitches for the series would be quicker and bouncier than usual, manifesting tensions between the new administration at the BCCI and its disinherited predecessors: Pune is the stronghold of former secretary Ajay Shirke, Ranchi the seat of former secretary Amitabh Choudhary, Dharamsala the fiefdom of erstwhile president Anurag Thakur.

India has form in this respect. Thirteen years ago, the Nagpur Test was played on, of all things, a green seamer, chalked up to tensions between the BCCI's poobah Jagmohan Dalmiya and restless rivals led by Sharad Pawar. Pawar's allies at the time included Nagpur's Shashank Manohar, since gone on to chair the ICC.

No wonder Shirke is now demanding the interim committee placed in charge of the BCCI by the Lodha Commission of India's Supreme Court refer the matter to the Central Bureau of Investigation: "Since the spot-fixing [in IPL 2013] came to light, the whole board has been thrown out. Now let us see what steps the court-appointed administrators take to get to the root of pitch-fixing."

Choudhary, meanwhile, is shortly to be heard in the Supreme Court on the plea that the interim committee is overstepping its remit of overseeing governance transition by "passing directions which give an impression that they are to administer the BCCI". Damned if you don't, damned if you do...

The team of Kohli and Kumble has done a remarkable job this summer of holding aloof from upheaval in Indian administrative circles. They may inadvertently have made themselves into an exhibit in the case against their new overseers. Certainly, the BCCI badly needs the story to go away, preferably under cover of a Kohli-led comeback by the Indians from this afternoon in Bengaluru; trouble is, under new measures agreed by the ICC chief executives' committee last month, it will, down the line, almost certainly result in an embarrassing fine, compounding the original ignominy of getting stuck in their own toilet.

Personally, I held no hardline objection to the pitch in Pune. Steve Smith made a fine hundred; nine wickets fell to pace; nobody was injured; the cricket was absorbing; the better team won. Where pitches are concerned, we can be too much like Goldilocks, anxious that everything be "just right".

Australians would do well not to be too pious in such matters too. It's not because Brisbane is pleasant at the time of year that Australia has traditionally commenced Test summers at Gabba: it happens to be a stronghold at which the hosts have not lost since 1988.

We have also rolled out our share of bad pitches. Comfortably the worst in Australia these past couple of years was the WACA's Nullarbor-flat surface 15 months ago, preluding a bore draw with New Zealand. Mitchell Johnson liked it so little that he retired. The most positive aspect of the CEC's new criteria for assessing pitches is that it also penalises those that display "little or no seam movement or turn at any stage in the match together with no significant bounce or carry, thereby depriving the bowlers of a fair contest between bat and ball". Hopefully Australian curators take note.

What pitches friendly to bowlers reveal, meanwhile, is the flipside of modern batting: batters have hardly been more explosive, innovative, virile; with that has come a disconcerting negativity and impotence faced with even minimal deviations, and almost neurotic frailty under pressure.

By *Cricinfo's* count, there were 29 batting collapses in 47 Tests in 2016, generally in perfectly fair conditions and under only standard pressure. Three innings defeats were incurred by teams that had accumulated more than 400 in their first innings — a fate that had befallen only four teams in the preceding 14 decades of Test cricket. So while India's fate in Pune of losing 7-11 in the first innings and 7-30 in the second reads grimly, it could hardly be deemed an outlier.

Administrators care little: the propensity has brought closer the four-day Test matches that many of them quietly favour. They might want to be careful what they wish for. Another feature of that toilet in Pune was noticeable: I never observed anyone trying to use it.

# India v Australia, Second Test, Bangalore
# THE GHOST IN THE MACHINE
## MARCH 2017

The only way to deal with an open can of worms is, proverbially, to obtain a much larger can. Thus this week's agreement between the Board of Control for Cricket in India and Cricket Australia, after they had issued violently clashing statements in support of their captains after the Second Test at Bangalore.

There had already been a conspicuous clatter as the International Cricket Council tucked its code of conduct can opener away in the disciplinary drawer, enjoining the antagonists to 'focus their energies on the third Test'. And people *did* just need to cool it, for as long as necessary for perspective to dawn.

Steve Smith was wrong; Peter Handscomb, while inexperienced and well-meaning, was wronger still. Indeed it beggars belief that modern cricketers could be so obtuse about the conduct of the game as to start surveilling player viewing areas for escape clauses. Under the circumstances, Kohli's suspicion was perfectly pardonable.

Yet this is also a grey area in the Playing Conditions. Consultation about a review, it is true, can only be on-field; but Bangalore was the first occasion anyone could recall umpires needing to define that line.

Some aspects of DRS protocols, moreover, remain ambiguous. In the Chappell-Hadlee Trophy thirteen months ago at Seddon Park, umpires referred a caught and bowled after a big screen replay revealed that Mitchell

Marsh had hit the ball into his boot and Brendon McCullum on seeing it reiterated his appeal.

Smith opted not to make an issue of this, but made a useful point: 'He was out, there was no doubt about that. But if I get hit on the pad next time and it's missing leg, do I stand there and wait until it's going to show that on the big screen?'

In a general sense, too, cricket's playing area is scarcely sealed. The modern field hosts a seemingly unregulated parade of reserves and helpmates, with drinks, gloves, tablets etc, and also, as we know, from time to time, messages. And messages can come in all forms. Cricket frowned on Hansie Cronje's earpiece; but boundaries have grown, if anything, more porous.

Under the circumstances, the umpires did very well, acting promptly, decisively and firmly. Virat Kohli did not need to say anything at all, during the incident or after the match. Regretably he could not contain himself.

Private suspicion is one thing; noisy public allegation of a pattern of behaviour, on the basis of assertion rather than evidence, is a leaf from Donald Trump's playbook. To let a journalist then interpolate the word 'cheat' was then just too cute. Had Smith acquiesced in a similar description of Kohli, one suspects that this might already have been ruled off as a two-Test series.

The only subsequent informal emanation from the Indian camp was disquiet about the response on the Australian balcony to Mitchell Marsh's first innings lbw. Yet this was almost certainly related to its occurrence to the last ball of the 80th over, shortly before the recharge of reviews. And, of course, it availed Marsh precisely nought.

Kohli is such a glorious cricketer and vivid personality that one is inclined to excuse his occasional verbal incontinence. But this was a lapse of taste and intelligence. The BCCI may have felt no choice but to back him — in the search for a minuscule patch of high moral ground after being caught in the act of cooking the Pune pitch — but succeeded in doubling down the crassness.

At the same time, there is a point or two to be made in India's favour. Such smug vindication has surrounded India's final assimilation of the DRS it has been overlooked that many of its initial criticisms were valid.

When the BCCI made its objections known nine years ago, the technology was inadequate, the protocols unclear, the adoption decidedly casual. It's thanks to the need to win Indian support that we have as effective a system as we do.

There have also remained solid grounds for objection, not least the mission creep of what started as a television gimmick being allowed to mutate into cricket's ultimate appeals court, and what was originally a means of redress for 'howlers' making welcome gamblers and chancers. The technology is still inconsistently applied, and subsidised by broadcasters rather than ICC.

On the field, DRS has become cricket's ghost in the machine, subtly distorting surrounding behaviour, essentially providing a legal channel for dissent, on which the game has traditionally frowned. Availability is unevenly distributed — the later you bat and bowl, the less likely reviews will be on offer. Benefit of the doubt is no longer extended to the batter — it accrues instead to the umpire.

These aren't necessarily arguments for its repeal. The best case for DRS is watching a game without it, like India's last Test defeat in Australia, when Cheteshwar Pujara was caught behind off his helmet and Ravi Ashwin off his thigh; or India's last win against England, when Joe Root was lbw despite virtually leaving a splinter in the ball.

But crude as he was, Kohli pointed up that the DRS is a conversation cricket has rather failed to have. And if there is sufficient of an incentive, every system will interest its users in gaming it. While denying his own team so indulged, Australian assistant coach David Saker conceded on Thursday that malpractice was perfectly conceivable: 'Because there is a lot of time, that could actually happen if you wanted to do it.'

The incident at Bangalore recalled a fleeting interlude in England's first innings in 2013's Old Trafford Test, when Australia hesitated to refer an lbw appeal against Kevin Pietersen — the confidence of bowler Shane Watson was insufficient for captain Michael Clarke and vice-captain Brad Haddin to seek a review.

At the time, Darren Lehmann was enjoying somewhat of a burlesque relationship with Sky, based on his ever-present earpiece: a reaction shot of the hearty Australian coach to commentary banter and on-field events had become almost a meme.

This reaction shot was different: on the player balcony, Lehmann was revealed signalling lugubriously with his right index finger. Clarke recalled the moment in his tour diary. 'It was out,' Haddin said. 'Who said that?' Clarke replied. The keeper gestured to the dressing room. Look in that direction today and you'd best have a big empty can handy...

# PART 3

## Conspiracies, Cock-Ups and a Tragedy

# The Big Three
## MEAN BUSINESS
FEBRUARY 2014

During the Second World War, it was Churchill, Stalin and Roosevelt. In the car industry, it used to be General Motors, Ford and Chrysler. But the world of cricket will remember 2014 as the year the game got its own Big Three — even if it was really a Big One (India), with two lesser parties (England and Australia) obediently in step.

In July, cement magnate Narayanaswami Srinivasan is set to become not simply cricket's most powerful figure, but the most powerful figure cricket has ever known. The president of the BCCI and owner of the IPL's Chennai Super Kings has arguably been cricket's Grand Poobah for some time, but his installation as ICC chairman will afford him unexampled pre-eminence in the game's governance — as well as unexampled conflicts of interest.

It says something that this was not even the most extraordinary aspect of the Big Three's campaign to revamp the ICC. That honour went, perhaps, to the notion of distribution of money raised by events such as the World Cup and World Twenty20 according to the size of the "contribution" made by the relevant member — massively enriching the BCCI, and somewhat benefiting the ECB and Cricket Australia. Or to the effective scrapping of the Future Tours Programme in favour of touring arrangements secured bilaterally. Or to a ranking system that ostensibly offered possible admission to Test cricket to the ICC's most advanced Associate Member, be it Ireland or Afghanistan. Take your pick: the so-called position paper, prepared by Srinivasan, the ECB's Giles Clarke and CA's Wally Edwards, made previous revamps look cosmetic.

It's not like there was nothing to fix, of course. The BCCI's economic heft has distorted cricket's finances to breaking point, with the health of other boards basically determined by how often their team played India — entailing, it must be said, an unwonted burden for India's cricketers. It was an environment that lent itself to temporary alliances, tit-for-tat wranglings, and negligible strategic thought.

The ICC's members and other stakeholders had condemned it out of their own mouths in 2011, when they participated in what became "An Independent Governance Review of the International Cricket Council". Its authors, former chief justice Lord Woolf and PricewaterhouseCoopers, found the organisation sunk in squabbles, and divided by financial imbalance, with "those in a strong financial position…using that strength to provide leverage to reach decisions that may be in individual members' interests rather than the interests of the majority of Full Members, or indeed international cricket as a whole".

Tabled before the executive board at the end of January 2012, the review made the case for a more active council, with a fully fledged chairman, independent directors and a funding model "based on need". Woolf and his colleagues argued: "The ICC react as though they are primarily a members' club; their interest in enhancing the global development of the game is secondary…The game is too big and globally important to permit continuation of Full Member boards using the ICC as a 'club.'" Sensitive to anything that might curb their influence, the BCCI rejected the review as "not appropriate". ICC chief executive Haroon Lorgat cleared his desk in June. The atmosphere at meetings grew tense, aggravated by Srinivasan's distaste for Dubai: he was once said to have complained loudly of his inability to find a burger at the airport. By January 2013, relations had broken down irretrievably, as Srinivasan informed other Full Members that he did not feel bound by the ICC's code of ethics to act in the body's fiduciary interests, and that the BCCI reserved the right to exit the FTP if any recommendation of the Woolf Review was even mooted. Further signs of restiveness at the BCCI were the foisting of Srinivasan's protege´, Laxman Sivaramakrishnan, on the ICC cricket committee, and manoeuvrings towards a life ban for his old enemy, Lalit Modi, because of alleged misdeeds in the management of the IPL.

Midway through 2013, Srinivasan experienced pressures of his own, temporarily standing aside from his BCCI and ICC roles when his son-in-law Gurunath Meiyappan was drawn into a new and different IPL corruption crisis. The sight of Srinivasan at bay emboldened both Modi, who plotted a return to the BCCI through his old power base at the Rajasthan Cricket Association, and Lorgat, whom Cricket South Africa, after some hesitation, felt free to appoint as their chief executive. If anything, though, this stiffened Srinivasan's resolve to reshape the ICC — a procedure which the ECB and CA could either collude in or face exclusion from. Pragmatically, they chose collusion. All the while the BCCI were foreshadowing the eclipse of the old FTP by dickering at length over a tour of South Africa to which they had previously committed.

The three-man working group met in London in October, in Mumbai in November, and in Perth in December, co-opting as their scriveners the IPL's chief operating officer Sundar Raman, and CA's legal and business affairs manager Dean Kino. The momentous changes envisioned by the group needed the support of eight of the ten Full Members, so various inducements were devised, from a Test-match fund — to provide grants to boards playing "unviable" Test series — to an understanding that Full Members could "enter into as many or as few FTP agreements as they wish". Lorgat's brainchild, the World Test Championship, was also to be scrapped, with the more lucrative Champions Trophy now restored.

But the Big Three's offer of leadership was mainly a means of entrenching their own position, embodied by a proposed executive committee made up of a representative from each and, a little grudgingly, one other board member: "ExCo would act as the sole recommendation committee...on all constitutional, personnel, integrity, ethics, development and nomination matters."

The Big Three also proposed rotating the chairs among themselves for the executive board, whose importance was now somewhat diminished, and the financial and commercial affairs subcommittee, whose importance was now considerably enhanced by their role in selling broadcast rights to the next eight-year cycle of ICC events (the hosting of which would be shared by the Big Three, with the option of embracing a co-host). It was on a handsome sale price for these — forecast to be in the region of $US2.5bn, a full $1bn more than in the previous cycle — that the new regime was predicated. The Big Three could then argue that, despite their additional rake-off of hundreds of millions of dollars, no Full Member would be significantly worse off — or not, at any rate, once they had been assured of binding and bankable bilateral tours.

When the paper was tabled at a special meeting of the executive board on January 9, curiosity quickly turned to consternation. In reference to the concentration of executive power among the mighty, the Pakistan Cricket Board's Najam Sethi was said to have asked: "So, are you doing a UN Security Council on us?" It was not denied. Not surprisingly, the paper was quickly leaked to ESPNcricinfo, who led coverage of developments. Other mainstream media, by contrast, veered between partisan and apathetic.

Initial comment, most of it indignant, focused on the Big Three's self-exemption from relegation in two divisions, which they first suggested, then ditched. It was actually a stipulation on which they could give way quite easily; likewise their absolute control of ExCo, now made into a transitional arrangement, and leavened with the addition of a further seat. The new distribution model remained stubbornly impenetrable, with "contribution costs" levied by the Big Three explained as recognising "the role of each Member in contributing to generating the ICC revenues required to sustain the game". There was no clarity as to their calculation, beyond the bland assurance: "The agreed principles are sound, and the break-up between categories appropriate." But on January 23, the contribution costs were rendered non-negotiable at a Chennai meeting of the BCCI's working committee, which magisterially pronounced them "in the interests of cricket at large".

Two days later came the first strong voice of opposition, as former ICC president Ehsan Mani went to the lengths of preparing his own paper, charging that the Big Three had "completely undermined the integrity and standing of the ICC...in promoting their own agenda". Mani wrote caustically: "BCCI, ECB and CA say in the paper that they will provide greater leadership and stability to the ICC and their members. They do not demonstrate how they will do this in any meaningful way." The biggest losers, he argued, were the ICC's Associate and Affiliate nations, some hundreds of millions of dollars worse off.

Mani's protest was joined by a variety of old ICC hands: Mani's predecessor Malcolm Gray, and their chief executive Malcolm Speed; former directors Sir John Anderson from New Zealand, Shaharyar Khan and Tauqir Zia from Pakistan, Saber Chowdhury of Bangladesh, and Ali Bacher from South Africa; and former international captains Clive Lloyd, Imran Khan and Martin Crowe.

Their prophecies of strife and division were lent credibility by Paul Marsh, head of the Federation of International Cricketers' Associations: "The result of this will be that the countries who need ICC income the most will receive the least, while the Big Three will get the lion's share, even though they are already financially healthy because of the value of the rights to their bilateral series. The role of ICC events should be to assist in levelling the financial playing field by distributing the proceeds fairly, rather than further widening the gap between the rich and poor."

The house of the other seven Full Members remained divided against itself. The three closest to their respective governments, the PCB, Sri Lanka Cricket and Cricket South Africa, felt the position paper's implicit slight on their stature most acutely. They gathered for the quarterly executive committee meeting on January 28 full of outward fight, and deferred a vote on the proposals, while further offers and threats were exchanged.

But India hadn't spent so long in the British Empire without learning something about dividing and ruling. Srinivasan, confined to his home for a period of mourning following his mother's death, participated in the meeting by Skype: shot slightly from below, and with the sun behind him, he loomed rather ominously. Pakistan's Zaka Ashraf stood firm, unmoved even by the offer of three series against India in eight years; South Africa's Chris Nenzani, however, settled mainly for a share of proceeds from the Test-match fund, previously denied to CSA. "It is not a perfect world," he mused. When Ashraf returned home, he probably found himself in agreement: he was sacked.

By mid-February 2014, many uncertainties remained about the new regime: how the calendar would look; how teams would be ranked; how what the authors euphemistically called "certain major domestic cricket events", such as the IPL and the Champions League, would be affected (only favourably, one suspected). The position paper's authors and advocates have justified the expedient on the basis of the dysfunctional relations between the BCCI and the ICC, arguing that, as the BCCI were not amenable to reform, the ICC had to reform instead.

The authors see the "contribution costs" as the price of concord and, even if that doesn't explain why the ECB and CA deserved their enrichments, some justification exists for this view. It's all very well to say that the world must stand up to India; frankly, the finances of world cricket are such that the smaller seven Full Member boards can barely stand up.

In the absence of many checks and any balances, however, a lot depends on the cordiality between ICC members, even the Big Three, and that requires a confluence of self-interests. It may not always be guaranteed. Personalities change; politics and economics are inherently unstable; and cricket, as they say, is a funny game.

# World T20 2014
## SHRINKING THE
## UNIVERSE
MARCH 2014

Mirpur, a suburb to the north-east of Bangladesh's capital city of Dhaka, is home to a zoo, a botanic gardens, the head office of the country's celebrated microfinance institution, and for the next two weeks to world cricket.

Half the group games and all the finals of the fifth World Twenty20, which begins on Friday, are to be played at Mirpur's well-equipped Sher-e-Bangla National Cricket Stadium, including all those involving Australia; the balance will be held at Chittagong's rather plainer ZA Chowdhury Stadium.

Both cities should be in for an excellent ensuing fortnight. In its short history, the World T20 has had greater gram-for-gram impact than any global cricket event.

India meeting Pakistan in the first game recalls the former's victory over the latter in the inaugural final in Johannesburg, which lit the T20 touchpaper in the sub-continent, leading indirectly to the Indian Premier and Champions Leagues.

Zimbabwe beating Australia in the same tournament established a tradition of upsets, and no competitor since has enjoyed an obvious, on-going ascendancy.

Each of the four tournaments has had a different winner, plumbing depths then scaling heights being the essence of T20, while home ground advantage has been undetectable.

In 2009, hosts England lost to the Netherlands, and Pakistan triumphed. In 2010, hosts West Indies fell apart in the last eight, and England prevailed.

Fifteen months ago, hosts Sri Lanka succumbed to the West Indies, ever more a cipher in other forms of cricket, but here ensuring the improbable inclusion in *Wisden* of the words 'Gangnam Style'. Which actually wasn't a bad description of the hitting in the tournament, no fewer than eight batsmen scoring at 150 per 100 balls or better.

In all, this World T20 promises to be an uplifting spectacle for a cricket-crazy country of more than 150 million people, being the first global event Bangladesh has hosted since the pathfinding ICC Knockout of 1998.

But it will also, on present indications, be the last — the last, in fact, to be held outside India, England and Australia for the next decade

Here's how the International Cricket Council's events schedule looks as its next commercial rights cycle approaches.

With New Zealand's help, Australia will host next year's World Cup, and also that tournament for stutterers, the 2020 Twenty20.

England will host two one-day international events, the 2017 Champions Trophy and 2019 World Cup, between times.

The 2016 World T20, the 2021 Champions Trophy and the 2023 World Cup will be held in India. And...errr...that's it.

This process was set in train nearly eight years ago, when India, Australia and England charmed and cajoled the other full members into granting them the next three Cups.

Strange to recall now but India were loath to participate in the first World T20, holding the format in contempt. The Board of Control for Cricket in India's representative at ICC was known for his repeated reverberating assertions: 'India will never play T20 cricket. *Never*!'

In the end, the BCCI consented only as a quid pro quo for getting their hands on the World Cup first, in cahoots with Pakistan, Sri Lanka and Bangladesh.

The rest is history: by winning that World T20 trophy, India turned it from a pewter tankard into a golden grail.

As ICC events have grown more valuable, so have hosting rights grown more coveted. As a result, we have entered into what might be described as the third stage in their history.

When the ICC was run out of Lord's, ICC events were also centered there: the first three World Cups and ICC Trophies were all held in England, with its natural advantages in infrastructure and distance.

The success of the fourth World Cup in India and Pakistan then preluded a period of globalisation: the Cup came to Australia and New Zealand in 1992, returned to Asia in 1996, visited Africa in 2003 and West Indies in 2007.

After its aforementioned start in Bangladesh, the ICC Knockout aka Champions Trophy visited Africa twice, England twice and Asia twice.

And, despite the Big Three's control of the Cup, just two and a half years ago, the ICC executive board signed off on a new strategic plan that not only proposed 'independent evaluation of the cost/benefits of Olympic participation' but countenanced an event in a 'targeted emerging market' — this was code for the possibility of a World T20 taking place in North America.

Gradually, all such murmurings have faded, and if they had not been abandoned by the time that India, England and Australia staged their Dubai palace coup last month they have now.

Interestingly, one of Cricket South Africa's 'demands' in return for its support of the Big Three was for the right to host the 2027 World Cup, it being 'patently unacceptable and unjustifiable for there to be no major ICC global event allocated to South Africa'. Answer came there none.

Furthermore, while Australia's World Cup is set to be a fourteen-team competition, the next two will feature only ten teams.

It used to be that the Champions Trophy was described as a 'mini-World Cup'; the World Cup looks ever more like a 'maxi-Champions Trophy.' Is it even right to call it a World Cup when more nations will compete in July's World Wheelchair Basketball Championship in South Korea?

There is method to this. Maximising commercial returns — which is, inevitably, the rationale for concentrating ICC events in the Big Three, as indeed it is the rationale for virtually everything in cricket these days — can legitimately be said to enhance distributions to the financially vulnerable full members.

Of course, under the new ICC regime of 'contribution costs', India, England and Australia have reserved for themselves the front of the profit queue, to be served more amply than everyone else. But in theory there should be more to go round generally. The loss, in the main, is cultural and moral — to cricket's pretensions as a global game, to its overall variety, accessibility and inclusiveness.

Denied a major ICC event for at least the next decade and possibly longer, fans outside the Big Three are effectively reduced to second-class citizens; actually, fans in Pakistan, denied international cricket since 2008 through no fault of their own, are already at that level anyway.

Of the Holy Roman Empire, Voltaire famously observed that it was neither holy nor Roman nor an empire. Perhaps the same will come to be said of the International Cricket Council — now barely a council, scarcely about cricket, and after this World T20 diminishingly international.

# The Big Three
# SRINIVASAN UNDER PRESSURE
## APRIL 2014

Australians follow global cricket politics apathetically — the doings of men with long names in hot countries. But last week, plans in which we have had a big say went seriously astray.

It started on Tuesday when India's Supreme Court called on cricket's most powerful man, Narayanaswami Srinivasan, to surrender his presidency of the Board of Control for Cricket in India.

Actually the court went further, mocking that Srinivasan had not already gone of his own volition after the publication of the court's damaging Mudgal Report into corrupt practices in the Indian Premier League. 'Why is Srinivasan not stepping aside?' fumed Justice AK Patnaik. 'It is so nauseating.'

Why the queasiness? Because Srinivasan remained in spite of his son-in-law, Gurunath Meiyappan, and his team, the Chennai Super Kings, being the chief focus of investigations.

That was not his fault, protested Srinivasan. Daughters, eh? Who knows who they'll marry? And you know hard it is to get good help these days...

So Srinivasan stayed put, as blase as Stuart Broad at Trent Bridge last year.

But on Thursday, the court returned in a fine fury. If Srinivasan continued in his obduracy, the judges would simply issue orders ousting him, and suspend from the IPL not just the Chennai Super Kings but also the Rajasthan Royals — it is a 2013 CSK-RR game that has detained investigators longest.

That got everyone's attention. At stake was suddenly the future of cricket's plushest playground, paying scores of Australians tens of millions of dollars.

In the end, the court decided to let the IPL proceed. But in confirming yesterday it would require Srinivasan to stand aside at the BCCI while the various corruption allegations were pursued, the judges left Cricket Australia and England Cricket Board in a predicament.

For who have they backed in as inaugural chairman of the brave new International Cricket Council, as part of root-and-branch reform of that body, but Srinivasan?

Last week I brushed the cobwebs off the ICC code of ethics — more, I dare say, than most of its directors have ever done.

Here's what it says at 2.1: 'Each Director shall act in an honest and ethical manner. In order to facilitate the transparent operation of the ICC, conduct that gives the appearance of impropriety will also be unacceptable. Directors shall not engage in any conduct that in any way denigrates the ICC or harms its public image.'

This will come as a surprise to directors who routinely wipe their feet on the council. And what my legally inexpert eye discerned at once was the disproval of not just unethical behaviour but on the 'appearance of impropriety.'

Let's recap briefly some highlights of Srinivasan's career. In January 2008, his family company India Cements bid successfully for the IPL's Chennai franchise.

At the time, he was secretary of the BCCI, whose constitution, at clause 6.2.4, read: 'No administrator shall have, directly or indirectly, any commercial interest in the matches and events conducted by the Board.'

The BCCI's reaction to this tank on the lawn was to put a bumper sticker on it. The aforementioned clause was retroactively altered by the addition of an exception for T20 franchises.

Interestingly, Srinivasan *has* shown a cognizance of appearances — he does not attend CSK games himself.

But an impact of this seems to have been to magnify the influence at CSK of the ebullient Meiyappan, who desported himself as 'team principal', becoming in effect Srini's proxy.

That, at any rate, was the inference of the Mudgal Report, charged with looking into Meiyappan's gambling offences.

The report concluded: 'It came to light that Mr. Meiyappan would be with the team during the practice sessions, would be present during team meetings, at the auction table, in the owners dug out, participated in the IPL owners meet, travelled with the team, participated in the IPL owners workshop representing himself to be the owner of CSK.'

In doing so, the report effectively dismissed the evidence of Srinivasan, amplified by MS Dhoni, that Meiyappan had 'nothing to do with the cricketing affairs of Chennai Super Kings and was a mere cricket enthusiast supporting CSK.'

Now if your robustly-given testimony had been so conclusively rejected on such an essential matter then chances are you might be checking out your personal appearance-of-impropriety-o-meter.

Well, not Srinivasan. And not CA's Wally Edwards or the ECB's Giles Clarke either.

But their joint plan for Srini's chairmanship is now, surely, a dead letter. Srinivasan has been credibly identified — not by a rival, not by a pundit, not by a politician, but by members of his country's apex court — as an obstacle to a thorough investigation of the gravest issue facing the game, that of corruption.

This may not worry the superbly haughty Clarke, who opined a couple of years ago that cricket's 'biggest danger' was from people watching pirate live streaming of games on the internet. The deuced curs!

But it should concern Edwards, trying to make the best of the busted arse that is global governance, left now to distinguish between degrees of dysfunctionality. Two other events last week are worth his noting.

On Monday, exiled IPL commissioner Lalit Modi trumpeted on Twitter that he had 'evidence to suggest there was fixing' in the T20 Champions League, on which the ICC's Anti-Corruption and Security Unit was sitting 'due to certain vested interests in world cricket', but which he pledged to reveal if the ACSU did not 'bring it out in public in a week.'

Modi is hardly an impartial source, but his information drops in the past have had a tendency to check out.

And coincidentally or not, the Metropolitan Police then detained Andrew Fitch-Holland, legal confidante to Chris Cairns, on suspicion of perverting the course of justice.

Cairns it was, of course, who won a bitter defamation action against Modi over fixing allegations in 2012. But he has acknowledged since being the subject of ongoing Met and ACSU investigations.

Ready or not, we seem about to learn a great deal more about corruption in cricket's midst, involving more cricketers across more jurisdictions in practices more pervasive than in the Pakistani spot-fixing affair.

Cricket's integrity apparatus will then be put to its sternest test yet. If it were to have to report to Srinivasan, at least under present circumstances, it would be more than absurd; it would, frankly, be 'nauseating'.

# The Lodha Commission
# FIXING INDIAN CRICKET
## JANUARY 2016

When he retired as India's Chief Justice in September 2014, Rajendra Mal Lodha, a frugal, pious Jain from Jodhpur who regards judicial office as a 'divine duty', had in mind a quiet life, during which he might write a book. A different literary work is about to make him among the most important men in cricket.

On Monday morning, Delhi time, Lodha and two other retired judges, Ashok Bhan and Raju Varadarajulu Raveendran, will present to the Supreme Court the final fruits of a year's examination of the workings of the Board of Control for Cricket in India, the de facto seat of power in world cricket.

Judges have been crawling all over the BCCI since the first allegations of corruption within the Indian Premier League franchises, the Chennai Super Kings and Rajasthan Royals, two and a half years ago.

The Lodha Committee is the final stage of the process, designed to impose sanctions and recommend redresses, reliant on a ruling by brother judges that while the BCCI is a 'private body' it performs 'public functions.'

It has already suspended CSK and the Royals, in the process putting the skids beneath the owner of the former, Narayanaswami Srinivasan. These days the Chennai industrialist who never met a conflicting interest he didn't like while lording it over the BCCI and the International Cricket Council plays a lot of golf.

For the last six months, Lodha and his colleagues have been peering at the governance of the BCCI, not stopping at the day-to-day functions of Cricket Centre at Mumbai's Wankhede Stadium, but drilling down to the level of the state associations represented on it, replete with parish pump politicians, crony capitalists and not-so-petty bureaucrats.

Their tin opener for this giant can of worms has been a simple questionnaire: six sections containing eight-two questions, seemingly bland, yet demanding in the way simplicity can be. Like this: 'Is the BCCI for profit or not-for profit? If the latter, how is this reconciled with its commercial engagements?'

And this: 'What is the financial oversight exercised by the BCCI over the income and expenditure of constituent bodies?' And: 'Who conducts an oversight of the various elections?' And: 'What records and papers of the state associations are available for inspection by BCCI and by the public?'

From all indications, there has been a lot of embarrassed rustling of papers, shuffling of feet, and 'I'll-get-back-to-yous'.

They could have asked more detailed questions. Like why did two teams turn up to represent Jammu & Kashmir in the Ranji Trophy against Himachal Pradesh in October, sent as they were by opposing factions of the JKCA?

Or why is the Gujarat CA doubling the size of Ahmedabad's Motera Stadium when it's never been full, and what might this have to do with the association being led by the president of the BJP and his son?

Or why did the Karnataka CA replace an effective administration run by Test great Anil Kumble in favour of one led by Brijesh Patel, who runs a company that is a big supplier of the association, owns his own private cricket academy, is CEO of Royal Challengers Bangalore in the IPL, and has a son in the state team?

But, well, asking such questions would have stretched deliberations out to kingdom come. Lodha and his colleagues have basically deemed the Augean stables not worth cleaning; what's required, they believe, are completely new stables.

Nobody knows in detail what reforms Lodha's report will recommend, but there are indications they are very serious indeed, including a rationalisation of the BCCI's membership and its revenue sharing. There is even talk of independent directors and a breaking of the nexus between Indian cricket and Indian politics — which would affect a good many of the most powerful figures in both.

The BCCI's new president Shashank Manohar met Lodha in November the day before he was elected ahead of Srinivasan, succeeding in the process to chairmanship of the ICC.

A private, conscientious man who abjures a mobile phone and computer, Manohar shares some qualities with the judge, and has made the Vidarbha he runs a model of its kind.

Since assuming office, Manohar has behaved like someone preparing for change, making available an unprecedented amount of information about the BCCI's workings, eliminating some of the more egregious conflicts of interest in its senior ranks, appointing an ombudsman to adjudicate others. He has pledged to 'try and implement as many things as possible from the [Lodha] report.' But he is one man, a concensus candidate, absent a true power base. The BCCI's ambitious young secretary Anurag Thakur, meanwhile, is the scion of a BJP dynasty from Himachal Pradesh.

Why does this matter so much, even in this country, where cricket issues run such a minuscule gamut. Look, a six!

Ten years ago certainly, and maybe even five, the currents of governance reform at the BCCI would have seemed of esoteric interest. That's changed: generally, because of the money the BCCI makes; specifically, because of the money the BCCI takes.

It's two years since the BCCI, abetted by Cricket Australia and the

England Cricket Board, voted itself a massive new rake-off from the ICC. That money was earned by cricket. To cricket it should rightly have returned. Contemplate it in the simple terms of the Lodha Committee: who is obtaining the benefit of cricket's relatively recent but rapidly expanding wealth?

The stakes are extremely high, and not only for cricket. In the last two months, one rotten Indian borough has stood out: the Delhi and District Cricket Association, whose president from 1999 to 2013 was the BJP power broker Arun Jaitley.

For much of this period, the DDCA was a byword for corruption and nepotism, colloquially known as the 'Delhi Daddies and Crooks Association', deflecting multiple efforts at reform.

Jaitley moved onward and upward: as Narendra Modi's finance minister, he is regarded by some as India's second most powerful man. The DDCA has since more or less collapsed, mysteriously denuded of funds. India's recent Delhi Test was overseen by a retired judge, Lodha's former colleague Mukul Mudgal. It earned a profit for the first time since the early 1980s. Just fancy that!

Now Arvind Kejriwal's Aam Aadmi Party, a popular anti-corruption movement that swept local government polls a year ago, has funnelled many of these allegations into a frenzied campaign, with Jaitley as its primary target. The volatile Kejriwal is independent of the Lodha committee, and chiefly motivated by his enmity for the BJP. But he is tapping a rich vein of discontent.

A system that has enriched so many will not pass without a struggle: for many, the current system works just fine. But aware of it or not, cricket around the world has a great deal invested in the outcome.

# The Big Three
# THE SHASHANK REDEMPTION

## FEBRUARY 2016

One of the challenges of writing about the chairman of the International Cricket Council, Shashank Manohar of the Board of Control for Cricket in India, is resisting the temptation to indulge in a lame pun about 'the Shashank redemption.'

Resistance today is futile. By mooting essentially a repeal of the 'Big Three' revamp of two years ago, Manohar has indeed acted as a redeemer, making it possible to regard the ICC with some semblance of seriousness. To be true, it's only the redress of a former wrong, but...well, baby steps, eh?

Thursday's communiqué from Dubai announcing that Manohar would head a five-member panel to conduct a 'complete review of the 2014 resolutions and constitutional changes with a view to establishing governance, finance, corporate and cricketing structures that are appropriate and effective for the strategic role and function of the ICC and all of its members' was not unexpected.

Almost as soon as he usurped his overmighty predecessor, Narayanaswami Srinivasan, Manohar has been openly critical of the the seizure of executive control and financial precedence at the ICC by the BCCI, Cricket Australia and the England Cricket Board, saying it was bound to 'make the rich richer and the poor poorer.'

Actually it was worse than that — it was a sick joke at cricket's expense, being chiefly about abetting Srinivasan's ambitions to establish a permanent, all-encompassing autocracy, and denuding the ICC of the powers necessary to be a credible governing body for cricket. The involvement of CA and the ECB was entirely to their discredit.

Its roots, moreover, were always shallow, being predicated on the friendly terms enjoyed by its chief sponsors: Srinivasan, CA's Wally Edwards and the ECB's Giles Clarke. Edwards basically echoed Margaret Thatcher on meeting Mikhail Gorbachev, proclaiming that Srinivasan was a man he could do business with. Clarke did as Clarke does, setting out to charm when unable to intimidate.

It's handy when powerful folk get on, but a governance system needs a firmer undergirding. People and circumstances change. Edwards, otherwise an effective chairman of CA, retired. Clarke, a lightning rod for controversy among his countrymen, was decanted from the ECB chairmanship into a ceremonial presidency.

Most importantly, Srinivasan came under attack in his own redoubt, the gambling scrapes of his son-in-law Gurunath Meiyappan intensifying scrutiny of his extraordinary remit: not only boss of the BCCI and the ICC but owner of cricket's richest club, the Chennai Super Kings in the Indian Premier League.

Srinivasan's co-conspirators made the call that somehow, in that way that things usually seem to work out for rich people, not least in India, it would all get sorted. It didn't and, at last, the Mudgal and Lodha committees of the Indian Supreme Court provided a bus big enough for his enemies to push Srinivasan under.

From the point the conservative, quietly-spoken Manohar took over, a counter-putsch against the reforms was in the stars. Not only was Manohar determined to repudiate Srinivasan's legacy, but lots of others were anxious to forget their previous toadyings, and the deal was an orphan: even those responsible for its detail, CA's legal affairs manager Dean Kino and the IPL's chief operating officer Sundar Raman, had left their respective employers.

A good deal was quietly accomplished by the way in Dubai last week, such as the end of the Big Three lock on the executive and finance committees, and the restoration of the requirement for full members to lodge their audited accounts with ICC — how this was ever not a condition of full membership beggars belief.

But a lot of heavy lifting will be required if the ICC executive board is to achieve its quoted bucket list, whose objectives range from improving 'the governance standards of, and transparency within, Member Boards' to 'a clearer cricket calendar with greater context, being underpinned by an appropriate funding model.'

The shortest route to the executive board achieving such ends would be, quite frankly, to sack themselves, or be required to stand down from the roles they also hold on their full member boards.

They have committed to electing an independent chairman at their annual meeting in June. If independence is deemed a virtue, why not make it a prerequisite?

Having been part of the problem at ICC, CA could here be part of the solution. It has patiently peeled its board away from the old state representative model, all the while failing to demonstrate why such a system would not suit the ICC just as well.

Sure, the ICC and CA are not identical. But they have at least as many similarities as differences. And what sort of organization can, like the ICC, have no say in who sits on its board?

Of course, the ICC has had a guide to governance reform in its bottom drawer since 2012, in the form of the expensively-generated and rapidly-rejected Woolf report, which, inter alia, advocated the introduction of independent directors.

The Woolf report went unmentioned in the ICC announcement, presumably because of the embarrassing reality that the council is back where it started five years ago: reviewing their governance after reviewing the governance that reviewed their governance.

That embarrassment will probably militate against the report being revived, at least under its own name. The report also offered no guide to a better direction of the ICC's distributions, which is chief among the concerns of most full members.

Yet Lord Woolf's premise, that the ICC should 'act in the best interests of cricket generally and promote, lead and develop the international game' rather than simply as a club of the full members, remains surely the overriding issue. These last two have been thwarted, ineffectual years for the ICC, but it is not too late to reverse the damage.

Surprisingly in this age of the motion picture franchise there has never been a *Son of Shawshank Redemption* ('This Time It's Personal'). But on the sequel to the Shashank Redemption may hinge the future of international cricket.

# The Big Three
# THANKS FOR JOINING US
FEBRUARY 2017

'Yours in cricket, Shashank': with these words last week ended what was
called a 'media release' by International Cricket Council chairman Shashank
Manohar, but which struck a curiously personal note for such a reticent
public figure.

With the ICC foregathering in Dubai ahead of a long-awaited
discussion of new competitive and financial structures for international
cricket, Manohar offered what is the nearest you are ever likely to hear
to a *nostra culpa* from anyone of his kind: 'Sport governance is under the
spotlight more than ever before and it is no secret that in our recent past
the ICC has taken decisions that were in retrospect not always in the best
interests of the game as a whole.'

'In retrospect'? Hardly: it needed no help from hindsight to
identify 2014's Big Three deal, a conspiracy of self-generosity by the boards
of India, England and Australia, as a squalid expedient.

Otherwise, though, pretty right: the interests of the 'game as a
whole' were altogether secondary to those of the Board of Control for
Cricket in India, and the placation of its majordomo Narayanaswami
Srinivasan by Cricket Australia and the England Cricket Board. Had the
confederates dropped fans a line at the time, the appropriate sign-off would
have been: 'Ours in cricket, Srini.'

Three years down the track, the so-called 'Manohar vision'
is taking shape. At meetings from Thursday through the weekend of

the ICC's chief executives committee, finance and commercial affairs committee, and executive board there will be discussions of two six-team conferences for Tests matches, a rolling 13-team league for one-day internationals, changes to the constitution that might alter the composition of the membership and the directors, and an ambitious pooling of overseas television rights for bilateral cricket, even if the last is not explicitly in the ICC's gift.

In his ruminations, Manohar explicitly promised decisions that 'support all of our members' from 'the largest nation to the smallest'.

The oddity in this is that such formulations are usually presented for the reassurances of the littlies — that, say, Slovenia and the Seychelles aren't about to get screwed. Yet, for once, the country in need of the most sensitive handling is Manohar's own.

A year ago, when Manohar was still BCCI president, he presided over a special general meeting which walked calmly back from the Big Three — a considerable feat of diplomacy, prefiguring his resignation three months later in order to become a properly independent chairman of the ICC.

Since then, however, life at the world's biggest cricket organization has become so chaotic that you could add Steve Bannon to the mix and the difference might not be appreciable.

The commencement of the ICC's review of the structure of international cricket coincided with orders by the Lodha Committee of the Indian's Supreme Court for top-to-bottom governance reform at the BCCI, sinking it into deep brooding. As a result, the influence on the ICC of its biggest member has waned, probably for the first time this century.

An end point of sorts was reached last month when the Lodha Committee by its new eligibility criteria for administrative office effectively ousted many of the BCCI's old guard, Srinivasan included.

Since then, the BCCI has assumed a hybrid identity: there is the cricket body being run on a day-to-day basis by CEO Rahul Johri, but there also remains a kind of ghost BCCI composed of malcontented ex-officials who by now probably wear 'Make India Great Again' trucker hats.

At the former, uncertainty prevails: a Deloitte report on widespread financial irregularities at state association level has gone unaddressed; the Indian Premier League auction has been repeatedly delayed; last week a selection meeting was held up six hours because it was unclear who was entitled to convene it.

At the latter, the Big Three deal has assumed a different context. A year ago, in the interests of the global game, a certain magnanimity was just palateable. Now repeal feels like a crowning indignity, especially given dark mutterings about what the BCCI might be foregoing, estimates exceeding $600 million over the next two ICC commercial rights cycles.

Of course, this money should never have been within the BCCI's reach in the first place. But it's asking a good deal now for the sum to be pushed back across the table with a philosophical smile.

Last week, at last, the Supreme Court appointed an interim committee for Johri to report to: an impressive quartet of former Auditor General Vinod Rai, former women's captain Diana Edulji, career banker Vikram Limaye and India's pre-eminent historian Ramachandra Guha, whose biography of Gandhi will have to wait a little longer.

In Dubai, however, the BCCI is being represented not only by Johri and Limaye, but also joint secretary Amitabh Choudhary, treasurer Anirudh Chaudhry and operations manager Maturi Sridhar, remnants of the former regime. The protocol is reportedly that only one can sit in the room at a time; the prospect is of a game of political musical chairs.

The ICC now badly needs the BCCI inside the tent, not only

because it presides over the world's biggest cricket market, but because it fields the world's best team. The irony, eh? The more upheaval at the BCCI, the more stability Virat Kohli's team have exuded...

But asking a newly-minted interim committee to make binding gestures leaving India's member associations demonstrably poorer will be a tall order. Declarations need captains to make them; Vinod Rai, nominally chairman of the BCCI, is calling himself a 'nightwatchman'.

One modest proposal seems worth making, in the spirit of the chairman's adieu, and also these post-Davos, populist times. The most cynical aspect of the Big Three, effectively conveyed in the documentary *Death of a Gentleman* (2015), was its 'move-along-nothing-to-see-here' secrecy and 'middle-aged-men-in-suits-always-know-best' contempt for the public.

If the ICC really wishes to argue that it is running cricket in the interests of great and small, its next step should be to make the game's future a truly public discussion, not just another fait accompli rolled out by a privileged elite. Unless there is a pressing reason for information about alternatives to remain confidential, every proposal before the ICC should be out in the open, discussion encouraged, engagement sought. It's all very well to say 'yours in cricket'; it's time for deeds to match.

# The Big Three
# THE SHASHANK RECONSIDERATION
## MARCH 2017

'Let's get on with the cricket' was last week's cry. The Ranchi Test could hardly come quickly enough, and in the end it didn't quite. At this rate, it will need to turn into Test cricket's third tie off the final ball of the last day to distract from events that continue unfolding off the field.

A recurrent complaint during the stand-off in the wake of the Bengaluru was about the lack of leadership at the International Cricket Council. Wednesday the complaint achieving literal truth: the ICC's chairman, Shashank Manohar, suddenly resigned, eight months into a two-year term, without a word to his fellow directors, without anointing a successor.

Manohar's resignation, 'for personal reasons', followed his meeting with representatives of the Board of Control for Cricket in India who advised that they could not support his mooted new ICC financial model. He denies any connection between the meeting and his departure, correlation is not causation etc etc. But, y'know, *c'mon*.

The connection between Manohar exiting meekly in Dubai and Virat Kohli standing astride India like a colossus isn't quite so obvious, but it's detectable. And unlike many of cricket's serial crises in recent years, both can be ascribed in their way to the BCCI being not too strong, but at the moment uneasily divided.

For the last few months, as a result of sweeping reforms mandated by the Lodha Committee of India's Supreme Court, the BCCI has been overseen by an interim committee of administration (CoA): former Indian auditor general Vinod Rai, former Indian women's captain Diana Edulji, banker Vikram Raye and historian Ramachandra Guha. Their chief responsibility is to oversee smooth transition to a new permanent governance structure.

Day-to-day issues are enlarging and elasticising their responsibilities. Most pressing of these has been reform of the ICC: a rolling back of the controversial Big Three deal engineered three years ago by the BCCI in cahoots with the England Cricket Board and Cricket Australia.

For the CoA, this rollback presents a problem. They are interim governors being asked to acquiesce in permanent measures substantially reducing the BCCI's rake-off — a rake-off the BCCI barely deserved and cynically obtained, of course, but to which, over the course of three years, the state associations that compose it have developed understandable sensations of entitlement.

The Lodha Committee's diktats have nominally swept aside many of BCCI's old power brokers, including president Anurag Thakur and secretary Ajay Shirke, not to mention the old Chennai warhorse Narayanaswami Srinivasan. But they remain vigilant, vigorous and in the vicinity.

So while the headlines of this Border-Gavaskar Trophy have pitted India against Australia, the back story has been the BCCI versus itself, with interim administrators accountable to the Supreme Court, state associations accountable to themselves, and a disgruntled ex-administrators accountable to nobody.

At the recent BCCI Awards, there were more representatives from Cricket Australia (one, Pat Howard) than from India's state cricket associations; at the Bengaluru Test, the atmosphere between the BCCI and the Karnataka State Cricket Association, the hosts, was chill.

When the BCCI became tangled in the Pune pitch fiasco, industrialist Shirke led the demands for an inquiry; no sooner had DRSgate erupted than

BJP politician Thakur darted into the Twitter fray: 'For years Australian ckt. team have been bullying world ckt. Not any more.' Exactly: that's India's job.

'Extremely proud of #TeamIndia (@BCCI ) and @imVkohli who reported the matter to umpires,' Thakur hashtagged and ampersaned on. 'We must stand by our captain and support him.'

Well, yes — extreme pride is the politically expedient position. One suspects, indeed, that part of the reason India's cricket establishment has turned so Kohlier-than-thou is the division elsewhere in its ranks.

Rallying round the skipper, describing his temper as passion and characterizing his word salads as witty ripostes, not only provides a pleasingly simple narrative, but makes the speaker sound bigger, tougher, more patriotic, more up-to-date.

Perhaps feeling a little relevance deprivation syndrome these days, for example, Sunil Gavaskar leapt to Kohli's defence with his umpteenth public jag about conspiracy and double standards, including the regulation disparagement of the Australian cricket media as serving the cricket team's interests — not bad from the member of a commentary panel who wear shirts that read 'India Cricket.'

When Gavaskar was in his cricketing pomp, one marvelled that such a small man could be such a champion. Now one marvels that such a champion can be such a small man.

Anyway, when Rai, Limaye and CEO Rahul Johri met Manohar this week, and advised their countryman that the BCCI's interim committee would not support the in-principle decision of the ICC's executive board made on 5 February, they recalled that famous negotiation exchange between Churchill and de Gaulle.

Shocked that the Frenchman was proving so intransigent from a terribly shaky position, Churchill asked: 'Cannot you make me any concessions?' Replied De Gaulle: 'No. I am too weak.'

Yet the BCCI's position is also not unjustified: the new financial model on the table might be more equitable, but by being cooked up from arbitrary numbers and opaque calculations invites the same criticism as the Big Three scam.

Nor should it have come as a surprise that the BCCI had drawn the boards of Sri Lanka, Bangladesh and Zimbabwe to its side, sufficient to throw into doubt next month's meeting to ratify the reforms.

Helpfully, the BCCI website now provides minutes of the CoA's meetings, where the motion agreed to on 25 February is there for all to see: 'The BCCI should take all steps necessary to protect the interests of BCCI including by engaging in negotiations/discussions with other ICC member countries as well as other concerned parties/individuals with proposals/ suggestions that could potentially garner their support for BCCI's position on the proposed changes.' Ambiguous, eh? You may disapprove the message, but it has the benefit of clarity and transparency.

Some argued that disarray at the BCCI was an opportunity to push the reform cause without the necessity for Indian support — there was, no doubt, an element of payback after the indignities inflicted by the Big Three. But as a tactic it always looked too clever by half, and right now appears misguided in the same proportion.

So, sure, on with the cricket, and it's been a tonic to watch this Test played in a keen and competitive spirit: go the tie, hopefully with laurels for both captains. But once it's over, cricket has lots of gaps to bridge, fences to mend and, now, places to fill.

# The World Cup
## GROWING UP FAST
MARCH 2015

Some games of cricket are remarkable because of what happens during them; a smaller category is occupied by those games that are remarkable for happening at all.

Australia played one of the former sort on Saturday, a knock 'em down, drag 'em out spectacular against New Zealand in Auckland; today they turn out for a game of the latter kind, at the very opposite end of this World Cup, in Perth, against Afghanistan.

One hundred years ago, Australians went to war alongside New Zealanders; just two months ago, Australians ended their country's longest war in Afghanistan.

Of course we were officially allied with Afghanistan in this conflict, or at least with its government, elected in insecurely democratic fashion.

But still: when the average one-day international is only slightly more meaningful than a game of Candy Crush, let's just say that Afghanistan in Australia after thirteen years of Australia in Afghanistan has to spare what these days is fashionably called 'context'.

Perhaps a little too much context for some. Around Afghanistan's involvement in this World Cup there seems on all parts something of a 'don't-mention-the-war' reticence. Afghanistan offering no electoral gain, no notable politician has yet seen fit to welcome their team. Liberal cricket fans who *do* welcome Afghanistan's presence here would probably prefer not to be reminded that it was in part rendered possible by a protracted, confusing, largely miserable military occupation.

These days, too, it takes only the vaguest mention of politics for cricket to start cringeing, like a craven tailender backing towards the square leg umpire. Most recently, the International Cricket Council put the kibosh on Moeen Ali wearing wristbands referring to the plight of Palestinians in Gaza, on grounds that their regulations did not 'permit the display of messages that relate to political, religious or racial activities or causes during an international match'. Hey Moeen, your job is the orderly and lucrative diffusion of corporate messages. Politics? Leave that to the big kids. Because, of course, politics and cricket administration overlap in a great many of the ICC's members, and no longer just the usual suspects.

When Tony Abbott heralded a mooted Australia-India free trade agreement last year, for example, he took Brett Lee and Adam Gilchrist with him to meet Sachin Tendulkar at Brabourne Stadium, then hosted new bestie Narendra Modi in the precincts of the MCG.

Frankly, this makes complete sense. Trying to build a sense of common purpose? Good idea to start on common ground. And cricket, where teams bear the names of the countries their athletes hail from and parade beneath their national flags, could actually do with facing its political reality more squarely.

Imagine if this World Cup was being fought out between teams that simply corresponded to the names of the organisations which assembled them — when it comes to it, arguably a truer reflection of their nature. Who would care if the Ashes pitted the Cricket Australia XI versus the England and Wales Cricket Board XI?

As 'Australia' and 'England', the teams partake of deep cultural and historic endowments. Eric Hobsbawm had football in mind when he penned his lovely line, but it is every bit as true of cricket: 'The imagined community of millions seems more real as a team of eleven named people.'

Nor does cricket immediately become obnoxious when it has a political dimension; on the contrary, its meanings can be enhanced, its edge sharpened. When India and Pakistan met in Adelaide Oval on 15 February, it was a political as well as a sporting event, and the more powerful and uplifting for being so, as the fans of both countries mixed with such good grace and high humour.

Afghanistan's astonishingly rapid rise in international cricket — from a country containing barely a score of players fifteen years ago to the world's twelfth ranked one-day international team today — is also a political story.

It was political rhetoric but it wasn't empty when Hilary Clinton contended five years ago: 'I might suggest that if we are searching for a model of how to meet tough international challenges with skill, dedication and teamwork, we need only look to the Afghan cricket team.'

That followed Afghanistan beating the United States in the World T20 Qualifier in Dubai — thrashing them, in fact. As Tim Wigmore recounts in the new book *2nd XI: Cricket In Its Outposts*, Afghanistan's match winner that day was the fast bowler Hamid Hassan who will take on David Warner and Aaron Finch today, and who cites Rocky as an influence.

'After yorking one player,' writes Wigmore, 'Hassan leapt to the floor, extending his arms and legs as he gloried on the wreckage he had made of the American's stumps.' The team dedicated their victory to a past player killed by American forces.

Politics can foul cricket as it can foul anything it touches. But one of difficulties besetting cricket at present is that, at least in one sense, it is not political enough. Many of its bilateral rivalries have stopped meaning anything much at all. New Zealand versus South Africa? Zimbabwe versus Pakistan? They are played because a system exists to expedite them not because they have any deeper meaning or ramifications.

England are lucky — the world still can't quite get enough of beating them. But which team has disintegrated most abjectly in the last twenty years ago? Step forward the West Indies, never a country, but once home to quite deep shades of political awareness — which might now, one suspects, court the ICC's displeasure. Yet a shower of Chris Gayle's sixes can't obscure the shambles of competing agendas and personal ambitions the team has become, devoid of any collective identity.

What's exciting about watching Afghanistan is not just the freewheeling brio of its cricketers, but the sense of them rising above their difficulties and differences, and helping in the process of defining their rickety nation. On the outcome of this World Cup, Afghanistan playing Australia today will have little bearing. But for the teams to play a common game on a level field in a global competition is a moment to absolutely cherish.

# The World Cup
# CRUMBS OF
# CONSOLATION

MARCH 2015

Small, isolated, quaintly old-fashioned battlers, never seriously competitive, they leave us at this World Cup with many happy memories, as the big boys settle down to duke it out in the finals beginning Wednesday...

But enough about England — boom-tish — who *did* provide many, many happy memories, at least in Bangladesh. Let's discuss the four associate members of the International Cricket Council, set to take their leave next week as the Cup sheds six of its fourteen participants.

Winless Scotland play Australia today in Hobart; winless United Arab Emirates then face West Indies in Napier. There's an outside chance Ireland will cling on if they can overcome Pakistan in Adelaide tomorrow, although Misbah ul Haq's mercurial band now loom menacingly for whoever faces them.

On the face of it, then, the failure of these three teams and Afghanistan to progress justifies the ICC's decision to confine the 2019 World Cup to ten teams, on the basis that, in CEO Dave Richardson's words, 'the premium event, without exception, should be played between teams that are evenly matched and competitive.'

Drill down a little and the evidence concerning these so-called associate members of ICC less definitive. Of evenness of matching, for example, Ireland v UAE and Scotland v Afghanistan were perhaps the tournament's outstanding examples.

Ireland, of course, disposed of two full members, West Indies and Zimbabwe, while two overs or less remained when Scotland, Afghanistan and UAE went down to Bangladesh, Sri Lanka and Zimbabwe respectively. For long passages of play, in fact, differences in quality have been barely discernable. Had you tuned in this week while Scotland's Preston Mommsen and Freddie Coleman were adding 118 off 124 deliveries against Sri Lanka or the UAE's Mohammad Tauqir and Amjad Javed were keeping South Africa to two boundaries in ten overs, you might have struggled to distinguish mackerel from sprat — just to vary the worn-out 'minnow' metaphor. Afghanistan's Hamid Hassan was the last bowler to make Kumar Sangakkara look human, while Najeebollah's sixes off Tim Southee and Narwoz Mangal's off Mitchell Marsh travelled just as far as any of Chris Gayle's.

There were blowouts, notably in Perth, whose unique microclimate told against Afghanistan (versus Australia) and UAE (versus India). But these were no more extreme, and arguably less so, than the monstering of England by New Zealand and West Indies by South Africa.

So it's been an encouraging showcase for associate member cricket, and thoughtful past and present players, from Martin Crowe and Aakash Chopra to Dan Vettori and Ryan Harris, have all pitched into the discussion. The debate so far has been on a pick-a-number basis, with Sachin Tendulkar, maintaining the habits of a lifetime, being the highest scorer, by mooting a twenty-five team World Cup.

It's been a useful conversation to have, because a ten-team, forty-seven-day World Cup, resembling a constipated version of the Champions Trophy, is a deeply stupid idea. Even with the fraying qualification rope ladder the full members dropped through their glass floor a couple of months ago, it's a squib, not so much the premium event of a global sport as a conference for accountants. It's as embarrassing to cricket as Giles

Clarke praising Alastair Cook's family and Kevin Pietersen meeting Taylor Swift rolled into one.

The problem with the conversation round it, however, is the risk of reducing cricket's global aspirations to something only thought about every four years, when what happens between times is every bit as integral to the game's spread. For associate members, the ICC is a little like joining a family of Victorian gentry with a cold and distant paterfamilias — it entitles one to certain privileges and comforts, with the occasional hint of some noblesse oblige, but a lot of the time is about nannies, boarding schools, cold showers and the occasional morally therapeutic flogging.

Before this World Cup, UAE had not played a full member for seven years; Scotland have enjoyed about one full member ODI a year for fifteen years; Afghanistan had had five in five years before they drew 2-2 with Zimbabwe in Bulawayo last year.

The trouble is that everyone knows the poorer full members and the better associates to be tightly matched. The former, however, have representation on the ICC executive board, and are naturally determined to protect their rake off — even if it means consenting to the Board of Control for Cricket in India, the England Cricket Board and Cricket Australia using bigger rakes. So incentives to provide opportunities for the next-best are negligible, especially in an organisation reshaped by its biggest members as an arena of competing self-interests.

'Context' and 'meritocracy' have become to cricket what Mark Twain used to say of the weather: everyone talks about it, but nobody does anything about it, with full member boards paying lip service to bilateral cricket for rankings of dwindling significance in order to preserve their entitlements.

Ironically, it is the junior membership, to whom every match played and every rung ascended or descended is a huge deal, that has become the bastion of 'context' and 'meritocracy'. And that should be celebrated every chance that cricket gets, because a sport not busy being born is busy dying.

So more inclusive big tournaments take us only so far towards a 'bigger, better global game' — which is what the ICC, in its last strategic plan, affected to desire.

What's also needed is international scheduling that reflects a desire to see cricket prosper, as distinct from a self-perpetuating elite. The old Future Tours Programme was basically voided a year ago on the say-so of the Board of Control for Cricket in India with the promise of its replacement by 'bankable' bilateral contracts. The FTP had its flaws, but what's eventuated is a mess — a system ripe for abuse by the powerful and subversion by the shrewd. Sorting out a better way is not something that can wait another four years.

# World T20, India v Pakistan, Mumbai
# THE MAIN EVENT
## MARCH 2016

Twenty20 is by nature a short game. Yet the India v Pakistan match in the World T20 scheduled at Eden Gardens tonight already feels like a kind of geopolitical Test series.

So far, it's run like this. When the tournament programme was published last year, the game was cautiously scheduled in Dharamshala, fiefdom of the secretary of the Board of Control for Cricket in India, Anurag Thakur. Then early in January, jihadists attacked Pathankot Air Force base 83km away, claiming the lives of six Indian soldiers.

That was enough for the local chief minister, a political rival of Thakur's, to disclaim responsibility for match security out of alleged solidarity with the military 'martyrs'. After lengthy shuttle diplomacy, the game was finally moved to its new venue, 1931km south east, a week ago — sorry about that, ticket holders/tourists!

When Pakistan's captain Shahid Afridi belatedly arrived, he tried smoothing his path with locals by remarking that he felt 'loved more in India' than at home. For this he was predictably excoriated back in Pakistan, including the issuance of a court order alleging 'treason'. Meanwhile, hundreds of thousands of fans from one country were swarming Facebook to pose in colours of the other as part of the #ProfilesforPeace initiative, earning an approving nod from Mark Zuckerberg.

So, yes, not your average T20I this, cricket being the connective tissue of two countries who once were one. The turmoil this time, unfortunately, reflects an inflammation of that tissue over which cricket has been struggling to exert control.

A look back over the history of cricket relations between these rivals reveals some counterintuitive features. Estimates of the death toll of partition in 1947 run as high as two million. Yet the partitioned fell quickly into Test competition, as though it assuaged various psychic wounds.

India and Pakistan played fifteen matches in the latter's first decade in international cricket, diplomatically drawing twelve in a row. There *were* small-scale protests by Hindu nationalists in India, but to eccentric and negligible effect. In general a remarkable goodwill prevailed. Wars in Kashmir and East Bengal then curtailed relations for sixteen years, and since that time a certain ingenuity has been required to provide as much cricket as there has been: 44 Tests, 127 one-day internationals and seven T20Is.

It was India and Pakistan, for instance, who led the way with neutral umpires, inviting England's John Hampshire and John Holder to officiate during India's visit to Pakistan in 1989-90, on the initiative of Imran Khan. It was India and Pakistan who pioneered the idea, now also familiar, of neutral venues, with no fewer than 70 ODIs between them held in third countries. One venue they effectively neutralised themselves, finishing a 1999 Test, in Kolkata as it happens, by emptying the stadium, whose spectators had rioted after a Sachin Tendulkar run out.

Back in the day, despite the periodic unravellings of their political ties, their boards cooperated closely at the International Cricket Council, successful joint bids for the World Cups of 1987 and 1996 manifesting the muscle of the 'Asian bloc'. Their rivalry, meanwhile, was paradigm shifting. It was when India beat Pakistan in the inaugural World T20 final in 2007 that the format began to go forth and multiply.

That's changed, for reasons partly economic, fast-growing India becoming its own bloc-of-one, and partly chauvinistic, the Board of Control for Cricket in India being based in Mumbai, seat of the Hindu nationalism that has moved from the lunatic fringe to the mainstream of Indian politics over the last twenty years.

Mumbai is the native heath not only of Tendulkar but of Bal Thackeray, the canny demagogue whose Shiv Sena is dedicated to simultaneously advancing Marathi pride and demonizing the world's second biggest Muslim population. The sprawling maidan of Shivaji Park where the Little Master learned his cricket in the 1980s is also where the Tiger of Maharastra was cremated in 2012 — after which Tendulkar paid Thackeray's family a condolence visit.

For Thackeray was, inevitably, a devotee of cricket, apt to borrow its terminology for political speeches: comparing the 1992 destruction of the Bari Mosque by Hindu rioters with the bombs that went off in retaliation, he acridly called it a contrast between Test match and one-day approaches.

Thackeray also conspicuously anointed Muslim players of whom he approved, calling Mohammad Azharuddin 'a true Indian Muslim' and Zaheer Khan 'a nationalist Muslim' in the same way as anti-Semites have been known to praise 'good Jews.'

Shivsenaites were hugely emboldened, and cricket concomittantly weakened, by the jihadist attacks on Mumbai just over seven years ago. Not only did the Indian government quickly rule out India's forthcoming tour of Pakistan, but their forebodings were vindicated when Sri Lanka visited in India's stead and came under a further jihadist attack near Lahore's Gaddafi Stadium.

Since having featured in the first Indian Premier League, Pakistani players have been effectively too hot for franchises to hold, while Shiv Sena has been growingly antagonistic to the possibility of a restoration of cricket ties between India and Pakistan in any form. In October, members stormed the BCCI's Wankhede Stadium offices in protest against Aleem Dar standing as umpire in the India-South Africa one-day series. Few noted the exquisite symmetry of Aleem, shot at alongside the Sri Lankans in Lahore, having now been targeted by extremists of two religions. He stood down, nonetheless — likewise commentators Wasim Akram and Shoaib Akhtar.

Political populism, then, is why international cricket's most compelling rivals have been able to meet in only one limited-overs head-to-head series in the last eight and a half years, and otherwise have been restricted to meeting under the auspices of the Asia Cup, and of ICC tournaments. Shiv Sena, ostensibly allied to Narendra Modi's BJP but quick to assail him when he recently visited 'that accursed land' of Pakistan, like it that way.

So tonight meet two great nations with a vast shared culture in a game they love at a classic juncture — India will be desperate, Pakistan confident. The irony is that were the Tiger still with us, there's no way he would not be watching the action even as he publicly disapproved of it.

What could better express the depths and possibilities of international cricket at a time it has never needed them more? That's worth all the trouble it has taken to bring it about.

# Doping in cricket
# THE GOOD GEAR
JANUARY 2016

Normally football rejoices in hogging airtime and column inches in summer. Last week not so much. Instead of one of those carefully choreographed pseudo-events in which it specialises, the Australian Football League was confronted with its own unflattering reflection.

Cricket, meanwhile, cruised serenely along, those unsightly Test matches tidied away, the Big Bash League and the VB Series alternating in prime time, further plenishing the coffers. Problems? Cricket's tend to be of a lower, less discordant if more lingering key, which thinking in relativities can drown out. At the moment the International Cricket Council could rebadge itself with the slogan: 'ICC: Not as Rubbish as FIFA and the IAAF, At Any Rate.'

Yet the issues in cricket's in tray commonly resemble those facing other sports: governance, corruption, the sway of mass media, the intrusions of politics. This suggests that if you want a sense of what's coming down the pike, check out other pikes. So what can said of cricket's drug risk profile?

A perennial backburner challenge, doping in cricket has smouldered more visibly since the ICC adopted WADA-compliant no-advance-notice out-of-competition testing in 2009. Between them, the ICC and its full members carry out 1200 tests per annum — not an exhaustively intensive programme, and some countries are more rigorous than others, but it is expanding, if not yet into blood doping.

In the last five years a dozen players have been quietly suspended for testing positive to prohibited substances — a range of anabolic steroids, masking agents, recreational stimulants and diet pills.

In the last two months have been confirmed two higher profile cases, yet to be resolved: Sri Lanka's exciting keeper-batman Kusal Perera, who tested positive to the steroid nandrolone in October, and Pakistan's mercurial leg-spinner Yasir Shah, who tested positive to the diuretic chlortalidone in November.

Both have been provisionally suspended by the ICC. Alternative hypotheses for their positive tests have been mooted in sympathetic media — Yasir was reported to have partaken of his wife's blood pressure medication, Perera (at first at least) to have been affected by a remedy for leech bite. Appeals are underway.

In Australia, of course, the issue will always be associated with Shane Warne, among whose many contributions to the game was the inadvertent one, thirteen years ago, of focusing attention on the responsibility of athletes to monitor their ingestions.

To that stage, Australian cricket's decade of drug screening had netted only two minor transgressors. After Warne's suspension, nobody could claim ignorance.

Warne's mea minima culpa, of course, involved a famous repudiation of the saying that mother knows best. While disclaiming any desire to enhance his performance, Warne confessed to the sin of vanity — the hankering to shed a little weight, to slough off an extra chin.

Credible or not, it continues to have some force. Young athletes today inhabit a world of mass and social media mirrors, in a culture hung up on appearances, in a professional environment involving constant bureaucratic surveillance of their physicality — the nag of the wellness form, the nip of the skinfold.

Nor are such hang-ups confined to a decadent west. In October 2013, a 22-year-old left-arm quick at the Delhi Daredevils, Pradeep Sangwan, copped an eighteen-month ban for steroid abuse.

In an interview with India's NDTV at the time, his coach blamed Sangwan's heedless pursuit of 'six-pack abs', despite the fact that his growing upper body had steadily nullified his ability to swing the ball.

Above all, however, doping is another part of cricket being complicated by the proliferation of T20, which is transforming it into ever more of a power game, in which the vogue skill is the big hit. Length hasn't been such a popular cricket subject since Joel Garner and Viv Richards were caught short on the Sydney Harbour Bridge.

The cost of the quest for the booming drive is now being seriously examined in golf, which these days returns a higher percentage of adverse analytical findings than athletics and cycling, while baseball may never live down its asterix era.

'Call God,' said Barry Bonds of the San Francisco Giants fifteen years ago when asked to explain the astonishing additional distances his drives were travelling. 'Ask him.' In fact, the call investigators had to make was a local one, to a Bay Area laboratory with an elite athletic clientele, BALCO, where the slogan was: 'Cheat or lose.'

Such a slogan would resonate with a young cricketer for whom the ability to regularly hit the ball an extra 20m might make all the difference. In a field of myriad aspirants, perhaps carrying a family's hopes, who would not be tempted to seek a tiny edge, to take a little short cut?

Indeed it's possible our thinking on doping in cricket is dated. We still regard it as a discrete offence rather than as a segment of the continuum of malpractice. Today's young cricketer is ever more so an individual athlete, faced with all manner of temptations and inducements, often encircled by instant friends and ingratiating helpers.

He glimpses a gilded world, but sporting life is short and nothing is certain. He receives warnings, but warnings are not welfare; he is advised of prohibitions, but prohibitions are not pastoral care.

Soon after Perera was suspended, it was reported that he had been approached by the emissary of a fixer in the guise of a net bowler, with the inference this may be related to his drug test.

True or not, who could doubt the tentacular reach of cricket corruption in a week in which it has been revealed in South African domestic T20 and associates cricket in Hong Kong?

Forces are massing in the shadows of cricket we barely understand, and may not until it is too late. If cricket is serious about heading doping off at the pass, a regime of testing alone may not sufficient; investigative support, of the kind that finally closed BALCO, could be required. As the benighted Bombers have demonstrated, it's all fun and games until someone loses a career.

# Fixing in cricket
# THE WAGES OF GREED
JANUARY 2016

Spot the odd man out: a/ Salim Malik; b/ Mohammed Azharuddin; c/ Hansie Cronje; d/ Gulam Bodi.

In the annals of cricket malpractice, the latest to be sanctioned makes a poor fit. a/, b/ and c/ were cricketers great and greedy. d/, who last week was suspended by Cricket South Africa for twenty years for attempting to pervert the country's domestic T20 Ram Slam, possessed only the latter quality — he was a modest cricketer nearing career's end in apparently straitened financial circumstances.

What he had, which would have appealed to gambling interests seeking an advantage, was access — entre to dressing rooms, relationships with players. He was known as a bit of a joker, which would keep the tone of exchanges light even as their implications darkened.

Bodi's inconspicuousness as a cricketer is also the salient fact about him. For it is at these levels of cricket — among the game's everyday Joe Sixpacks whose domestic matches are increasingly broadcast into the sub-continent — where for many years the game's greatest vulnerabilities have lain.

The first generation of fixers, in the 1990s, were audacious, subverting closely-watched Test matches and one-day internationals. So, of course, did Salman Butt, Mohammad Asif and Mohammad Amir, who served time for the injudicious rigging of events in a Lord's Test in 2010.

Yet that last great 'fix' — which was, of course, a well-orchestrated sting by a little-less-shady, now-defunct tabloid newspaper — obscured as much as it revealed.

The days of big occasion, broad-daylight heists were already over, thanks in part to the system of anti-corruption surveillances created in response to that earlier generation of scandals.

Opportunities and susceptibilities were growing greatest in the twilight world since described by malefactor turned informer Lou Vincent. Vincent's 2014 confessions covered matches between 2008 and 2011 that frankly nobody could remember — short-form county cricket in England, domestic T20 in India and Bangladesh.

Mervyn Westfield, Naved Arif, Mohnish Mishra, Shalabh Srivastava, TP Sudhindra, Harmeet Singh, Abhinav Bali, Ajit Chandila, Ankeet Chavan, Kaushal Lokuarachchi, Anusha Samaranayake, Gayan Vishwajith, Irfan Ahmed etc: these are among the names in the households of absolutely nobody who have been fingered in England, India, Bangladesh, Sri Lanka and Hong Kong over the last five years for fixing-related offences.

The vast majority have been poorer paid players in a cricket world fast getting richer at very different rates, where an elite make seven-figure sums in six weeks of Indian Premier League but the vast majority don't.

The foregoing sample, by the way, is assuming sizeable proportions, and it's been instructive to contrast the reactions in this last week to tennis's travails and cricket's.

Tennis is in a shock similar to cricket's fifteen years ago. Cricket has gone dangerously close to normalising corrupt practice: another day, another cricketer you've never heard of, move along, nothing to see here.

In an interview last week, the ICC's chief executive David Richardson went so far as saying that cases like Bodi's were encouraging because they showed that 'education is working' — not unlike being gratified by a building burning down because it vindicates investment in a fire brigade.

Richardson has a point, that cricket can never be rendered safe from corruption, but it is a small point worn out from overuse, indicative of an administration in the habit of treating symptoms rather than addressing causes. And the preconditions of corruption in cricket are hardly far to seek.

You have a game that has been glutted with money in a short period of time with a fast-growing gap between rich and poor, individuals and nations.

You have an emergent set of domestic T20 competitions, even the largest of which, the IPL, is chaotically if not corruptly run (and operating, in the IPL's case, in a country where most forms of gambling are illegal).

These competitions have vastly discrepant standards of administration and anti-corruption measures. In the Bangladesh Premier League, players have routinely gone unpaid. In the Sri Lankan Premier League, one franchise emerged as actually owned by bookmakers. The first impresario of T20 cricket in the Caribbean will live out his days in jail.

And never mind, for a moment, swarthy figures on cricket's shadowy fringes; particularly in Australia and England, cricket has welcomed colossal legal betting apparatuses, increasingly regarded as a lucrative source of revenue. Approximately $3 billion was gambled on the recent BBL — officially anyway.

What's underestimated, above all, is that the modern cricketer is increasingly an income-insecure independent contractor tugged hither and yon by multiple employers, bonds of loyalty no deeper than the provision of agreed services.

Trade unions, where they exist at all, are generally weak. Manager accreditation is recent and remains loose. Players' protection is — what? — 'education'.

Are the ICC's full members addressing these factors? Are they, bollocks. For they are the sponsors of these self-same forces, having into the bargain weakened the council's authority, further skewed the playing field to the advantage of the strong, and raced one another to the bottom of governance standards. The family of Cricket Sri Lanka's new president, a powerful politician elected recently in a curiously abrupt landslide, owns a betting shop chain. Pub test anyone?

In his interview last week, Richardson passed one another poignant remark. 'Certainly when we find [out] about it,' he said, 'no stone will be left unturned to make sure the matter is investigated proactively, and if necessary, prosecutions are made."

Well, yeah, you can't investigate something you don't find out about. But isn't it also possible to *look*, to turn a few stones over yourself? If your chief resource is player tip-offs, you're showing a flimsy grasp of human nature, and Richardson knows this better than anybody.

Twenty years ago this year, Richardson was one of the South African players who was privy to MK Gupta's approaches to Hansie Cronje, and who not only said nothing but thought it kinda cool. As Richardson told the King Commission: 'We had heard that other teams had been approached and when we got this offer we thought, "We're one of the big boys at last".'

Cricket has changed a lot since; cricketers too, in some respects; but human nature, maybe not so much. Gulam Bodi probably thought he was a pretty big boy too.

# Fixing in cricket
# FORGIVABLE?
DECEMBER 2016

On 23 June this year, preluding his first Test appearance in nearly six years, Mohammad Amir posted a Twitpic of himself in his team apparel looking wistfully from the dressing room towards the middle of Southampton's Ageas Bowl. 'Back to white :), read the simple caption.

It was a poignant image. The whiteness, on one who not long before had been clad in prison greys, took on connotations of purification and redemption; in combination with the green, it hinted at the hues of Pakistan's flag. And it summed up Amir's uniqueness: the 24-year-old opening bowler is the first cricketer the game has striven to rehabilitate after his confessing to its most heinous crime, of accepting money to influence the course of a match.

Before the affair that enmeshed Amir and his co-conspirators Salman Butt and Mohammad Asif in that 2010 Lord's Test, life sentences had been more or less mandatory since the career of the great all-round cricketer William Lambert was ended by his being deemed to have tried 'less hard than he might' for England against Nottinghamshire almost two centuries ago.

During international cricket's first brush with match-fixing around the turn of the millennium, exemplary justice was meted out to three Test captains in Saleem Malik, Hansie Cronje and Mohammad Azharuddin. Permanent excommunication has been the fate of more recent malefactors such as Maurice Odumbe, Lou Vincent and Danish Kaneria.

Amir, Butt and Asif, however, all received finite sentences, in jail and from cricket, which they have now served. Other suspensions are also due to end in the next couple of years, including those of Bangladesh's Mohammad

Ashraful to Essex's Mervyn Westfield. And about this, not everyone is content.

'I don't feel badly towards them and I wish them well in their lives, but the game is bigger than us, the game will be around a lot longer than us, and we don't have the right to steal from it,' Kevin Pietersen has insisted. 'There's no place in the game for corruption, and if you get caught you have to be given a life ban.'

'We were led to believe there was a zero-tolerance policy and that anyone found guilty of corruption would be banned for life,' agreed another England captain, Michael Vaughan, insisting that not even Amir's youth excused him: 'Amir is a young kid and many feel that giving him a life ban would have been too harsh, but I feel it is the only way to clear corruption out of the game.'

Lest this be thought an English prejudice, former Pakistan captain Ramiz Raja has also chimed in: 'I am all for rehabilitation and for finding ways to set a young man back on course in his life. But it just can't be in the very game that he sullied and brought disrepute to.' When Amir returned to the fold at a training camp a year ago, those reservations were also shared by at least a couple of teammates.

Unlike in New Zealand, where a Wellington ground announcer punctuated a bowling spell with the sound effect of a cash register, Amir has been cordially received in Australia, not a soul at the Gabba wishing him other than well when he went to ground on Thursday.

But his rehabilitation has emboldened others. In the last few months, possible recalls for Butt and Asif have been mooted, while even Malik has emerged from the darkness to play the world's smallest violin: 'I played so many matches for Pakistan, I took part in so many great wins and even single-handedly won and saved matches for my country so why can't I be given a second chance as others have been?'

Deodorizing reputations is big business too. Hansie Cronje and Mohammad Azharuddin, who in their playing days shared bookmakers, have since then shared the fate of having their lives made into whitewashing biopics, *Hansie* (2008), supported by the Cronje family, and *Azhar* (2016), directed by loyal fan Tony D'Souza. And if it is too late for a Cronje comeback, Azharuddin, for the last seven years an Indian parliamentarian, can argue that he's hardly been away.

Just over fifteen years ago, he confessed to India's Central Bureau of Investigation having fixed one-day internationals against South Africa, Sri Lanka and Pakistan between 1996 and 1999 on behalf of three different bookmakers. 'It is clear Azharuddin contributed substantially to the expanding player/bookie nexus in Indian cricket,' the CBI's report concluded.

Four years ago, however, a home town court voided Azharuddin's life ban on a technicality, and he is now running for the presidency of the Hyderabad Cricket Association, a notorious rotten borough. Had he captained India, O. J. Simpson would probably have been asked to endorse a brand of gloves.

Amir? His story is more nuanced than commonly imagined. Not only was he a callow 18-year-old when he transgressed, but he appears to have been effectively entrapped within an entrapment.

During Pakistan's 2010 tour of England, he began to be plagued on the phone by a 'businessman' he knew only as 'Ali', who had introduced himself as a friend of Butt.

Amir has always maintained that he resisted Ali's invitations to influence a 'bracket' — a five- or ten-over period on the events of which bets are placed. But when Butt and player agent Mazhar Majeed told Amir that the ICC had been tapping his phone, and he accepted their urgings that the only way to make amends was to follow instructions to bowl no balls.

In fact, Butt and Majeed were themselves being played, by the *News of the World*'s journalist of a thousand faces Mazher Mahmood. The affair, of course, boded ill for all concerned — entangled by their own illegalities, the newspaper has since closed and Mahmood been jailed. But Amir emerged with a tiny speck of credit by pleading guilty at a pre-trial hearing, and later cooperating with ICC.

Butt, the captain, and Asif, the senior seam bowler, emerged with none, repeating denials until it served no purpose, confessing only when it became expedient. Investigators six years ago, moreover, shone only a very narrow beam of light into a disturbingly dark room. If there is room to debate the forgiveness of Amir, cricket should never forget the treacheries of his teammates.

In the modern climate of every man for himself, cricket is in danger of relegating fixing to a mere compliance issue, rather than regarding it, properly, as the ultimate taboo. As disturbing as the evidence Brendon McCullum gave last year in the Cairns case was the testimony he gave about the apathy and ineptitude of the ICC's anti-corruption unit. Yet a sport is defined not only by the values it mouths but the behaviours it anathematises. Mohammad Amir is an exception, and that is the way he should stay.

# The death of Phillip Hughes
# SHOCK AND HORROR
## NOVEMBER 2014

It always takes you slightly aback when you see a Test cricketer close up.

Normally you observe them from afar, when they're involved in what they do best, and trying mighty hard at it. Then they're usually a little flushed. They're suncreamed, stubbly, slightly grim.

But in repose, whether in a hotel lobby, or boarding a bus, or traipsing to training, or simply tapping on their phones, they look astonishing young, taut from the discipline of their various physical regimes, but still almost teenage in their gawkiness.

To excel in sport, of course, involves a kind of indefinite extending of youth, with its boundless horizons of future possibility. Watching Phillip Hughes, so boyish, cheerful and amiable, was all about the future. There was barely any past. I remember a press conference on the 2009 Ashes tour. Twenty-year-old Hughes was asked what he recalled about the preceding Ashes in England. Not much, he said. He'd been in Year 10 at the time, and hadn't been allowed to stay up and watch it.

Long-headed critics looked askance at his homespun technique, so raw, so original, so seemingly ingenuous. But it came underpinned by a prodigy's record, and a knack for hundreds, which few in his generation shared.

Hughes played the First Test of that series at Sophia Gardens in Cardiff. He cut his eighth ball for four. The journalist in front of me, a good Aussie patriot, said aloud with lip-smacking satisfaction: 'The first of many!' He seemed vindicated when the next one was despatched identically.

Eighteen months ago, I watched Hughes bat with enormous maturity and poise at Trent Bridge in the Test match now remembered for the spectacular strokeplay of Ashton Agar. I speculated at the time that his unbeaten 81 would in the long-term be more significant than Agar's star-spangled 98, being as Australian cricket was in sorer need of top-order stoicism than tailend heroics.

In each case, in 2009 and 2013, the selectors left Hughes out after another Test. There *was* work for him to do on that technique, not at that stage quite secure enough for the lures, baits and pitfalls of the top level. But we were all of us — peers, pundits, selectors, spectators — dealing in blue sky with Hughes. He had the attitude. He had the look. Here was a cricketer, we told ourselves, with time on his side. Perhaps he assuaged his disappointments the same way. Certainly, he handled himself as first reserve with dignity, patience and enthusiasm.

Thus the intensity of the shock at his loss. Hughes is the tomorrow cricketer who will now form part of history. He is not the youngest Test cricketer to die. That tragic mantle still belongs to Manjural Islam Rana, the Bangladeshi spinner who was 22 when he died in a traffic accident in March 2007. But Hughes has become the first to be cut down, as it were, before our very eyes — in the act, in full bloom, in the presence of his mother and sister, by a delivery from a bowler who just six week ago was his teammate in a one-day series in the Gulf. Every line of that is torture to write, and I simply watched him play cricket. What can palliate the blow for his immediate circle?

There will be analyses, repurcussions, maybe even recriminations. When our modern bubble of safety is pricked, we ache for objects of ire, and some have already been lined up as potentially blameworthy: the bouncer, the helmet, the medics, an anonymous ABC tweeter.

But please, not yet. Why sour tragedy with anger? That the world has turned topsy-turvy is enough to cope with for the present. A Test match is scheduled for next Thursday. In all likelihood, Hughes would there have resumed his Test career. What just days ago we looked forward to we now dread.

The longer term? Cricket reserves a corner of its mythology for the unheard melody — always, as Keats wrote, the sweeter. Bradman's well-loved contemporary Archie Jackson, twenty-three when he perished of tuberculosis, played just eight Test matches but is remembered today.

Google 'Archie Jackson' and the face that looks out is as fresh and youthful as Hughes's. That is how this good young man, Phillip Hughes, will remain: good and young forever.

# The death of Phillip Hughes
# LEGACY OF A DEATH
## NOVEMBER 2014

The communiqué concerning Phillip Hughes that touched me most deeply last week was an email circulated on Wednesday, while his life still hung in the balance, by Cricket Australia public affairs.

Beneath the slightly severe subject heading of 'Media Protocols', it laid out in plain language the arrangements for public announcements regarding Hughes's condition. And it included the request from his parents, fond but firm, that journalists refer to their son not as 'Phil' but as 'Phillip.'

I cannot speak for others, but it was probably at this point I first felt the full force of events, the yearning to exert a tiny measure of control over runaway events, the whole domestic backdrop to the unfolding sorrow. I could sense the love and the pride, and hear the insistent but caring parental voice: 'Phillip, we're running late for school.' 'Phillip, do you have your lunch money?' 'Phillip, there's more to life than cricket.'

'Cricket was Phillip's life', acknowledged the family, via Michael Clarke, on Thursday: they had, of course, known it all along, and let him live his dearest wish. But his death is a tragedy of a kind seldom if ever exampled in the game, reaching far beyond its immediate confines.

Most obvious, and public, have been expressions of grief on social media — a reminder of one of Phillip Hughes' peculiar distinctions, that he introduced many of the travelling press corps to Twitter. On the first morning of the Birmingham Test in 2009, I arrived in the media centre to find many of its older and fustier occupants clustered round laptops while younger and more with-it colleagues showed them a 'Tweet' under Hughes' name expressing disappointment at his omission from the Australian team — a team not yet publicly named.

It proved to be a gaffe by the manager who ran Hughes' Twitter account, but it also seemed to locate him as a cricketer of the new, albeit with pleasing dashes of the old from his rural roots and sunny nature.

On Thursday, Twitter took on a different guise in the Hughes story, as the chief means of public mourning. And it actually served this purpose admirably. People hankered to connect, to say something — but not, perhaps, to say all that much, words feeling so inadequate in the circumstances. The important privacies, meanwhile, remained untrespassed.

*Cricinfo* compiled tweets from cricketers of Hughes' acquaintance in eleven countries, including Ireland. You experienced the overwhelmed helplessness of those closest, such as long-time New South Wales teammate Daniel Smith: 'I love you little brother. I'm so sorry I couldn't help you'. You also sensed the universal quality of the death from those far away, like the young New Zealand all-rounder Jimmy Neesham: 'I've never felt so keenly the loss of someone I'd never met'.

And that, of course, spoke for the great majority, social media being merely a narrow promontory of the continent of feeling and opinion. Many, many more watched Phillip Hughes than he ever knew or ever knew him, and yet his cricket forged with them a robust link.

Here was a cricketer, let us remember, who elicited firm views. He enacted the debate at the centre of cricket between the natural and the trained, the spontaneous and the orthodox. He provoked the abiding question: can attitude conquer all, and talent and temperament make up shortcomings of technique? It is a question to which in his case we will now never know the answer. Yet if ever a batsman was capable of such development, I suspect, it would have been Hughes, with his stockwhip batspeed and guillotine-clean square cuts.

And, then, he was a boy also: eager, lively, likeable *Phillip*, who should have turned twenty-six tomorrow, but who lived with the simple unguardedness of one half that age. It says something about the embeddedness of cricket in the national imagination that the boy or girl with a bat has such a transcendant appeal: it is youth, freedom, generational change, continuity. 'We all have children, don't we?' a cricket official said to me on Wednesday by way of explaining the desperation of the vigil. There was nothing very much to add.

Nor is there now. On a personal note, it has been one of those weeks where as a journalist you badly feel the futility of your task — being asked to make sense of something that doesn't really, being required to speak of that which is all but unspeakable. Yet it's also been a week to be buoyed, every so often, by the way the worst of events can bring out the best in people. Kudos to Michael Clarke; kudos to the Indian cricket team; kudos to the many, many schools and clubs involved in tributes; kudos to the pace bowler who bounced me first up at training on Thursday night and followed through with a chorus of: 'Sorry, sorry, sorry.'

I'd like to conclude with two other cameos, among many. My friend Pam Newton, writer of excellent detective fiction, was at the SCG on Tuesday with her 92-year-old mother. It's the way they like cricket now: as Pam says, 'no queues, no crowd, no crush, no blaring music, and a car park at the front gate.'

The incident, naturally, has left them both shaken. Almost as bad was the sense yesterday that she and her mother should have been packing the picnic for the fourth day of the Shield game, perhaps to watch Hughes further his case for selection in the Brisbane Test. But — and it's the but, I hope, of cricket people more broadly — Pam and her family have their tickets, flights and accommodation booked for the Adelaide Test. 'It's going to be an emotional summer,' she signed off her email. 'And that's fitting.'

I also awoke Friday to the news from my old friend and erstwhile coach Andrew Walton, now at Plenty Valley CC in the Victoria Women's Cricket Association, that his partner Carolyn had given birth to a son late on Thursday. Naturally, I hope that son will play cricket. But I hope that whatever he does, he'll give his parents cause to be as proud as Phillip Hughes did.

# Risk in cricket
# WILDNESS IN WAIT
## NOVEMBER 2014

Our awareness of danger in sport can change in an instant. A racing car crashes. A skier falls. A bull fighter is gored. Suddenly the possibilities are obvious. Until we forget again.

A week ago, being a batsman in cricket was as safe as milk. Now, with the shattering death of a gifted, popular and hugely promising young player, it seems impossibly dangerous.

In actuality, batting is probably best regarded as meeting a third description: an activity that is very close to completely safe. But it was in that very closeness that the danger lurked, because the possibility of total safety in any endeavor is illusory and deceptive.

The safety of batting is manifest. The helmet is standard at all levels from junior ranks. Protective gear has never been better. At the top level, pitches are like tarmacs and bats like claymores. Bowlers of genuine pace are few and far between. Umpiring errors are often as not rescinded.

It is hard to discern the danger in such a landscape, and we'd probably prefer not to: a sense of danger might beget fear, which these days is an almost impermissibly negative emotion.

Before the present day of super safety we weren't, perhaps, as afraid of fear. We factored it in. We sensed its menace. In his timeless textbook, *The Art of Cricket* (1958), Sir Donald Bradman illustrated the pull/hook stroke, which Phillip Hughes was playing last week when he suffered his lethal blow, with four photographs of batsmen getting hit. Twice he discussed the 'danger of being struck by the ball'; he firmly counseled against 'making a shot' when the ball was at head height.

There have traditionally been two means of disposing of the short-pitched ball to leg. To the delivery arriving at between waist and chest height on the line of the stumps, the recommended stroke was the pull, played chest-on in front of yourself with a full extension of the arms, dispatching the ball roughly through square leg. To the rising ball directed somewhat to leg, the prescribed response was the hook, played from inside the line and sending the ball to deep fine leg. Both shots involved a back and across step, and a pivot of the body; both shots involved rolling the wrists to keep the ball down. Bradman called this 'the safest method, physically and cricket-wise'.

Descriptions of the pull and hook in the classic old Australian cricket manual of the 1960s, *Calling All Cricketers,* contained cautions both for players ('Never attempt the stroke unless your feet are in the correct positions') and for coaches ('Many eminent players and coaches consider that the pull and hook strokes should not be encouraged in the early stages of tuition for young boys').

Frank Tyson's advice about the pull and hook in his popular *Complete Cricket Coaching* (1976), written on the brink of the helmet age, was scattered with words like 'dangerous', 'risk of injury', and 'the ball may strike your head and face'. Tyson wrote with some authority, having survived a blow to the back of the head inflicted by Ray Lindwall in a Sydney Test twenty years earlier.

To modern eyes, footage of batsmen in the pre-helmet age is vaguely unsettling. Yet none of the English batsmen who faced Lillee and Thomson in Australia forty years ago were hit on the head. And for all their apparent vulnerability, serious injuries were comparatively few, albeit the more memorable for being so.

So what happened? Chiefly the helmet, although also the aforementioned environmental factors tilting the game in the batsman's favour.

For one thing, the hook and pull, which Bradman insisted be played off the back foot, became incorporated into the popular initial movement of the forward press. Executed by Ricky Ponting, the front foot pull from in front of the face was one of the great sights of the age: magisterial, disdainful. Adam Gilchrist's feet scarcely moved at all when he played with a cross bat to leg: a pivot on the spot, a whirl of hands and bat, and the ball was sent soaring seemingly to the clouds. Keeping the ball down — it was so twentieth century.

The pull and the hook, too, are now a hybrid. In his canonical *Art and Science of Cricket* (2008), Bob Woolmer distinguished them not by line of the ball but by height: below the chin was a pull, above the chin a hook. Woolmer also included an admonition that's hard not to read without a pang of horrified recognition after last week's events: 'Hooking requires perfect concentration. Watch the ball as it comes to you. Keep your head and eyes very still. Do not blink, flinch or look away! The moment you take your eyes off the ball, you are effectively blind and a sitting duck, liable to be hit on the helmet or the back of the neck.'

So warnings were still being issued, but were they being heeded? Steve Waugh famously forswore the hook on grounds of risk, to wicket rather than health, but the attitude made him seem a little antique. The observable reality was that superior exponents were pulling and hooking off their eyebrows without compromise, without fear.

The other observable reality, to which we paid ever less attention, was that batsman were being hit on their heads far more often than of yore. We saw it. We even rather reveled in it. How often has the bouncer from Steve Harmison which split open Ponting's cheek at Lord's in 2005 been reshown, offering red-blooded cricket fans the sight of real red blood? But we trusted the technology, and it was kind of miraculous the way batsmen bounced back from impacts, like football players bouncing up from a tackle.

When Brett Lee hit Shivnarine Chanderpaul on the back of the helmet during the Sabina Park Test of 2008, for example, the West Indian fell on the spot like a tree under the axe. 'I did not know where I was,' he confessed afterwards. 'My entire body went numb. I could not move my hands and I could not move my feet.' Yet after being helped up and receiving a few minutes' treatment, he batted another hour, carrying on from 86 to 118, finally succumbing to a full toss from Stuart MacGill — which seemed almost a cosmic joke.

In the Port Elizabeth Test in February, South Africa's Ryan McLaren was hit a sickening blow by Mitchell Johnson, which caused him to suffer twenty-four hours of headaches and nausea. Yet at the time he carried on batting — a bravery that was saluted, at the same time as seeming almost de rigueur.

Then, of course, there was the television japester Piers Morgan who volunteered to face Brett Lee in the nets at the SCG for the edification of Channel 9 last summer, a stunt that now seems shockingly crass. What were they thinking, assuming they were thinking at all?

At a certain level, this apparent impunity of batsmen could not but seep into the collective consciousness, reinforcing the idea that the headblow was little more than an everyday hazard of a lesser order, something from which you walked away with a slight ringing in the ears and a sketchy leg bye.

In hindsight, as they say, everything is inevitable. But something is perhaps clear in retrospect: that we had lapsed into a fantasy that danger had been eliminated from cricket, when a minuscule but irreducible residue remained, and was closer than we knew.

As Sean Abbott ran in on Monday at 2.23pm, Phillip Hughes had batted more than two and a half careful hours. The time was ripe to do as batsmen now are encouraged to do at all events — take the initiative, move the game on, give the bowler something to think about. Now all of us are left something to think about.

# Aggression in cricket
## SMALL STEPS
DECEMBER 2014

The cricket ball is a beautiful object. It slots exquisitely into the hand, leaves the bat with a lovely crack, somehow connects you to the whole antiquity of the game: where bats have changed so much in the last decade, a cricket ball has had essentially the same features and physical properties for 250 years.

Yet since the death of Phillip Hughes, that perfection of leather and cork is feeling a little differently in the hands of its users, its potential lethality suddenly made manifest. Nor have helmets sat so securely as we've been used to, or even uncertainty seemed quite so glorious.

'Where now? Who now? When now?' The three questions with which Samuel Beckett begins The *Unnamable* would probably occur first to Australian cricketers in the context their summer schedule, but they've come to mind this week too.

In simple terms, we now know the answers: Adelaide, India, Tuesday. But in what spirit do we go forward? It is already not quite the same as before: witness the mixture of sorrow and pride with which New Zealand and Pakistan resumed their delayed Test in Sharjah.

Yet this was also a week in which, for the first time in a good while, Australian cricket saw itself, stripped of artifice and ostentation, and the reflection was not unbecoming. Without anything much to tell or sell them, the marketeers and media professionals stepped back, leaving the voice of the game to be heard — and the voice was clear, true and caring.

It was a week in which words like 'spirit', 'community' and even 'society' were used, as distinct from 'audience', 'market' and 'cricket consumer'. Everyone seemed aware of the restraints of tact and taste, nobody tried to flog any memorabilia or a new show, and the hashtags that mattered, #putoutyourbats and #63notout, arose and spread organically — a world away from #OrangeNation, #ThunderNation and photos of blokes dressing as Monty Panesar.

It was a week in which local and junior cricket, of the kind where eight-year-old Phillip Hughes scored 25 in an under-10 match and was at once smitten with the game, carried the torch and lit the way. It was a week in which probably more fans were gained than lost. Cricket in Australia has quietly impressive charitable instincts and credentials, and has often been a means of regrouping after disasters and tragedies. It did not fail to rally in its own cause.

Cricket's renewed sense of itself may not pass quickly either. There are new and frankly welcome sensitivities. Not only do things not feel the same, they do not sound the same. In the foreword to Michael Clarke's new Ashes diary, for example, Shane Warne opines that Clarke's defining gesture last summer was his threat to James Anderson in Brisbane: 'Get ready for a broken fuckin' arm'. Says Warne: 'This was the moment I believe Australia saw the very competitive, tough Michael Clarke I know, and accepted him as an Australian hero.'

Seriously? Was that *really* the stuff of twenty-first century Aussie heroism? Some fans probably did warm more to Clarke afterwards — the same noisy fans who regard his metrosexual airs as effete and suspect.

But a fair few, the serious and thoughtful ones, just heard the kind of phony machismo on which Australian sport is inclined to fall back at its most clueless. They're a great deal more impressed by the Clarke they have seen the last ten days, culminating at Macksville on Wednesday: he has been more than a captain; he has been a leader.

This sets a challenge for the sporting media, dutiful propagator of the hyperbole, chauvinism, contrived confrontation and martial allusion which under present circumstances rings so falsely. It will be a good challenge too, and worth meeting.

Australian cricket does not only seem changed in our own eyes. It has been seen in different light abroad. To other countries over time we have been an object of affection, animosity, respect and fear, but never before, or at least in such measure, sympathy.

The breadth and depth of the response abroad has been striking evidence of cricket's interconnectedness. Hughes represented three English counties and an IPL franchise, made friends everywhere. In his career, compressed with ins and outs, ups and downs, he was easy for peers to identify with.

Stuart Broad, vilified the length and breadth of Australia last summer, gave an emotional interview to *The Guardian*, in which he described learning of Hughes' injury then his death from his weeping mother, of finding it hard to look at a photograph in which he and James Anderson were pictured alongside Hughes walking onto Trent Bridge.

The Indian team, as guests not always easiest to embrace, was strongly represented in Macksville on Wednesday, and international cricket has continued with a lump in its collective throat — and it *was*, after all, what Hughes passionately aspired to be part of.

Now and again the question has been heard about how that first bouncer will feel come Tuesday — the effect of the trauma of the last fortnight on the aggression we're prepared to sanction.

It would be as well to remember that the bouncer is not what it was. In the hands of a relative few is it a weapon of genuine intimidation today, being as much about disrupting a batsman's rhythm, moving them around the crease, restricting their options in the modern free-scoring game: in T20 the bouncer has developed undreamed-of varieties.

It would also be as well to remember that cricketers are actually also good at this stuff. Cricket has a venerable statute book and a bulging code of conduct, but in lots of areas the participants still draw their own limits. As Ashis Nandy has noted, cricket is 'almost unique in providing ample scope for unjust play as well as having strong taboos against such play.' Given that, it's remarkable how, much more often than not, cricketers find a means of striking sparks off one another without igniting the undergrowth round them.

Which is why we should trust them to make their way again, to rediscover cricket's satisfactions and solaces. It will be trying at times, haunting at others, but undertaken, perhaps, in the same spirit as that of the speaker at the end of *The Unnameable*: 'You must go on, I can't go on, I'll go on.'

# Australia v India, First Test, Adelaide, 2014, Day 2
# CLARKE FIGHTS ON

DECEMBER 2014

'Johnson' said the world's loveliest scoreboard yesterday morning in the corner that tracks the running total and the current batsmen, with a pardonable desire to keep patrons informed ahead of the game.

It was perfectly plausible, a wicket having fallen from the last ball of the previous day, and Mitchell Johnson being the next batsman in the nominal order. Michael Clarke? Well, he had not so much 'retired hurt' the previous day as withdrawn into seclusion, visibly distraught, barely able to put one foot in front of the other. What price his return, for the day, the game, the series, the summer?

And then, with one bound, ten minutes of throwdowns, and an all-but sleepless night of treatment, Australia's captain was free. Well, perhaps not free — more properly the opposite, actually, having himself lashed to his fate, as naval captains would have themselves lashed to their helms during storms, entwining their fates with those of their ships.

Was that Clarke coming to bat? It was Clarke. Compared to publicly and privately farewelling your dearest friend in cricket, perhaps resuming this innings was a cinch. It wasn't, of course: it was the pursuit of a Test century with a peculiar sort of valiance, physical and mental.

During his death-before-dishonour 161 in Cape Town earlier this year, Clarke visibly earned his fractured shoulder and other contusions, and came to wear them as medals of valour. Here the enemy was within, from an injury incurred in the course of a tiny sideways jink, and part of an innings always on the brink of a repeat mishap.

As the bowler approached, Clarke stood tall and still at the crease, the tap-tap that keeps the beat of his batting now a thready pulse. His torso was thickened by some supporting garment, his feet confined to a tiny square of activity, leaving his arms and hands do almost all the work; you saw him wince every so often, and found yourself doing the same; you heard his occasional groan through the stump mic, and wondered how long he might last.

The former England captain Tony Lewis tells a story about Majid Khan when he played at Glamorgan in the early 1970s, who settled a debate about the insignificance of footwork in batsmanship by undertaking a half hour net in which he did not shift from a standing position, and nonetheless met every ball in the middle of the bat.

For the limitations to be involuntary...well, that is something else. We are used to the idea of bowlers being injured by their explosive exertions; batsmen, still as pillars, are what teams are built on. Clarke here reminded us of the physical vagaries of batting's movements, its swivels, pivots and levers, its calls on agility, endurance, ability to generate power and capacity to weather blows, because they were all in his case restricted. When he directed Mohammed Shami over the slip cordon and shovelled Karn Sharma through mid-wicket yesterday from a standing position, they were epics of minimalism. When he jogged between wickets and gingerly dabbed his bat into the crease, they were testaments of frailty.

It was, of course, a personal sense of mission that drove Clarke on, the physical pain of success paling before the mental pain of failure. Clarke lost some of his future with the death of Phillip Hughes: it was possible to envision him going on to be a mentor to the younger man of whom he prophesied so much, a hundred Tests and more. One day, in all probably, Clarke will be a father, and know paternal pride; in his relationship with Hughes, I suspect, he experienced a sporting equivalent.

Runs will not have remotely made good the loss, but they are a currency in which Hughes jubilantly transcated, and thus part of their bond.

A hundred was all Clarke could do, just as he had said all the words that could be said. It was grim all the same. Clarke began his Test career with among the sunniest smiles in cricket; he is approaching that career's conclusion with teeth often gritted, lips pursed and bitten. On reaching his hundred, and upon dismissal, his responses were, in the context of recent effusions, almost austere — calm of mind, all passion spent.

It is hard to be overshadowed whilst passing 150 for the first time, but that was almost Steve Smith's fate, even if this was partly an outcome of expectations of his batting he himself has raised. His bearing was once as fresh and spry as that of a PMG boy bearing telegrams; he now appears as reliably as the postman with the daily delivery. His back and across step is slightly more pronounced than last season, and his bat sponsor new. Otherwise he continues on the smoothest of ascents, having averaged 62 in his last dozen Tests.

Smith solemnised his century with a steady and deliberate step towards the '408' embossed on the outfield, then celebrated it with strokes that composed their own sort of tribute, clearing his front leg and smashing overhanded down the ground. Radar timed the deliveries from Varun Aaron at in excess of 140kmh; it was a shame there was no reverse radar to measure their speed coming back.

Flailing cuts and reverse sweeps ensued, with hints of a declaration. All the Australians have batted in this match with Hughes on their mind; these were the shots perhaps closest to the Hughes spirit, full of generous abandon, including the chance Smith offered to slip from Karn Sharma from a metre wide of leg stump.

The beginning was the end, the scoreboard finally having to drag the nameboard for Johnson out at 5.51pm, just ahead of the gloom's descent. With two days elapsed and more than 500 runs hoarded, it's probably time to see his name on the other side of the scoreboard. But that's up to the captain — a man very sure of his own mind.

# Australia v India, First Test, Adelaide, Day 3
## A SICKENING BLOW
DECEMBER 2014

It was perfect — in the absence of consequences, it is allowable to say so.

Mitchell Johnson's first ball to Virat Kohli at Adelaide Oval yesterday was the kind of short delivery every pace bowler would wish to reproduce to a fresh batsman: fast, straight, rearing, deceptive.

Kohli played it badly too — that, thankfully, it is also possible to report.

India's captain pressed forward, went up on his toes too early, ducked too late, took his eyes off the ball when he was squared up, and absorbed the impact flush on the crest of his helmet, the symbol of the Board of Control for Cricket in India.

I can digress from here to tell you that the aforementioned crest is derived from the Most Exalted Order of the Star of India, a chivalric order founded in 1861, dormant for the last five years. Interesting, huh?

I have the licence to do so because, as the technology of the helmet means it to be, nothing happened — the way nothing, or at least nothing much, has been happening for a good many years, at least until the tragedy whose ghostly imprint is embossed on the outfield here, and commemorated in the very black band round Johnson's bowling arm.

Nothing happened in a vaguely chilling fashion, of course. Johnson himself was visibly anxious, approaching reticently, and being consoled by his captain Michael Clarke as he withdrew. The umpires converged. Fielders came in solicitous relays.

Four years ago, Kohli was a burr beneath Australia's saddle, chock full of chat, the kind of opponent you would hardly have minded seeing roughed up a little. But it's only eight days since he attended Phillip Hughes's funeral.

There was relief, therefore, as Kohli removed his helmet with all the nonchalance of a shopper scanning a piece of fruit for bruising, then donned it again with apparent satisfaction. And so the game moved on — a little step closer to normality, if not without a jitter.

This was always going to happen, and probably sooner than later. People wondered how the first bouncer would feel after the tragedy of Hughes; head blows have grown so normalised in recent times that an actual impact was never destined to be far behind.

The real test was the next ball, and the participants passed it well. Johnson again bowled short and fast; Kohli tucked in defensively behind it. They were, at least momentarily, protagonists rather than antagonists, taking cricket forward together, out of its dark weeks and despondent thoughts.

Since Hughes' death, Johnson has pronounced himself 'ready to go', and Kohli described the bouncer as 'part of cricket' and 'every bowler's right'. Their deeds here spoke still louder. Two deliveries later, Kohli eased forward then punched confidently down the ground.

In the main, it was a day of mild cricket in mild weather before a mild crowd. Bowling was made challenging by blustery conditions, brisk enough to blow off bails. There was hard work for fielders without competitive cricket in their legs. The convalescent Clarke avoided slip, spending much of the day at mid-on, a position Sir Robert Menzies once described as 'the last refuge of mankind', turning to chase only as long as it took him to detect a younger and more mobile fielder in the vicinity.

The benignity of the pitch was encapsulated in two early cuts by Pujara off Harris, the first square as the ball sat up, the second fine as the ball came back slightly — adjustment made easy.

Suitably reassured, Indian batsmen exorcised some of the demons by which they were possessed in the northern summer. Pujara, troubled in England by the ball that came back as he tried to cover deliveries going away, faced no risk of such whipsawing by seam here. Kohli, for whom a fourth stump line in England might nearly have been surrounded by crime scene tape, looked ever more secure and authoritative.

A determination to assert himself was most obvious in Ajinkya Rahane, who tried to sweep from outside off, pull from above head height, slash square, hit over the top and drive on the up all in his first twenty-five balls, before settling down.

The short ball, nonetheless, remained a useful threat. After tea, Siddle bowled a waspish and accurate spell, encouraging the pull shot, menacing the helmeted heads, and Rahane's top edge landed in space between equidistant fielders.

In his day's concluding sally, Johnson then slipped himself, and looked again like the bowler who a year ago made it almost look necessary to wear two helmets. Kohli, who in reaching a hundred kissed his badge as if to atone for its earlier rough treatment, was suddenly defending it again, and fell to a cramped pull shot. With a leg gully and short leg in close attendance, Wriddhiman Saha had eleven deliveries to negotiate from the world's fastest bowler, and handled them well, remaining inside the line, keeping his eye on the ball, timing his sway, on guard for the fuller variation — hostility handled with skill. The Australians bristled, the crowd crowed, and everyone, perhaps, felt a little better afterwards.

# The death of Phillip Hughes
# UNHAPPY
# ANNIVERSARY
## NOVEMBER 2015

The anniversary has rolled around quickly. Unpleasant anniversaries always do, as the events that give rise to them never quite leave our minds.

Next Wednesday will be a year since Philip Hughes suffered his mortal blow while batting at the Sydney Cricket Ground; Friday will be a year since he died. By then, the Australian team will be back where they regrouped last season, playing a Test match at the Adelaide Oval. They won't simply be absorbed in the behaviours of the pink ball. There will be Sheffield Shield matches in progress at Bellerive Oval, the WACA and the SCG itself involving many others in Hughes' circle too.

The splendid new official biography of Hughes by my esteemed colleagues Peter Lalor and Malcolm Knox stops almost at the instant of his death, dealing with the astonishing public reaction simply by montages of photographs. The effect is not unlike that achieved in Boston at the John F. Kennedy Presidential Museum and Library, where the president's assassination is dealt with by a muted video loop of Walter Cronkite's CBS newsflash.

To the Hughes story, because it is still so recent and raw, you instinctively add the detail yourself. As the death of Kennedy had a way of freezing one generation in the act of what they were doing when they heard the news, so in its smaller, narrower but still profound way did Hughes' ours.

I was sitting where I am now and doing much the same thing, following the summer's cricket by various means, wondering what subjects might present themselves for discussion — only to face one for which the journalistic palette felt entirely inadequate. To be frank it still does.

To read through the new book, and sample its great many voices, is to appreciate the magnitude of the direct loss. The Hughes family lie at its centre. From there emanate concentric circles of clubmates, teammates, coaches, support staff and even opponents whose lives Hughes enriched, and whose lives have therefore been irrevocably the poorer this last year.

The rebuilding of these circles without him is the work of lifetimes, but it has begun. To its great credit, Cricket Australia implemented a broad-based programme to help the effected cope with grief and trauma, involving lead psychologist Dr Michael Lloyd, specialists at state level, and employee assistance provider Davidson Trahaire Corpsych.

Strategies devised in response to sporting deaths in cycling and horse racing have been applied. The emphasis has been on enabling those in need to feel both 'supported and personally resourceful', to stay engaged in circumstances that can encourage withdrawal, to remain open when there are social and cultural expectations of stoicism.

It cannot have been easy. Sport is somewhere we look in optimism. In playing and watching it we celebrate our good health and good fortune. A lot of the preparation of modern athletes is about placing them in a positive frame of mind, reinforcing sensations of security and well-being.

What to do under the opposite circumstances? For players especially, surrounded by cues associated with their beloved comrade and deeply involved in the activity that claimed his life, respite must have been especially hard to find.

During his ruminations this week, Mitchell Johnson placed his retirement frankly in the context of his role as a fast bowler in the post-Hughes environment: 'It made me think, was I doing the right thing? You know, was I playing in the spirit of the game?'

The circumstances of response need not be so explicit either. Grief is volatile, intrusive, demanding, debilitating, and sometimes intensely isolating. Although Michael Clarke mainly staves off thoughts of Phillip Hughes in his new *Ashes Diary,* there is a moving passage, composed shortly before his retirement Test at The Oval, where he meditates on the loss of his friend.

It is not maudlin or bathetic; it even contains even a hint of self-reproach, in that he 'never thought Hughesy's death would affect me as much as it has for so long.' As trauma gave way to mourning, Clarke reflects that perhaps he missed a step: 'I don't think I had time to grieve personally. Maybe that was a mistake, because now that I think about it, since his death, I'm not sure I've loved cricket in the same way.'

After giving way to a brief, fond recollection of Hughes on tour, Clarke takes a breath, lest he be thought to be excusing himself for his run of outs.

'None of that has anything to do with it,' Clarke says, sternly, and perhaps to himself as much as anyone. 'I'm just thinking of the good times, which must be a sign that I'm getting old, at least for a cricketer.'

I suspect that the passage, understated and personal as it is, speaks for more than a few of Hughes' contemporaries, at least in those spaces available for solitary reflection, often far from the solaces of home, which are naturally sewn in to the structures of the modern game.

Maybe take a moment to think of them now — the young men, and also women, in and around Australia's cricket team, not only trying to be the best at what they do, but also, in hotel suites, departure lounges, team buses and dressing rooms, striving to occupy their free time without dread thoughts crowding in.

Salute them also. Australia's elite cricketers engender both a lot of hyperbolic gush and a fair degree of quibbling censure — to a degree, the two are related, each perhaps a compensation for the other, if seldom in what seems like ideal proportion.

They have had an up and down time of it these last twelve months, winning a World Cup, losing the Ashes, changing a captain, blooding new talent — partly, in the last case, to make good the absence of the hugely-gifted, long-groomed Hughes. They have provided us, in other words, with something like normal cricket in a year that could hardly have felt more abnormal, when at times they must have felt far from a frame of mind conducive to it. For them, getting through to another Adelaide Test should feel like a triumph.

Australians, sporting and otherwise, take a good many cues from their cricketers. Of this group, they have reason to be proud.

# Sixes
# LE DELUGE
### DECEMBER 2016

The running total of sixes in the Big Bash League spiralled towards 250. In one Test, an Australian scored a Test hundred in 82 deliveries without raising a sweat. In another, two Englishmen put on 400 at seven an over then saw their team almost lose. A 15-year-old Indian made 1000 in two afternoons. It was just another crazy week in batting.

Batting is a craft that has evolved gradually, over centuries. We're in the throes of what looks more like revolution. Had you returned to cricket watching after a decade away, you'd assume the foregoing were misprints: instead they are becoming the norm.

It is not all about T20. The returnee from 2005, having watched that year's Ashes, with its unprecedented fifty-two sixes, would have recognised the brute force entering into batting from all sides even then.

Batting is also being reshaped in large part by our tools of trade. Modern bats — extracting more mass from less weight by greater dryness — would have regrooved batting had T20 never been invented.

T20's contribution has been to make a bazaar of the skills of power hitting, visible in every slap, scoop and switch hit, audible in every collective 'wooooooooah' of the BBL commentariat as balls disappear from view. Yet it is about more, I think, than eye-catching technical innovations: these, instead, express changes in batting's underlying philosophies.

In his *Cricinfo* column a couple of weeks ago, Ian Chappell argued that case that 'a solid all-round technique is easily adaptable to T20 cricket'.

Full as usual of common sense, Chappell argued that there's 'a lot to be said for the old-fashioned method of simply advocating a solid defence and then encouraging a youngster to spend hours playing in match situations'. His case in point was old man Swan River, Mike Hussey, still rolling along at forty years of age, cascading lovely cricket shots, flickering between wickets.

There are also, however, counterexamples, the three clearest being the very best batsmen of their generations, in Ricky Ponting, Sachin Tendulkar and Kumar Sangakkara, whose T20 statistics add up unremarkably: just over 300 games, average less than 30, strike rate around 120.

The perceptive Ponting has explained this as an outgrowing of his unrelentingly disciplined junior regime: 'When I began an innings I was batting until a bowler got me out. If it took them a week, that's how long it took...Everything about my development, on the field, in the nets and in the backyard, was about setting me up so I could bat forever.' T20 required accommodations with getting out he could not countenance.

The youthful cast of mind Hussey describes in his autobiography is not all that dissimilar. He recalls being a youngster who 'blocked the living daylights out of it' and 'didn't know where I was going to get my next run from'; further, that he took the same approach into the Test arena, where he stayed 'the boy I was.' He recalled enjoying Test batting only when partnered with the tail, there not being 'too much time to think.' T20 encourages similar abandon.

Think of the distinction as one of time. Ponting reveled in duration, in establishing lasting dominances; Hussey found duration an agony, albeit that his anxieties drove him on. For Ponting, T20 was a frustration, cutting him off from his favourite part of the game; for Hussey, T20 was a disinhibition, relieving him of the hardest part.

Generally we're in a swirl of theory: all we can really tell is that T20 is redefining core practices in batting. While Chappell's point about the ubiquity of a 'solid all-round technique' remains sound, techniques can clearly now be built different ways: where strokes were once grafted onto a defence, more and more coaches talk of adding a defence to a foundation of strokes.

To long-form batting, premeditation is fatal; to T20 batting, it is integral. In the long run, one must survive in order to score; across the shorter distance, where teams are hardly ever bowled out, scoring *is* survival.

In the longer term, convergence of methods is in some degree inevitable. Test and T20 cricket are poles, but of the same magnet. They draw on the same player pool, utilise the same equipment, occur in the same dimensions and involve the same number of opponents. Test batting already appears more brittle (Trent Bridge 2015) and more explosive (Gabba 2015).

In one respect, however, the demarcations remains quite sizeable. In contemporary Test cricket, failure seems to matter immensely: techniques are monotonously drilled by coaches, surgically scrutinised by media; batsmen's last half-dozen scores are accorded outsized significance, as evidence of their proximity to that mysterious state of 'form.' The view abides that life begins at 40.00.

Batting failure in T20 is far less psychologically injurious. At least publicly it tends to be lost in the whole, swallowed up in the generally greater number of failures that naturally accrue amid the randomness, and the overall carnival air. Games pass quickly, succeeded by others, leaving faint traces. Fans are bombarded with numbers of ambiguous significance: what matters, rather, is the capacity to succeed at telling moments.

In Brendon McCullum's invaluable short primer, *Inside Twenty20* (2010), New Zealand's captain talks about this being one of the aspects of the format that first engaged him.

McCullum was an instinctive aggressor who felt slightly held back by the gauntlet of criticism such players run — celebrated one day, censured the next. In T20, McCullum explains, he loved the feeling that 'you were able to give it a decent crack and people were not going to get too hot and bothered if it didn't come off.'

'Fear of failure can be a driver in Test cricket,' McCullum observes. 'It is an impediment in T20.' And 'form'? To cite one of McCullum's slogans: 'Form is irrelevant, confidence is important.' We have tended to see confidence as founded in 'form'; T20 is revealing the relationship as more elastic than we had supposed.

A lot of the forces that drive T20 are economic, with profound implications for cricket's structures and institutions. But its internal dynamics and priorities are also reshaping the game, in ways we can hardly guess at. Come back in 2026, when the generation now establishing themselves have passed through, and almost everything we once held true of batting may have been rethought.

# The game and the players
# THE CONTROL BOARD
## DECEMBER 2016

Cricket is a game strewn with interludes in which nothing much can seem to be happening while quite a lot is. The negotiations between Cricket Australia and the Australian Cricketers' Association over male and female players' forthcoming employment terms have unfolded likewise.

After months of barely perceptible movement, last week they halted altogether, following stories in *The Australian* on consecutive days drawing on the parties' opening submissions. This caused CA to decree icily that it would "not take part in a process which seeks to draw its players into a public dispute".

To quote the press release: "Players deserve the opportunity to focus on the game, rather than being distracted by a negotiation that should be conducted in a professional and confidential manner."

You might think this disingenuous from the directors who courted Steve Smith and David Warner over dinner on December 7 in the middle of an ODI series against New Zealand.

You might think it paternalistic for an organisation to opine about players being "distracted" by a negotiation profoundly impacting their futures.

You might even consider it a bit naive for an organisation with a sizeable media arm employing a good many journalists and a public affairs department run by a former newspaper editor to object so primly to official but widely-circulated documents becoming public.

If CA wants discussions, as CEO James Sutherland puts it, "behind closed doors and in an appropriate fashion", that's its prerogative. But it cannot control absolutely everyone and everything. Although it would seemingly like to.

From CA's public pique, one obtains a hint of what these negotiations are *really* about — not money but power. It's 43 years since CA was known as the Australian Board of Control for International Cricket, but its urge to do so has seldom been so apparent.

Not quite 20 years ago, CA and the nascent ACA agreed a memorandum of understanding that walked back from the adversarial us-and-them industrial relations model that had operated since World War I, temporarily destabilised by World Series Cricket.

After a long and rancorous negotiation, with much appealing to public sentiment on both sides, it was agreed that Australia's international and first-class cricketers should share directly in a fixed proportion of the game's revenue.

Notwithstanding that the dispute was "painful and distracting", Sutherland's predecessor Malcolm Speed described the outcome as "a triumph for both sides", who could "look back...with satisfaction and without bitterness". It may even, Speed observed, have been "a process that had to be undergone in order to take the board-player relationship into the modern era".

Some at CA, however, have never quite come to terms with such modernity. While the boards of New Zealand, South Africa and West Indies have also moved to revenue-sharing models, CA has continued kvetching privately about cricketers enjoying only upside and bearing none of the game's growing cost, while bemoaning inhibitions the arrangements place on their allocation of resources — even if said restrictions hardly seem to have checked personnel growth in Australian cricket administration.

CA would essentially like to revert to the former ways, with unilateral control of the exchequer. Under its proposal, only a core of "international men" would share the big bucks, while the earnings of "domestic men", whom it has basically concluded are overpaid, would be reined in.

"International women" and "domestic women" — not the politest nomenclature, perhaps — would remain dependent on CA's indulgence. And the ACA, really, would exist only in vestigial form. It's noticeable, in fact, how much less often the ACA features in CA's submission than vice versa, except where CA questions "the appropriateness of CA directly funding the ACA". Few organisations brandish the word "appropriate" to such chill effect as CA.

CA does have a point about changing labour dynamics. Revenue sharing was devised in an era before domestic T20 portended a revolution in the game's finances and rewards: a proportion of players, albeit still not huge, now earn sizeably outside their CA contracts. Nor is CA mistaken in noting resource challenges at lower levels of the game that need alleviation; although let's just say that this illumination seems rather recent.

Yet on its proposition for "domestic men", CA is really talking out of both corners of its mouth, exalting the prospects of the Big Bash League while aspiring to cut participants out of a direct share of the further growth in a competition they have helped build. For were it not for the skill, athleticism, commitment and adaptability of the "domestic men", the BBL would not be half the attraction it is today.

This, of course, is the way of the world. CA is exhibiting merely the inexorable tendency of all commercial organisations towards, as far as possible, pervading their market, dictating all terms and shaping all messages. The process has been steady, stretching back, in a way, to CA regaining marketing rights to the game from PBL in 1995 and absorbing Women's Cricket Australia in 2003.

In recent years CA has centralised coaching resources and management in the National Cricket Centre while lavishing funds on its high-performance programs, even to the extent of endowing its own eponymous XI

— all as established domestic competitions have been allowed to atrophy.

It is steadily reducing to branch offices the state associations that once regarded themselves as CA's owners, eliminating them as a check on its ambitions.

Its large public affairs team seems to issue a press release if someone at Jolimont is scalded at the tea urn. Its media arm gushes content — of, to be fair, passable quality although one wonders if it will be "appropriate" for cricket.com.au to cover these pay negotiations?

Which other counterweight to its influence might CA see as needing to be subdued? Oh yes, the players, despite the "international men" already being on a schedule so relentless, under monitorings so minute and contractual restrictions so binding that their lives border on a form of amply-compensated house arrest.

Yet, with the best will in the world, no organisation is so wise and benevolent that it should enjoy concentrated and untrammelled authority, least of all of a game so embedded in the life of the nation, and evolving so rapidly that nobody has all the questions let alone all the answers.

Nor are athletes readily reduced to the status of mere employees, fulfilling as they do the dual role of worker and product: "the shoemaker and the shoe", as the shrewd American sportswriter Dave Zirin puts it. And, in ways administrators never will, they risk their reputations and livelihoods every time they take the field.

For nearly two decades, CA and the ACA have enjoyed an *entente* that has effectively aligned their interests, contained tensions, allowed for constructive disagreement and mutual accountability, and correlated with a period of on-field success. When events resume moving, CA will need to present better arguments for change than it has made so far, and be prepared to defend them.

# The game and the players
# TWO AUSTRALIAS
## JANUARY 2017

Some sentiments in cricket are never to be heard. Such as: what the world really needs is more banter between commentators. Or: how profoundly cricket has been enriched by the involvement of gaming companies. And: that is really, really great scheduling.

In the context of the last subject, of course, more often the view is opposite. And Australia's vice-captain David Warner had his say last week in an interview with Fox Sports by holding Cricket Australia accountable for 'very, very poor scheduling' in its forthcoming Test/T20 fixture clash.

For those still unaware, a team bearing the name 'Australia' is scheduled to play Sri Lanka in T20 internationals on 17, 19 and 22 February. Another team also called 'Australia' will commence a Test match against India in Pune on 23 February.

Resemblance between these teams will be largely coincidental. Although chosen by the same selectors, they will contain not only different players in different formats but answer to different coaches: the former composite will jog between their witches' hats at the behest of Justin Langer, Jason Gillespie and Ricky Ponting, possibly the most decorated coaching bench ever assembled.

Frankly, though, that trio might as well play, because their team will not, by any objective measure, be composed of the eleven best T20 players in the country. While short-form cricket selection here might as well have been determined by the zodiac for all its recent coherence, Steve Smith remains officially the T20 skipper, while Australia's last T20 XI featured Warner,

Mitchell Starc, Usman Khawaja, Matthew Wade, Adam Zampa and Glenn Maxwell, all of whom will or might be required in Pune.

So good on Warner for responding to the question with something other than the statutory 'not ideal' and 'it is what it is', and enunciating the basic principle that 'you want to be putting your best team on the park all the time' — statements that derived an additional context from the argy-bargy between CA and the Australian Cricketers' Association over the players' next pay deal. Interestingly, and probably sensibly, CA issued no response, while the comments went unreported by CA's official media arm, cricket.com.au. Fancy that.

To be true, T20Is have long been viewed as opportunities to rest senior players and to audition newbies. We have also abided twin Australias before. While Michael Clarke's Australians skulked home from Test defeat in the UAE in November 2014, an Australian team led by Aaron Finch and coached by Trevor Bayliss played South Africa in three T20Is, from which honest sweats Ben Dunk and Nathan Reardon took home caps.

Yet at least Finch *was* the national T20 captain at the time, and the games *did* prelude a full-fledged five-match ODI series accented to the impending World Cup. Putting a second-string version of the world's sixth-ranked T20 side into the field against the eighth-ranked three times in six days next month hardly seems worth the frequent flier miles, unless it's to give Chris Lynn range hitting practice.

The technical explanation for the scheduling is that Australia 'owes' Sri Lanka as part of bilateral arrangements that also included last year's tour there. Originally mooted for January, the games were pushed into February by Sri Lanka's ongoing tour of South Africa.

The outcome of parallel Australian teams, however, illuminates an issue a little larger even than distended schedules and competitive contexts, which is the peculiar status of cricket boards, and their entitlement to parade beneath national flags when they are not branches of the state but self-constituted monopolies.

The 'Australian cricket team' and Cricket Australia are not synonymous. The former predates the latter by 27 years. The foundational totems, such as the green and gold, were actually originated by the players; the swirl of modern patriotic displays, from the singing of national anthems to the welcomes to country, are actually relatively recent. For a long time, in fact, the notion of the nation's embodiment by its best eleven cricketers needed no remark, reinforcement or elaboration — indeed it was somehow more compelling, more wholesome, for the general lack of ostentation.

The cricket team's claims to representing Australia were lent further legitimacy by the vaguely democratic underpinnings of the game's structure. Admittedly more in theory than in practice, anyone could rise to the level of a director of CA and its antecedent bodies: the only prerequisite was election by a first-grade club to the role of state association delegate.

It was a structure sub-optimal in many ways, inefficient, conflicted, exclusionary and sometimes reactionary. But it possessed a rough-and-ready representativeness, and none doubted that the nation in rallying behind an Australian team could feel as though it was cheering itself on.

This has changed. With its independent boards and bureaucratic bulk, CA has acquired the ambitions, appurtenances and impersonality of a sizeable commercial organization. It's an evolution that is in some respects inevitable. But it renders more important resisting flippant and frivolous notions like simultaneous Australian teams, which endanger the sense of CA holding cricket in trust for all, by reducing 'Australia' to a brand name unrolled for corporate purposes, courting contempt for international cricket, and introducing ambiguities to established hierarchies.

In the early days of the old Big Bash, when finishing in the top two smoothed a path to the lucrative Champions League, states were apt to grumble when key players were chosen for national duties — and were usually slapped down. What would the reaction be now were Chris Lynn required for a second-string 'Australia' in a T20I that coincided with the Brisbane Heat hosting a Big Bash League final? Lynn may already feel he's slumming it by playing ODIs against Pakistan.

One CA director with a better feel for this than most would be Mark Taylor who as Australia's captain 22 years ago was averse to a rather less obtrusive concept, the involvement of an Australia A team in the World Series Cup. The Australian cricket team, he argued with some force, deserved undiluted support: the experiment was not repeated. Look forward to some quality banter in the Nine box next month.

This has been an uneasy few weeks for international cricket more generally. Attempts to bring it back to Pakistan faltered again; more West Indians forsook national contracts; South Africans Kyle Abbott, Rilee Roussow and David Wiese joined the steady stream of countrymen taking the Kolpak shilling, following a trail blazed after the World Cup by Zimbabwe's Brendan Taylor.

All the more reason, one would have thought, to defend the principle of international cricket being 'best against best'. Otherwise we might as well add another to the log of unheard sentiments: the administrators have really thought this through.

# The game and the players
# CHRIS VERSUS SAM
## MARCH 2017

Chris Hartley and Sam Heazlett have a few things in common. Both are from Queensland. Both are left-handers. Both grew up chasing the dream of playing for Australia.

Hartley, 34, retired last week after a career as honourable as it was long: 131 first-class, 96 List A and 55 domestic T20 games, including a record for Sheffield Shield dismissals. He was a better player at the end than the beginning, topping the season's Shield batting averages with 535 runs at 76.4. Not to mention an excellent fellow.

You might remember 21-year-old Heazlett from a few months ago, when the national selectors inserted him a line-up for a Chappell-Hadlee Trophy match in Auckland. Heazlett has, indeed, shown glimpses of promise, making a hundred on his Sheffield Shield debut in November 2015, but in sixteen first-class matches since has averaged 25.8, and is yet to represent his state in the Matador Cup. That's OK, of course: it's early days yet.

So despite their similarities, it's hard to compare these two Queensland Hs. Except that this week Cricket Australia did just that, in its pay proposal to Australia's cricketers — and it was a comparison in which the older man came off the worse.

CA said essentially that a Hartley, a top-drawer domestic cricketer unlucky that only one wicketkeeper can represent Australia, was less valuable than a Heazlett, for his having fleetingly entered the gilded circle of international cricket.

For CA wishes to scrap the 20-year-old revenue sharing model that through the Australian Cricketers' Association has encompassed all interstate and international cricketers; to its way of thinking, only internationals deserve to benefit directly from revenues, because only they contribute to their generation.

CA's argument is simple: it wants more money. Broadcast rights deals impend. Allocating a fixed proportion to first-class cricketers cramps its style.

It wishes, for example, to apportion more to women's cricketers. Indeed it has invited female internationals into its newly plush and exclusive revenue sharing penthouse suite on the grounds that, in executive general manager Kevin Roberts' catchy phrase, 'a cover drive is a cover drive, no matter who plays it.' It has even mooted, as a 'landmark commitment', a 'gender pay equity model' under which all players will 'earn the same hourly base rate of pay.'

This sounds great, until you appreciate that women only play 20- and 50-over cricket, so that equity is not exactly a synonym for equality. Nor, if we're going to go all Chicago School economics on this, does the idea of cricket-by-the-hour reconcile readily with the general trend towards shorter games being of disproportionate commercial value. Rather does it have the makings of a cartoon in which a captain remonstrates with a fast bowler standing by a set of broken stumps. Caption: 'Stop taking wickets you fool — the quicker we win the less we're paid.'

CA's other worthy cause is 'grassroots cricket', which it has worked out receives just 12 per cent of its revenues — a damning statistic which, perversely, it can now roll out almost as a boast.

Now, everyone can unite in the name of 'grassroots cricket', including me, whose club is today pursuing a B-grade flag that's personally every bit as important and more than what might occur in Dharamsala.

But CA's plans on this front remain compellingly vague, save for another stat Roberts has tossed off that 'more support for junior cricket communities' was essential in the light of the AFL having '450 people on the ground to support its grassroots compared to just 170 people in cricket.'

All this does is confirm CA's permanent squint and neck kink from the effort of staring at Docklands from Jolimont, and savours of an organization more concerned with processes than outcomes. If you were a bunch of cricketers being asked to sacrifice tens of millions of dollars of upside, moreover, you might want to know a little more about how and where it will be allocated.

The proposition deserves a fair hearing, even if CEO James Sutherland's comment that negotiations now contain 'a fair degree of urgency' sits uneasily with CA's months of dickering about this proposal, and the release of it on the eve of a crucial Test match in India seems strange after all CA's 'the-players-must-not-be-distracted' pieties ahead of the Boxing Day Test.

It's true enough: cricketers have done well financially in recent years. Domestic T20 worldwide has also offered them unexampled scope; women closing the gap on men is a heartening sight in any context.

But through the relevant period, cricket, especially in certain lucrative markets like Australia, has grown extraordinarily rich. To feed this beast, ever more has been asked of players at all levels, from premier and grade cricket upwards. They have attained unexampled standards of versatility, innovation, athleticism, organizational flexibility and public responsiveness. Nor is it a small matter that Australia cricketers have remained remarkably, perhaps even a tad boringly, scandal-free, even David Warner stepping out from the behavioural shadow seemingly cast by the first five letters of his surname.

Players have done this willingly, even eagerly, partly because of the sense they have developed of a direct stake in the game's expansion, with its recognition that a Chris Hartley, by his consistent excellence, by his undismayed commitment, by his loyalty, sportsmanship, example to teammates and contribution to culture enriches Australian cricket without wearing an Australian cap.

Sutherland calls this model 'out of date' on the basis that 'international cricket actually funds the game'. But nobody is born an international cricketer. And in progress to that goal, merit and dedication are hardly the only factors. Opportunity, fashion, prejudice, luck, general standard and selectorial brainstorm — see under Heazlett, Sam — exert huge sway.

For five of the last ten years, for example, Chris Rogers scored more first-class runs than any other player in the world. But when he turned thirty-five, it seemed likeliest that he would remain a one-Test wonder. Industrial logics have decidedly limited application to a game so full of complexities and caprices.

In threatening to kibosh the revenue share, furthermore, CA places all the weight on 'revenue' and none on 'share'. The sense of Australian cricket being a shared enterprise has been hard-won and valuable, containing and diffusing many of the tensions inherent in a fast-changing game increasingly distorted by the dictates of consumer capitalism. Kevin Roberts makes a fair point: there isn't much to pick between cover drives. Which is why privileging Sam Heazlett's over Chris Hartley's is such a retrograde step.

# The game and the players
# AUSTRALIA VERSUS ITSELF
MAY 2017

For the last six months, Cricket Australia has been making an excellent case in its representations regarding a new Memorandum of Understanding — an excellent case for its counterpart in discussions, the Australian Cricketers' Association.

At times in its existence, it's been possible to wonder what the ACA has been all about. The machine has seemed to run itself, with a sluice off the fast-growing channel of CA's revenue directing a healthy fixed proportion to the players. It's not been so easy, of course. But in most respects, relations have been harmonious and mutually beneficial.

In arguing for the end of the revenue-sharing model after nearly twenty years, however, CA has behaved as unchecked monopolies are apt to. It has postured, obfuscated, delayed, intrigued. It has sought to divide the players among themselves: women from men; international from domestic; just recently, senior internationals, to whom it offered extended contracts, from their colleagues. That having failed, it has escalated to outright intimidation.

David Warner has been tut-tutted for his statement that Australia 'might not have a team for the Ashes' — it is believed that Warner lives in a nice house and owns a nice car, placing him in a category that some believe invalidates his opinions. Yet Warner's remarks merely translated for a lay audience last week's ultimatum from CA's CEO James Sutherland, who threatened the ACA's rank in file with an uncontracted void come 30

June — a lock-out, by any other name.

Bear in mind, too, that under CA's offer, Warner and his elite circle actually stood to be paid a good deal more. His objections signify disquiet about the impact of the offer not on himself but on others, and in some ways on the status of cricketers generally.

For it would be a mistake to regard this dispute as solely about the division of a sport's spoils. For players, the mechanisms of revenue sharing have been a recognition of their position in the game — as not just skilled practitioners but also national embodiments, as producers and product, as custodians and conscience.

With that status in Australia has come both a certain dignity and a sense of responsibility. In fact, where football codes have been wracked regularly by behavioural and ethical crises, Steve O'Keefe has become the exception that proves the rule of cricketers' squeaky-cleanliness.

Why does CA want to end this *entente cordiale*? Obviously it wants more money, even if to what precise end is unclear, notwithstanding bromides about 'grassroots' investment and foreshadowing of significant increases in CA's media and game development headcounts. Yet it concerns more than that: a tell-tale paragraph in Sutherland's letter complains of the ACA's 'reluctance to recognise the necessity of change and innovation as circumstances change', reflected in its push back on matters such as scheduling, and a reticent embrace of concepts like day/night Test concept.

In fact, the players have prevented none of these 'changes and innovations'. Rather have they acquiesced in them after expressing perfectly reasonable reservations. Had players been habitually and capriciously vetoing matters of significant cricket policy then there might be some grounds for Sutherland's complaint. But they have not. On the contrary: the sustainability of Australia's eight-day-a-week international treadmill and the vitality of the men's and women's Big Bash Leagues testify to their wholehearted commitment.

More than a few of their views, too, have struck a public chord, such as misgivings expressed last season about the degradation of the Sheffield Shield and the debasement of national representation inherent in separate Australian teams playing simultaneously at home and in India. It seems, however, that what sticks in CA's craw is the inconvenience of considering any view but its own. How dare the players express opinions? How dare they do anything but obey? This is the voice of authoritarianism and it has no place in a modern game.

It's not too late to turn this back. For once, in a way, the money part is the less difficult. If the apportionment of expenses is complex, the revenue is ample and growing — at least it is, both parties might note, in an environment of industrial accord. Even now, I suspect, players would be open to an MOU that, providing it respected the integrity of a revenue-sharing model, freed up significant funds for an identified greater good. After all, it is only two years since Australia's international cricketers forewent tens of millions of dollars for the sake of welfare and wellbeing schemes benefiting past and future players less fortunate.

The deeper issue is the philosophical question of the players' relations to the game, whether they should be partners in it or merely vassals. It would doubtless suit CA's short-term corporate purposes better had it no administrative counterweight in the form of the ACA. But a certain contention is valuable in any sphere: in the long run, such mechanisms diffuse tension, build consensus, and actually promote the 'change and innovation' on which CA is so keen.

Some have identified this as the power play of a board longer on corporate experience than on sensitivity to cricket's unique mesh of overlapping stakeholders. To the man with a hammer, everything looks like a nail; to the representative of commerce, everything looks like a business.

But CA's directors might want to be careful what they wish for. In shredding twenty years of accumulated goodwill, they stand to leave players as disaffected as they were forty years ago. Back then there was no player union. There were no dispute mechanisms. There was a sense among players of being stood over and taken for granted — and that disaffection, as much as financial motivation, was a factor when Kerry Packer hove into view.

CA's approach in the last six months, then, has been a glimpse for the players of what life totally at Jolimont's behest would be like. Administrators are at risk of turning themselves from partners in cricket's progress into employers for whom few would work ungrudgingly.

# The game and the players
# MEMO FROM THE
# CHAIRMAN
## JULY 2017

Marshall McLuhan's maxim that 'the medium is the message' remains so beloved of op ed pundits that it's overdue a run in the sports pages. And this week's contribution to the game's pay dispute by Cricket Australia's chairman David Peever could hardly be improved on as an illustration.

For those who dimly recollect a McLuhan bowling seam-up for Western Suburbs or playing on the half-forward flank for Carlton, he was a Canadian philosopher who argued that the form of a message is every bit as significant as its content.

And that, in a dispute as much about authority as it is money, should guide our interpretation of Peever's having his say via a column published in this newspaper yesterday: that is, he chose not to appear, not to answer questions, not to incur the risk of interruption or contradiction, but simply to publish, in order to control.

Peever said some things — we'll get to those. Yet the step itself was almost as self-revelatory as the moment a couple of months ago when CA condemned the Australian Cricketers' Association for issuing a press release by issuing a press release.

The first four paragraphs foamed with indignation — 'most tawdry', 'complete myth', 'deeply insulting', 'deliberately fabricated', 'disrespects all those involved across the cricket community'— about the role of ACA adviser Greg Combet in portraying cricket as 'an industrial relations battleground.'

Well, heaven forfend that one should perceive a collective bargaining agreement as having anything to do with industrial relations. But to quote Peever: 'The suggestion that CA's push to modify the player payments model has nothing to do with genuine issues facing the game is an insult to everyone involved at CA, including other members of the Board. It is also an insult to all those from across the State and Territory Associations who understand and support the need for change.'

Goodness me — everyone's so insulted. But this is the vigorous threshing of a straw man. Precisely nobody says the dispute has 'nothing to do with genuine issues facing the game'; they merely sniff the unmistakeable bouquet of bullshit when CA insists that this is *all* the dispute is about.

'I recognise the place of collective bargaining,' Peever continues proleptically, 'and I accept the industrial relations framework in Australia.' Yet this is a bit like saying that he recognises the place of the speed limit and accepts the custom of driving on the left hand side of the road. All anyone worth listening to in this debate has argued — as my colleague Peter Lalor did recently — is that the relationship of the professional athlete to modern sport makes a problematic fit with the conventional relationship of employee to employer because the athlete represents both producer and product.

It's a simple enough idea. CA has acquiesced in it for twenty years by paying cricketers out of a share of revenue. Those cricketers are entitled to ask what has changed, especially when they see athletes in other competitions, rightly or wrongly, agitating for similar status.

Let's be fair to the chairman. His merely having worked for Rio Tinto should not make of CA a 'union basher'. But what CA is doing is behaving as a monopoly. And of monopolies a wariness is always justified, especially when they assert their market power, as CA has in escalating this dispute.

Not that you'd guess this from the victimhood that oozes from

Peever's screed. By his account, CA has always respected the ACA; it has been 'very generous'; it has endured a campaign against it of 'sustained ferocity' waged by others with a 'reckless stategy'.

Yet an express principle of CA's proposal, unchanged from the very beginning, was that it cease its indirect provision of a portion of the ACA's funding — a hitherto uncontroversial convention, in recognition of the union covering 100 per cent of Australia's male and female international and domestic cricketers. What could have been more adversarial?

As for CA's generosity, its proposed package, stripped of payroll tax, rolled-over adjustment ledger and pie-eyed prize money projections then stretched across a greater number of players reflecting the inclusion of women, actually looks a bit parsimonious.

Finally, who did what to whom? For even if one accepted every other aspect of Peever's position — and of his commitment to grassroots cricket I would never doubt his sincerity — it is CA that has kept turning up the dial in this dispute.

It is CA that attempted to turn the top international cricketers against the rest by seeking to buy the former off with turbocharged rewards. It is CA that has tried to turn female cricketers against male, with, among other things, an attempt last week to make a big deal out of the last adjustment ledger that was lamer than a three-legged dog.

It is CA that has sought to turn grassroots cricket against elite cricketers — an entirely bizarre gambit when the success of both are so strongly linked.

And in the end it was CA that walked away from the cricketers, not the other way around, that terminated their relations with extreme prejudice, that isn't paying them now, that threatens not to back pay them ever, that opposes them pursuing their livelihoods anywhere else.

In instituting the lock-out, CA also caused the players' intellectual property to revert to the ACA. Yet Peever now criticises the ACA for its decision to 'lock up player IP into its own business ventures'. Precisely what was the ACA meant it do? Put in the fridge? To surrender something so valuable was the very definition of a 'reckless strategy'. And CA's commercial and broadcasting partners will, one imagines, be letting it know.

In the meantime, players have demonstrated their good faith by continuing to train, keeping their own counsel, and hoping for resolution, while CA have gone on blaming everyone but themselves. And while the message of Peever's communiqué yesterday may have strained for the odd conciliatory sentiment, the medium tells otherwise — that CA remains no closer to understanding how clumsily it has gone about its work.

# The game and the players
# PEACE IN OUR TIME?
AUGUST 2017

Thursday was a good news day for Australian cricket. An all-inclusive memorandum of understanding. Respectable pay rises for men, hearty pay rises for women. Industrial peace ahead of a long and potentially intriguing summer.

It's a measure of the sheer strangeness of the last ten months that the general impression was of abject defeat for Cricket Australia. After all, they had anathematised the idea of a pay model partaking of revenue, asserted that the majority of players were being rewarded unsustainably, ridiculed the idea of cricketers being partners in the game.

Grassroots? What would players know about grassroots? Apart from, you know, having sprung from them, and usually not so long ago...

How did CA end up in a position of such extremity, where all but seventy male players and every female player was out of contract, training for nothing, living on subsistence?

How did they end having figure-eights skated run around them by an Australian Cricketers' Association so small it does not even have a receptionist, and whose 16 staff have been on short rations since 30 June?

We may never have the complete answer to this question. But it looked suspiciously like George Santayana's definition of fanaticism — redoubling one's efforts after losing sight of one's aims.

So much about CA's approach to this dispute smacked of someone's cock-eyed idea of cleverness: courting Steve Smith and David Warner over the banquet table; turning the ACA away from the first scheduled meeting because of objections to this newspaper reporting the 'pregnancy clause' in female contracts; the huffy 'players-must-not-be-distracted' charade around the Boxing Day Test; the paradoxical delay in tabling a formal offer until the eve of the decisive Dharamsala Test.

There was the shameless stunt of allocating the players' foregone pay to 'grassroots' — which must now be dealt with. There was the brazen attempt to spin the adjustment ledger as something male players were greedily keeping from females — which few people grasped anyway. Above all, perhaps, there was the ploy of holding CEO James Sutherland back from negotiation, as though Nicholson was just a monkey who had no business socialising with organ grinders.

A result of this, however, was that while the ACA had a variety of credible and effective spokespersons, nobody owned CA's message. It was an empty suit, seemingly hung on chairman David Peever's coathanger — an irony given that the ostensible purpose of the exercise was to reclaim money for the egalitariat.

In the end, CA could not even stay on terms with its corporate peers. These sponsored cricket in order to align with well-known and popular players, not to fund a campaign to position those same individuals as an impediment to cricket's future. So much for those hand-picked top-end-of-towners who were going to shake sleepy cricket out of its fusty old ways.

What was learned about the players? Obviously that, as the Wobblies sang, there is power in a union, even if the ACA is of a very particular kind — with its relatively small membership and total coverage, as much an old-fashioned craft guild as a modern industrial grouping.

If the rhetoric of labour was widely used, the solidarity probably arose more simply. It is instilled from the first in Australian cricketers that the team comes first, and that senior players set the example. That can sometimes make for a dull conformity; but who would have wanted to be the first player to break ranks in this dispute?

Not that there weren't enticements. This was the first Australian sport-industrial relations dust-up to feature women in a significant role. CA offered them every incentive to look after themselves, and male players have not in the past gone out of their way for female colleagues. Had the cricketers fissured along gender lines, the optics for the ACA would have been challenging. But, led by Meg Lanning and Alex Blackwell, Australia's women showed remarkable collegiality, especially given their lesser resources and alternative prospects.

What now? There is justifiable concern about the impact on cricket of whole laundries of dirty linen being publicly aired. At the same time, it's not clear that the public took sides so much as held tighter to existing prejudices.

A certain proportion of fans will always feel that players are overpaid prima donnas, a certain proportion that administrators have cloven hooves. Neither is true, of course; fortunately, neither is inconsistent with a love of cricket. The Ashes is also a great unifier. It cannot come quickly enough.

Between CA and the ACA, the administration and the players, tensions will be longer abating. That their joint press conference had to convene on neutral ground, that CA's chairman left his luckless CEO to mouth the necessary pieties, reflected a marked departure from previous days of accord.

These tensions were foreordained, regardless of outcome. They were allowed to worsen heedlessly. Peever's haughty communiqué three weeks ago and Sutherland's awkward doorstop last week sounded like the political phenomenon to which John McCain referred a week ago in his floor statement on bipartisanship, where being seen to 'win' is felt more important that any outcome. Cricket will bear the cost of those eroded bonds of trust.

But let us all try to concentrate on the good to which I first referred. Certainly it is not a bad thing that male, female, international and first-class cricketers have been reminded of their reciprocal obligations, and even that cricketers at lower levels have a stake in what they do.

In divisions of sporting spoils, the community often receives short shrift, because it is too dispersed to be represented. CA's attempts to redress that here were crude, but not meaningless.

A vow might be worth contemplating: ask not what your club can do for you, but what you can do for your club. In fact, I've hardly met a player who did not care deeply about where they were from. But more can always be done. If cricket has not been the winner these last ten months, it need not have lost so badly.